Market Society

Market Society

Markets and Modern Social Theory

Don Slater and Fran Tonkiss

Polity

First published in 2001 by Polity Press in association with Blackwell Publishers Ltd

Editorial office:
Polity Press
65 Bridge Street
Cambridge CV2 1UR, UK

Marketing and production:
Blackwell Publishers Ltd
108 Cowley Road
Oxford OX4 1JF, UK

Published in the USA by
Blackwell Publishers Inc.
350 Main Street
Malden, MA 02148, USA

A catalogue record for this book is available from the British Library.

Library of Congress Cataloging-in-Publication Data
Slater, Don.
    Market society: markets and modern social theory / Don Slater and Fran Tonkiss.
       p. cm.
    Includes bibliographical references and index.
    ISBN 0-7456-2026-4—ISBN 0-7456-2027-2 (pbk.)
       1. Economics—Sociological aspects. 2. Markets—Sociological aspects. 3. Sociology—Economic aspects. I. Tonkiss, Fran. II. Title.
    HM548 .S55 2000
    306.3—dc21   00-040088

Typeset in 10½ on 12 pt Sabon
by SetSystems Ltd, Saffron Walden, Essex
Printed in Great Britain by MPG Books, Bodmin, Cornwall

This book is printed on acid-free paper

Contents

Acknowledgements   vi

Introduction   1

1   The Emergence of Market Society   6

2   Markets and Economic Order   36

3   Rationality, the Individual and Social Order   63

4   Markets and Social Structures   92

5   States and Markets   117

6   Commerce and Culture   149

7   The Cultural Turn   174

Conclusion: Markets versus Market Society   197

Bibliography   204

Index   225

Acknowledgements

After another hard slog to the finishing line, Don Slater would like to thank Jo Entwistle for her support and encouragement, and to apologize for a few miserable months along the way. He would also like to thank Danny Miller for comments gratefully received.

Fran Tonkiss is grateful for the support of colleagues in the Department of Sociology, Goldsmiths College, University of London. In particular, Les Back, Monica Greco, Caroline Ramazanoglu and Dave Walsh offered teaching and administrative cover that allowed for a term's study leave while the book was being written.

Introduction

Ideas of the market play a primary role in contemporary approaches to social and economic organization. Whether within the neoliberal restructuring of advanced capitalist economies, the economics of transition in post-communist societies, or programmes of structural adjustment in developing regions, market models have in recent decades dominated the strategies and the rhetoric of social and economic governance. In an extended way, a market logic has come to provide a means of thinking about social institutions and individuals more generally, such that notions of competition, enterprise, utility and choice can be applied to various aspects of people's working lives, access to public services and even private pursuits. Different versions of the market are invoked in an array of sites: from the practical concepts of the advertising agent ('what is our market?'), to the health manager applying a market model to relations between hospital departments, to the formal calculations of econometrics. If it is sometimes hard to see how these different markets relate to each other, it seems clear that the *market idea* goes beyond models of economic co-ordination to touch on broader principles of social regulation and social action.

This book examines key ways in which markets have been conceived within modern social theory. In thinking about 'market society', we are concerned with markets and market relations as frameworks for understanding social order. The notion that market exchange can provide an organizing principle for diverse spheres of social life – if this has been especially prominent within recent neoliberal politics – has a rather long history. The emergence and extension of market forms is central to accounts of 'modernity', such that the contemporary world could be viewed as 'a whole society

embedded in the mechanism of its own economy – a market society'
(Polanyi 1977: 9). Modern social theory, moreover, has had an
enduring concern with the origins and limits of order in complex
societies: in this context, markets have appeared as both problem
and solution. To certain thinkers, market relations exemplify the
competitive struggle between atomized modern individuals; to others,
market mechanisms work to secure social harmony between diverse
private interests. In either case, a theory of markets always implies a
larger theory of social integration and regulation.

Market theory in this sense offers a broad set of responses to the
problem of whether and how social processes can be co-ordinated
(Thompson et al. 1991: 1). Different approaches to the market have
been bound up with competing modern projects – both intellectual
and political – aiming to explain and govern the social. These
concerns run across the boundaries of different social science disciplines. The history of the social sciences has been marked by struggles
to set out distinct areas of inquiry – that of economics from that of
sociology, for example; or of sociology from psychology. In the
division of labour that resulted, market analysis became the special
task of economics, and came to focus on a specific version of order.
Put simply, economic approaches to the market centre on the way
that networks of exchange between buyers and sellers, mediated by
agreements on price, provide an efficient model of allocation under
conditions of scarcity. However, an interest in the market as a
principle of co-ordination is not confined to economists. Our aim in
this book is to take the market seriously as an object of social theory,
broadly construed. In the chapters that follow, we consider
approaches to markets from a range of theoretical perspectives.
Economics, in this context, sits within a larger tradition of thought
in which market forms feature as means of explaining social processes and relations.

'The term market', as Frances et al. (1991: 6) put it, 'seems obvious
enough.' Yet this self-evident ring belies the different forms that
markets take, and the diverse meanings that attach to the market as
an idea. If within modern economics 'the market' has had the same
kind of axiomatic status as 'society' within sociology or 'culture'
within anthropology, like these other categories it has come under
serious criticism. In particular, a range of critiques from within and
outside economics have targeted neoclassical approaches to the formal
modelling of markets, aiming either to refine the economic analysis,
or to shift this analysis into multidisciplinary frameworks within
economic anthropology or sociology (see, for example, Ferber and
Nelson 1993; Friedland and Robertson 1990; Granovetter and Swed-

berg 1992; Smelser and Swedberg 1994; Stiglitz 1994). The point of the present book is not to rehearse these critiques of neoclassical economics, but to address theories of the market in a more lateral way, in terms of what markets and market behaviour might mean in relation to the production and reproduction of modern social order.

It is not, then, a question of being 'for' or 'against' markets as such. Our argument is that markets are not simply good or bad, because they are highly variable. We are saying not that one should suspend judgement as to the effects of market failure (or success), or the import of market values in specific cases, but that it is analytically and politically weak to do so *carte blanche*. There is an important tension here between the complex range of transactions that take place in actual market settings and the market *ideal*, which tends to focus the attention of its advocates and critics alike. Put baldly, the market is both less good and less bad than is often claimed, because it is a less definite thing than we might think. Part of the reason why market models have been so portable to other areas of social life is because notions of the market tend to be so pliable. A simple model of free exchange between buyer and seller at an agreed price, and the way that such exchanges are knitted into a complex network, opens on to a range of substantive markets, abstract theories and critical ideas. Economists have pointed to the variety of market models within their own discipline (see, for example, Brittan 1988; Hodgson 1988); and other theorists have outlined extended conceptions of markets as social institutions, often in pursuit of larger arguments about the 'social' nature of economic life (see, in particular, Polanyi 1957 [1944]; see also Lane 1991). In what follows, we do not pin down a preferred version of the market, but examine how market concepts have been taken up at different moments within social theory as a means of analysing questions of social order, rationality and action.

Modern approaches to markets have frequently turned upon an opposition between pro- and anti-market positions – liberal versus romantic, capitalist versus socialist, populist versus conservative. The neoliberal ascendancy that has taken hold in so many national contexts since the 1970s, the collapse of an 'actually existing' socialist alternative, and the global extension of markets in commodities, labour, finance and images seem to render these oppositions untenable. This is not because the market has in some simple sense 'triumphed'. Rather, such oppositions beg the question of what type of market is at stake in different cases – and exactly which social groups, ideas and programmes 'triumph', as it were, in the guise of an abstract market. Recent political and economic orthodoxies treat markets as self-evident, permanent and incontestable. Imagining alternatives can be difficult given the density and obviousness of an apparently endless market 'present'. However, taking account of the variety of market histories, of the different ways in which markets have been instituted and analysed, brings into question the inevitability of market 'imperatives', the specific forms in which markets currently operate, and the role of market values within political rhetoric and economic ideology.

Plan of the book

The book is organized around those themes and questions that have proved central in attempts to understand markets as broadly social – as well as strictly economic – phenomena. Chapter 1 takes up historical approaches to markets. We begin with market relations as a practical mode of exchange and with the marketplace as a social and cultural site. This substantive conception of markets contrasts with our historical analysis of 'marketization' – the complex processes of commodification and monetarization through which diverse aspects of modern social life became integrated into market arrangements. The chapter goes on to consider responses from within political philosophy to the extension of market forms, as a range of modern thinkers from Hobbes and Locke to Bentham and Mill sought to analyse the roots of social order in an emergent market society.

Chapter 2 centres on the market as a more formal model of economic order, examining major perspectives within economic theory. Our interest is in how the ideas of such thinkers as Smith, Walras and Hayek offer reflections on social questions even as they define a specialist field of economics. Modern economic theory has been characterized by market models in which both market outcomes and social order arise from the rational decisions of individuals seeking to maximize their interests. This model of co-ordination and this account of agency have, however, been subject to contest. Here, we consider economic perspectives on market failure and *disorder*, as well as critiques of market rationality as a model of social action. While assumptions concerning market order and private interests have in this way been open to internal criticism, they have also been challenged by arguments from other disciplines against the very formalism of economic approaches. Chapter 3 examines the efforts of classical sociology to grasp the logic of a modern market society. To what extent – and at what cost – might a social order be founded on market exchange and on the individual pursuit of self-interest? In different ways, thinkers such as Marx, Weber, Simmel, Durkheim and Parsons criticized market society as promoting a dubious and reductive version of the individual, and of a normative social order.

Chapter 4 considers arguments in economic anthropology and sociology which hold that market behaviour and relations are 'embedded' in a wider context of social interaction. Our discussion here focuses on attempts to connect markets to broader accounts of social relations and institutions. Chapter 5 is concerned with problems of political order, examining perspectives on the link between markets and states. We consider how these ideas have helped to shape political and economic arrangements, as competing theories of welfarism, corporatism and neoliberalism have been taken up within changing government programmes for the management of market societies.

Chapter 6 draws on cultural and critical theory to address the variety of connections between economy and culture that have animated modern social thought. These range from enduring concerns that market society debases or destroys cultural coherence and values, to more contemporary concerns with the cultural dimensions of market processes. We examine market forms in relation to different definitions of 'culture' – as a broadly meaningful social world; as a distinct realm of aesthetic or expressive practices; and as an increasingly commodified sphere of social distinction and economic value. Finally, chapter 7 engages with the 'cultural turn' in contemporary theory, in which markets are increasingly seen in terms of processes of signification and identity. If the emergence and extension of markets have been central to our understanding of modernity, the logic of marketization is even more pronounced in the analysis of late modern social and economic forms.

1

The Emergence of
Market Society

Introduction

Modern social thought arose in response to the complex transformations that produced the conditions of modernity. From at least the
eighteenth century, these transformations have been thought about in
terms of such developments as industrialization, capitalism, scientific
revolution, the rise of democracy and the modern nation-state, and
urbanization. Bound up with all of these is another overriding characterization of modern society as a market society or commercial
society: that is to say, one which was increasingly dominated in all its
aspects by the monetarized exchange of goods. The new centrality of
market exchange seemed to introduce a quite new principle of social
order, of social integration and co-ordination, that was both specific
to modern societies and tied to its most profound values. Moreover,
this new principle of social order was not narrowly economic – though
of course it was that, too – but rather promised new patterns of
political, social and cultural organization. The notion of market
society particularly marks a transition from an older order, literally
an *ancien régime*, regulated by traditional rights and obligations
rooted in ascribed status and a cosmological order (the 'great chain of
being'), to one in which social order emerges from the independent
actions of autonomous individuals. The individual's sphere of action
was circumscribed solely by their material means and the rationality
with which they could deploy their market power. Such a transition
could be understood either as the liberation of reason, freedom and
progress from the irrational constraints of tradition, or else as the
erosion of communal life and the decline of all social values that might
stand above the merely economic measure of price.

This chapter explores the emergent social features that have been central to the understanding of modernity in terms of a market society. While we can consider market exchange in relation to a range of types of exchange, market society is characterized by the dominance of one mode. This can be registered in the contrast between markets as places and markets as disembedded processes. As markets came to take on a central importance in the modern West, social thinkers focused on several features that seemed to typify a new social and economic order: an extensive division of labour, commodification and monetary calculation. These developments raised profound issues concerning individual freedom, social values and political order. The latter part of the chapter maps out some of the initial positions taken up within modern social thought, particularly in terms of the relationship between the individual and society.

Markets and exchange

Social life – indeed, human life – is inconceivable without exchange: people are not – nor do they want to be – self-sufficient monads who produce for themselves all that they need or desire. At the limit case, social reproduction depends on the complex forms of domestic provision that allow infants to survive to adulthood: we *give* our children food. The social forms that exchange may take are enormously diverse, not only historically or cross-culturally, but at any one moment within a culture. Today I might filch some stationery from work, buy food at the grocery store, pay my mortgage by direct debit, invite some friends round for a dinner that reciprocates one they gave me last week, lend money to a friend, donate to a charity through a sponsored bike ride, carry on an email correspondence, get my salary paid, pay my kids' allowances, be paid by the thousand words for a magazine article while submitting a paper (unpaid) to an academic journal in the hope of promotion, and pay for a shareware licence over the Internet by cybercash or credit card. The list is seemingly endless, and yet all the items on it belong together as recognized ways in which things and services are passed along between social members.

Indeed, a complete categorization of a society's modes of exchange (just like a categorization of the material culture that is exchanged) would give us a rather vivid map of a particular social order, of its social relations and networks, values and meanings, ethics and cultures. A person's involvement in the full 'repertoire' of exchange types – as Davis (1992) calls it – can also tell us something about what it means to have a 'full life' or to be a 'whole person' in a particular society: 'In my view it is this image of what a whole person is, and the desire to be considered good of one's kind, that leads us to try to be market-wise in commerce, reciprocal with our friends, a little bit charitable, and altruistic up to a point' (p. 46). Conversely, to define all social life in terms of one sort of exchange alone – to be entirely altruistic or to quantify *all* social transactions in profit/price terms – would be deemed pathological.

Moreover, these different forms of exchange are appropriate to quite different social relationships that they each play a part in reproducing or affirming: to do a favour for a friend is different from selling a service to a client, and a dispute over whether what I did was a favour or a service is always also a dispute over whether our relationship is friendship or commerce. Modes of exchange are therefore central to reproducing particular patterns of relationships, and co-ordinating social identities, functions and actions. The exchange of goods, services, information and other social forms links people up in culturally specific ways. At a more global level, a society in which, say, personal services predominate over commerce will have not only a different economy, but a quite different social order. Anthropologists have produced a huge literature on societies in which goods tend to be circulated in terms of kinship relations (see chapter 4). As noted, this does not mean that other forms of exchange are not also present, but it does mean that the bulk of economic and social life is co-ordinated by family ties rather than, say, market transactions between independent individuals. These different modes of exchange are important not only in distributing resources and meeting material needs, but in promoting certain ways of understanding social relations and values.

From this perspective, thinking about modern social order in terms of 'market society' implies the primacy of one mode of exchange – based on market transactions – which has come to dominate, restructure or marginalize all others. The real extent of this dominance is disputable. On the one hand, market behaviours and institutions are themselves quite various, rather than reducible to a single type. On the other hand, a wide range of other forms of exchange persist in modern societies (in households, public and non-profit bodies and social networks), which can significantly mediate market relations (Carrier 1994; Gibson-Graham 1996). Whether total domination by market exchange gives an accurate picture of contemporary social life is therefore dubious, but the point is that it represents a specifi- cally *modern* view of social action and relations. The idea that modern social order is dominated or even defined by market relations has been a central preoccupation of modern social thought, generally supported by what Carrier (1997) has called 'the Market Idea'. By this he means that representations of the market – the 'meanings of the market' – have had a central role in organizing the modern West's conceptual and normative universe. Indeed, Carrier argues that the market idea is central to western 'cosmology' – the way in which normative notions of social actors, actions and institutions are organized as modern social myths. The power of such myths, for instance, has been especially evident in the neoliberal restructuring of advanced capitalist and transitional economies since the 1980s.

Marketplaces and markets

One way of tracing the transition to market society is via a distinction between marketplaces and more abstract modern markets. 'Marketplaces' are visible public events that happen at a regular time and place, with buildings, rules, governing institutions and other social structures: the marketplace is what happens under the market cross or in the covered market square every Saturday morning in a market town, or in the floor of a bourse or exchange, or on the school car park that hosts a car-boot sale every weekend, or in the extensive architecture of a shopping mall. The spatial and temporal location of marketplaces is a crucial feature; indeed, the geography of market timing and location is a significant area of study in its own right, particularly in the form of 'central place theory' (Plattner 1989; Smith 1983), which looks at how markets are spatially distributed in order to concentrate a maximum of demand given the time and transport costs involved for dispersed populations in getting to markets at given distances.

Marketplaces are found in an extremely wide range of societies, both historically and globally, and seem both to be embedded in their particular culture and to comprise very diverse forms of exchange and interaction, only some of which are simply commodity transactions. By contrast, with the rise of modern markets, as we shall see, the very idea of a market comes to be detached from particular places and people and takes on ever more abstract senses such as 'demand', 'opportunities for buying and selling' and 'the trade in a specified commodity' (all from the *Concise Oxford Dictionary*). Such formulations point to the market as a conceptual space, to the ways in which consumers, economists or enterprises might map out the world of exchange in terms of their own commercial aims. In other words, the modern market seems to comprise a single, economic form of exchange that transcends any particular cultural setting.

A marketplace, on the other hand, is never simply a meeting of buyers and sellers. Being an embodied event, it always has a specific cultural character, and involves a multitude of social actions and relations. The social density and richness of the marketplace unfolds on a number of levels. First, as the congregation of a populace, market-goers may conclude a vast range of business other than exchanging commodities: for example, Braudel (1982) notes that many kinds of legal contracts (such as marriage contracts) and processes were concluded on market days, thus providing a business opportunity for lawyers, letter-writers and notaries. The marketplace as a congregation of a public also provides a place for political and religious communications (for example, proselytising and rabble rousing) as well as flows of information and gossip that may be consequential in political, social or commercial terms.

Second, this range of activity testifies to what Shields (1992) dubs the 'social centrality' of the marketplace: the market focuses the attention of a wide range of individuals, each pursuing diverse interests and desires, on to a place that they identify with the public life of the locality. This focusing of the attention of the market crowd can be thought of in terms of both amenities and spectacles (Slater 1993). For example, the marketplace is often seen as a cornucopia, drawing a wealth of goods from all over the world, orchestrated into a vast range of images and sensations, and indeed often providing a utopian image of a world beyond scarcity. The goods are themselves presented spectacularly, drawing attention through the hawker's songs or calls, through display, advertising or demonstrations that are also theatrical performances or the salesperson's artful conversations and the ritualized agonistics of bargaining. The sense that all the goods of the world come to the market, as well as traders from far afield, constitutes the market as both an exotic and a dangerous place (Agnew 1986), a representation of the strangeness yet wondrousness of the world as seen through the 'dream world' of circulating things and people (Williams 1982). Moreover, the attractions of the marketplace make it seem a spontaneous and rather explosive congregation of crowds. They seem to spring up at any opportunity and then gather ever-larger crowds until they become problems of public order. For example, whenever the Thames froze over in the eighteenth century, there was an immediate appearance of entertainers and stalls selling food, drink and trinkets.

Third, marketplaces emerge in often complex relationship to local urban governance. For example, marketplaces come to the fore in European history with the general revival of trade, politics and communications in the twelfth century, after which, in England, large numbers of Royal Charters to hold markets were granted. Some of these grants gave legal recognition to existing, unofficial markets. Others gave a local political or ecclesiastical ruler the right to establish a new marketplace to support a more recent population centre, or even to construct a new town by building a fixed market-place with attached houses, workshops and shops. Either way, as Braudel (1981: 479) put it, 'No town is without its market, and there can be no regional or national markets without towns . . . : the town in other words *generalizes* the market into a widespread phenomenon.' Possession of a market charter gave the local ruler a very wide range of advantages, including the ability to provision a growing urban centre, lucrative revenues (tolls, duties and taxes, rents on stalls) and an extension of regional power through the legal privileges that flowed from market ownership. Marketplaces are never 'free markets', but involve regulations, prohibitions and policing functions which, in European history, provided an important basis for local law making and enforcing, for establishing local courts and policing. Yet, at the same time that the marketplace pioneered forms of aristocratic freedom and power, it was also the forging ground for bourgeois civic freedoms: town-based crafts, commercial and trade enterprises and financial services all involved freedoms of movement, information and interaction that were foreign to the feudal system.

Fourth, although marketplaces are bound up with local culture, identity and power, they are also 'liminal' spaces, as Agnew (1986) puts it; they are the point at which the community is permeable. Foreign merchants – especially members of the great ethnic and familial trading networks, such as Jews and Armenians – come and go, able to escape local surveillance and accountability: they can always disappear into the exotic nowhere land from whence they and their goods appeared. The merchant appears throughout litera-ture as a trickster, a figure of comic or admirable guile, but also more dangerously as one who profits by famine and disaster, or one who brings along with his foreign goods the contagion of foreign ideas and religions, desires and luxuries, and the corruption represented by cosmopolitanism in a world regulated by local loyalties. At the same time, the local population of buyers on entering the market also enters a liminal space in which local norms and scrutiny are loosened, a place of liberty and licence, of desires and fun: hence carnivalesque disruptions are events of the marketplace (Bakhtin 1984; Stallybrass and White 1986).

Fifth, the marketplace is always both dangerous and highly regulated, as we have indicated, involving policing, regulation and law or enforced custom. The kinds of protections or prohibitions commonly secured by marketplaces and their courts are significant: policing against adulteration, forestalling, engrossing and regrating (offences by which middlemen manipulated market supplies and prices), and enforcement of fair or just prices (Braudel 1982: 30; also Adburgham 1979: 18). Many of these regulations aim to secure adequate provision for a population in times of shortage or even famine: the fury over the high prices that might result from engrossment are intimately connected, well into the nineteenth century, with the fear of actual starvation, or the fear that merchants may not only take advantage of shortage, but actually create it through hoarding. Hence many traditional markets were regulated to ensure provision, at just prices, to the local population: for example, in Preston market, 1795, 'none but the town's-people are permitted to buy during the first hour, which is from eight to nine in the morning: at nine others may purchase: but nothing unsold must be withdrawn from the market till one o'clock, fish excepted' (Thompson 1971: 84; see also Randall and Charlesworth 1996).

A final aspect of marketplaces is their very publicness. There is a generally egalitarian imagery attached to the marketplace: all classes of people have access to it and might rub shoulders there. Moreover. marketplaces – such as the ancient Greek *agora*, which is defined as both marketplace and place of civic assembly – may combine economic, political and social senses of the public. Of course, different money resources entail quite different kinds of participation in marketplaces. The apparent democracy of the market is often belied by the hierarchical differentiation of shopping spaces: for example, there may be differentiated spheres of exchange in which certain kinds of exchange are legally restricted to certain classes of people; or there may be different marketplaces catering to different sectors of the population. Samuel Pepys' diary records that he spent much of his day moving between the Royal Exchange and the shops in Westminster, both of which provided him with luxury goods (stationery, fine clothing) as well as political and commercial 'intelligence'. This was an entirely different kind of marketplace and activity ('shopping') from the provision markets for fish, meat and vegetables down by the Thames, which were the focus for the activity of 'marketing', the basis of domestic reproduction as opposed to political and commercial networking. Once, when their maid was away, Pepys and his wife went marketing in the provision markets. They made of it a kind of pastoral or masque, playing at being servant girl and lackey, a costume drama of class inversion. They were careful, however, to hire a real servant girl to carry their basket home for them, lest a neighbour might see (Adburgham 1979).

Modern markets

Marketplaces exhibit a concrete and public sociality in which exchange is embedded in localized cultural, social and political relationships. Braudel (1977) uses a distinction between this 'public market' and what he calls the 'private market' to structure his magisterial work, *Civilization and Capitalism*. In Braudel's powerful imagery, the public marketplaces formed a 'layer' or membrane stretched over the vast landscape of everyday material life, or a gate through which local actors, actions and objects passed – occasionally – into 'economic life' as opposed to self-sufficient domestic or village production. That is to say, it embedded market exchange within fundamentally non-market societies.

Braudel distinguishes this marketplace from the networks of global trade, finance, information, wholesaling and vertical integration of trading up and down lines of supply that became increasingly important to modern western society. These networks operate above, behind and between marketplaces and are populated by quite different people and classes. These actors make up 'private markets', in the sense that they do not comprise a public assembled in full view of each other and in direct communication. Rather, their connections, meetings and activities are largely hidden from those who cannot operate at this level. Indeed, Braudel characterizes the private market in terms of economic behaviours that concern long 'chains' of supply and circulation – an Antwerp merchant linking Chinese silk to the Parisian court via Spitalfields workshops. These merchants, financiers and commercial explorers see the world from a God's-eye view, operate across economic sectors and regions, and talk directly with political rulers. They meet each other in fairs, exchanges and courts, later in clubs and boardrooms, rather than in marketplaces or streets. But they are – Braudel argues – the engine of modernization, the market level at which capital, energy, facilities and techniques gather into the critical mass of modern capitalism.

There is 'no simple linear history of the development of markets' (Braudel 1982: 26). Nonetheless, the centre of power increasingly passes from local, public marketplaces to the ever more sophisticated private markets. Discussing the English case, Braudel argues that the expansion of London markets to draw on all of England plus foreign trade led to the dislocation . . . of the traditional open market, the public market where nothing could be concealed, where producer-vendor and buyer-consumer met face to face. The distance between the [public and private market] was becoming too great to be travelled by ordinary people. The merchant, or middleman, had already, from at least the thirteenth century, made his appearance in England as a go-between for town and country, particularly in the corn trade. Gradually, chains of intermediaries were set up between producer and merchant on the one hand, and between merchant and retailer on the other; . . . Traditional habits and customs were lost or smashed. (p. 42)

Braudel traces this spread of the private market firstly through the great fairs that culminate in the sixteenth- and seventeenth-century currency and credit markets in Antwerp, Frankfurt or Besançon. Often the public/private market division takes a literal form at such fairs: while the public enjoys the visible spectacle of an international jamboree of things and entertainments, the international merchants meet behind closed doors to settle payments and bills of exchange, to make markets in currencies, or to circulate funds that might furnish voyages of discovery and trade or might, through Genoese financiers, pay off a king's creditors or sustain his military adventures.

The fairs themselves were in decline by the seventeenth century, giving way to more sophisticated private institutions such as banks and stock markets that, from the eighteenth century onwards, increasingly constitute, as Braudel puts it (1982: 136), an *anti-market*, a range of activities operating in parallel to 'the ancient nucleus of trade, which they crush'. In many respects this shift in the centre of economic gravity from public to private markets is a move of increasing abstraction, a move from the marketplace as concrete and embodied to the market as a conceptual, strategic, abstract space of calculation and commercial opportunity. Markets could now be defined abstractly as opportunities for buying and selling: to point to a market in cotton futures or a niche market in Ferraris simply denotes the possibility of profitable transactions rather than to a specific place or time or institution. In this sense of a market, the most developed enterprise – just as in the days of Fugger – is the financial capitalist, whose money is ever fluid, moving rapidly from opportunity to opportunity, committed to no use value, loyal to no community or ruler. Certainly this is how economics tends to see the market, as do business and management studies, marketing and other forms of market knowledge: a structure of supply and demand that can be quantified and mapped, a space of calculation. Moreover, the modern abstract market is not visible as an event, but constituted through an instrumental gaze concerned with 'opportunities to buy and sell'. For example, the concept of 'marketing' later develops as a set of practices, organizational forms and discourses that operate to 'make markets', to co-ordinate distribution channels, product identities, sales forces, media, public relations, retailers and so on.

To be clear, the private market must be grounded in very concrete practices and events: the most abstract financial markets, like the old medieval fairs, are embodied in particular trading rooms with particular architectures, modes of communication and sociality, technologies of information flow, means of socializing informally and formally, bonds of trust, honour, obligation and so on (Callon 1998a; Lazar 1990). Nonetheless, these modern senses of the market involve a quite different organization of economic action from the old public marketplace. Indeed, the distinction between public and private markets, or marketplaces and modern markets, is fraught with ironies. Above all, although the private market appears to be the engine and exemplar of modern capitalist market society, it offends against basic principles of the 'market idea' in ways that the traditional or archaic marketplace does not. On the one hand, although the public market involves intensive regulation, it is nonetheless based on 'transparent exchanges' between a large number of buyers and sellers, none of whom is able to dominate the market for long. Hence, although ancient, the public market could be construed as based on open competition between autonomous individuals rather than collusion between connected ones, and hence closer to the modern model of a market. The private market, on the other hand, emerges from attempts to escape precisely the kinds of regulation that made public markets competitive and transparent: access to the private market is restricted, and membership comprises a limited number of large merchants and financiers who know each other and who operate behind the back of the competitive market by buying directly from producers at the point of production or in inns (rather than on the market like everyone else).

Braudel likens his distinction between public and private markets to the conventional eighteenth-century distinction between natural and artificial markets. For example, at the birth of modern economic liberalism, Adam Smith, although noted for his robust advocacy of the repeal of all restrictions on free trade, makes this argument on decidedly traditional grounds: 'Consumption is the sole end and purpose of all production and the interest of the producer ought to be attended to, only so far as it may be necessary for promoting that of the consumer' (Smith 1991 [1776] II: 155). The consumer that Smith has in mind is the local populace that relies on the marketplace for basic necessities such as grain and that has an ancient hatred and distrust of anyone who gets between the farmer and the citizenry. Middlemen, as we have noted, were traditionally seen as bloodsuckers and privateers, who drove prices up by creating artificial scarcity and who operated at a global level that allowed them to make unearned profits from arbitrage (taking advantage of price differences between markets). On the same grounds, Smith is concerned that there should be no collusion between producers or middlemen, as expressed in his famous statement: 'People of the same trade seldom meet together, even for merriment and diversion, but the conversation ends in a conspiracy against the public, or in some contrivance to raise prices' (Smith 1991 [1776]: 117). Although, as he goes on to say, no law can prevent this, some laws encourage it. Smith therefore opposes guilds and corporations, as well as public registers of traders which will make them known and accessible to each other. Here again, Braudel's private market – the engine of capitalist reorganization of the world – may be associated with artificial prices and collusion against the public, whereas the more ancient marketplace provides a normative model of economic co-ordination.

While the private market becomes an engine of modernization and central to a new social order, what happens to the marketplace? It could be argued (see, for example, Slater 1993) that the public market persists in the realm of consumption, shopping and retailing. It is part of the spectacle of modern economic and social life: it persists in the themed shopping mall (Ritzer 1999), in the simulation of market-like imagery in the supermarket, in the transformation of the market stalls into the different counters of a department store. That is to say, images drawn from the marketplace become the basis for arcades, emporia, department stores, supermarkets and now shopping malls, all of which draw upon the vivid profusion of goods, the gathering of crowds, the range of spectacles and entertainments, the immediacy of markets. Modern shopping spaces often do this through conscious replication of market spaces: for example, the replication of the oriental market in the 'chaotic-exotic' displays of nineteenth-century department stores (Williams 1982); or the medievalist organicism of the postmodern shopping mall (Jameson 1984). At the same time, this new concretization of market experiences can also be seen in terms of extreme abstraction: behind the department store or mall most definitely stand the private markets for finance and capital, the strategic calculations of the marketers and urban planners, the networks of power-brokers. As opposed to the early modern period that concerned Braudel, or Adam Smith for that matter, the connections between the public and the private market may well be more direct today: the shopping mall or high street, and their chain-store tenants, are likely to be owned by large-scale organizations. Indeed, there must be few people in the world unable to draw a straight conceptual line from their local Mc-Donald's to the huge multinational empire that owns it, if not beyond that to rainforests, global warming and global inequalities. On the other hand, these lines of sight may well be quite obscured: it took massive publicity campaigns to begin building a public understanding of the connections between Nike's participation in the market for street style and Nike as a massive recruiter of sweated labour from the Third World (Ross 1997).

From marketplace to market society

Whereas marketplaces can be seen as embedded within local social orders, the extended market system seemed to operate at a higher level, above and across any particular social settings. What is meant, then, by 'market society' in this context? The basic image in much modern social thought is founded in a sharp opposition between traditional and modern society, often characterized in such binaries as status versus contract, *Gemeinschaft* versus *Gesellschaft* or community versus corporate order. In these conceptions, premodern life is governed by values largely derived from outside the economic order, such as status, lineage, kinship and religion. These place the sources of social value not in the individual, but in communal social forms that extend over time and generations. Though often romanticized in notions of organic or natural community, they were also understood within Enlightenment thought as fundamentally irrational and oppressive. By contrast, emerging market spheres of action were seen as both rational and oriented to the individual. The market was therefore paradigmatic of new principles of action and order in which the individual acted independently in the pursuit of his (*sic*) self-defined desires and values, unrestricted by received or social obligations. He did so, moreover, by rationally calculating and allocating his own interests and means.

Traditional social order can be characterized in terms of fixed and ascribed relationships between people, along the model of status. Formally, at least, one could neither choose nor buy one's status; one was born into a rank, a place within a communal order to which particular sources of income and styles of life were 'naturally' appropriate. Exchange relations within the status order therefore followed lines of historical lineage and obligation: for example, relationships of patronage within households (including the extended ones of the powerful), and ancient rights and obligations between lords and their dependants, and between landlords and their tenants. The payment of dues to one's superiors, and their obligations to inferiors, were forms of exchange that both economically and symbolically reproduced a status order. Not only were social relationships conceptualized as fixed but so too were forms of property: the idea that land could be sold – literally, that it was 'alienable' and could be separated from the current possessor – was anathema, a betrayal of the fixed order, in that the possessor was seen not as an owner but merely as one embodiment of an ancient relationship of lineage to land.

The transition to market society was revolutionary in the way that social obligations came to be mediated by contract. Parties to a market transaction are individuals who enter into a limited agreement, of their own choosing. Indeed, a contract entered into under duress is legally void. It involves stated obligations; once the terms of the contract are honoured, the parties go their separate ways with no further obligation. Whereas status relationships are *reproduced* through the meeting of obligations, contractual relationships (at least in principle) are thereby *ended*. The individuals simply go on to make further contracts with whomever they wish. As a principle of order, market contracts are not only individual but impersonal. The only social relationship they affirm is the formal freedom of individuals, rather than the place of those individuals within a cultural order. Moreover, the role of money is crucial in this kind of relationship, for it marks the extreme point of 'alienation' in the traditional sense: not only can any good be sold, but it can be translated into formal terms of calculation – can be given a price or monetary value. Land, to use the earlier example, is not only divorced from lineage, but can be reduced to an abstract value, another form of capital.

Whether these new principles were seen as progress or corruption, they were generally understood, from at least the late seventeenth century onwards, as inevitably corrosive of the old order. If anyone could buy or sell anything simply according to their own desire and means, then no status obligations could conceivably survive. Nor could the values underlying the old order (tradition, honour, religion) resist the rule of economic values of price and money. The eighteenth and nineteenth centuries were rife with fears and hopes about the levelling character of the market society; about the ability of anyone with money to buy things like land, titles, culture, education, mobility, power and all the other goods that had previously been allocated through a quite different order. Indeed, the first half of the eighteenth century was preoccupied with market society as a kind of collective insanity, exemplified by financial bubbles and market hysteria; and nineteenth-century novelists such as Dickens often structured their narratives around the sudden fall of bourgeois to pauper, or rise of clerk to magnate, that was consequent on a financial speculation or business venture.

In marking the contrast between traditional and modern market society, modern social thought foregrounded three key features that seemed definitive of the emerging social order: the division of labour, commodification, and monetarization and calculation. We will take each of these in turn.

Division of labour and social integration

Adam Smith famously noted that the growth of markets depended on the extent of the division of labour, on the sheer scale of separated yet interdependent productive operations that must be co-ordinated via trade. In fact, the term 'division of labour' points to two different developments. On the one hand, an increasing *social* division of labour means that in place of the production of numerous different goods by one unit – say, a household that makes clothes, grows food, brews beer, etc. – there are numerous different units each specializing in one commodity: each unit trades the single good it produces for the other goods it needs. Specialized production is associated with increased productivity (through greater efficiency, scale and skill), but also with increased interdependence: each unit *depends* on mechanisms such as markets through which they can exchange with other actors.

On the other hand, an increasing *technical* division of labour means that the work process within a production unit – say, the making of clothes – is divided up into specialist operations, each to be carried out by a single person. This process has to do with rational planning and control of labour processes, and is in many senses more a consequence than a cause of marketization, as producers seek to increase productivity and efficiency in order to be more competitive in markets. However, the huge increases in output brought about by the technical division of labour mean that firms need to sell more goods and they therefore seek more and larger markets. The classic case is Fordism, in which the intensive rationalization of assembly-line production was linked to the need for mass consumption markets and marketing.

The idea that a division of labour entails interdependence, and that all these specialized units are connected through market exchange, promotes the view that markets are a means for achieving social and economic integration. Figures as divergent and even opposed as Montesquieu and Adam Smith in the eighteenth century, Durkheim in the nineteenth century, and Simmel and Hayek in the twentieth century have all argued that, in a modern society characterized by a complex division of labour, people see themselves as both more individual (characterized by their specialized social functions) *and* more connected to each other. As Hirschman (1977) has argued, many of these thinkers consequently understood the market as a vehicle for achieving a society of peaceful co-operation. Indeed, a number of nineteenth-century thinkers used organic or ecological metaphors to analyse market society. The specialized parts within the division of labour fit together functionally, like the organs of a body, in order to make a functioning whole. In other words, such views of market society stressed social integration rather than competition. Similarly, market co-ordination of an intensified division of labour is identified with the geographical spread of markets as systems of economic co-ordination. Merchants operating across often vast distances between local markets have been a feature of most historical periods: for example, bringing high-priced luxury items such as spices or silks, taking advantage of price differences and local scarcities. However, such merchants historically served urban elites rather than reaching deeply into local populations. Market society, on the other hand, is identified with developments that routinely interconnect markets and economic activity on a global scale: the development of facilities such as transport and communications, money instruments, packaging and branding, retail policies and infrastructures that allow firms to treat wide regions as single selling spaces.

These developments were driven not only by the desire to sell an increased output of goods within an ever more complex division of labour to ever larger markets, but also by the need to procure raw materials and components for ever more rationalized production processes. The development of modern markets is closely tied to the 'discovery', conquest and colonization of the world by European empires, as in the complex and far from peaceful division of labour in the Atlantic trade which knitted together geographically dispersed sites of (slave) labour supply, raw materials and manufacture. The contemporary legacy of such a history – the North–South divide – also takes the form of trade that integrates regions on the basis of a division of labour between raw materials producers, dispersed manufacturers and service and financial enterprises. In other words, the relation between markets and the division of labour was not just part of a story of social integration, but also a story about new global social orders based on institutionalized power and domination.

Capitalism and commodification

While the concept of division of labour stresses the market as a mechanism based on social and technical interdependence, market society has also been understood in terms of the systemic drive to profit and accumulation that is typical of capitalism. Although markets are compatible with basically non-capitalist economic systems, these tend to be marginal or unofficial. For example, owing to low levels of division of labour, productivity and monetarization, the vast majority of a population may only infrequently purchase from the market and then only luxuries or specific manufactured or raw materials (tools or seeds, for example).

However, it is impossible to conceive of capitalism without markets. The classic Marxist formulation is as good as any in this context: whereas 'primitive' modes of production may involve market exchange at their fringes, this generally involves the marketing of surplus goods – that is, goods which were not produced *for* market exchange (as commodities) but rather are simply surplus to a need for which they were originally produced. Marketplaces throughout the world are filled with (generally) women who lay out before them a few tomatoes, some plantain, a half kilo of rice, etc., which they market for some cash or for goods they do not produce domestically. Production, however, is not oriented to the market (and is therefore not generally reckoned in money terms).

Capitalism, on the other hand, is entirely oriented to production for the market with the purpose of making a profit. Interestingly the word 'capitalism' had very little currency in western thought until after Sombart's (1902) *Modern Capitalism* (see Berger 1986: 18); Marx rarely used the word, Adam Smith not at all. The word 'capital', on the other hand, has a long and busy history from the twelfth century onwards (and 'capitalist', as an owner of capital, from the seventeenth century). Defined as 'the stock (including property and equipment) and/or money used for carrying on a business' (*Chambers*), capital comprises either goods converted into money or money converted into goods, and which is 'productive'. That is to say, capital is a sum of value which is not consumed, but which circulates through cycles of production and exchange in order to create ever more value. Capital must continually change form: for example, from money into means of production into a stock of produced commodities and back again into (hopefully) more money realized through the sale of those goods. Hence, capital indicates a close integration of production and marketization.

The significant move here is not to capitalism simply as a preponderance of market activity, but rather to the entrepreneur's calculation of 'capital' as productive wealth across a reproductive cycle that ineluctably includes markets. For Marx, markets constituted the 'leap' that every capitalist dreads, the moment in which they attempt to realize through sales all the capital put at risk through investment in production. Indeed, theories of monopoly capitalism (Galbraith 1972, most famously, but also Marxists such as Lenin, Luxemburg, Baran and Sweezy 1977 [1966], and Mandel 1976) focus largely on the ways in which capitalists seek to control or evade this terrifying moment, to control or bypass markets, to administer prices or to gain political patronage so as to evade market competition altogether.

The relation between capitalism and markets foregrounds the fact that all factors of production – labour, land and capital – become treated as commodities that can be competitively bought and sold on markets with a view to reducing costs and increasing profit and productive wealth. Hence, the history of modern markets is bound up with not merely the functional specialization of productive activities, but also the commodification of all that goes into these activities. This means attending to what Marx called the social relations of production that lay beneath the market itself. Modern thought, and not just the Marxist tradition (see also feminist work on the decoupling of paid 'productive' work from the household, such as Jennings 1993; Nicholson 1986), has placed central importance on a major historical shift from household production for domestic consumption to a situation in which household members work for employers in exchange for wages; they are therefore said to secure the livelihood of themselves and their co-dependants by 'selling their labour' as a commodity within the labour market, rather than producing goods that satisfy their own immediate needs. This development is itself part of a broader separation or dispossession of people from the means of production. Unable to produce their own goods for immediate consumption, modern workers (or their 'breadwinners') must sell their labour on labour markets in exchange for the cash to purchase goods on consumer markets.

Labour and land (which, as we have seen, is increasingly 'alienable') become as fluid, mobile and competitive as is capital itself, and are regulated through the market mechanism rather than traditional social structures. Hence, modern labour markets can be traced back to changes in agricultural tenures such as the abolition of serfdom, allowing for both freedom of movement off the land and extraction of money rents, and the enclosure of previously public lands, providing the basis for large agricultural enterprises as well as producing landless labourers to work for them or to move on into industrial wage labour. These developments can be seen as part of a process of liberalization, deregulation and modernization: employment relations are decoupled from personal or customary obligations, from status, from ties to land or community, such that the labourer is 'free' to sell his or her labour anywhere to anyone at the going market price. But what is experienced as liberalization by some is a new apparatus of compulsion for others, a loss of traditional rights, protections and securities, a gain in others' rights to exploit one (Randall and Charlesworth 1996). As a commodity sold in markets and possessing no productive capital itself, labour has to compete for wages, can be hired or fired according to market conditions, and must fit into rationalized work processes over which it has little or no control. Finally, under capitalism, the price of labour (its wages) is linked to market competition between workers and not to the profits that are made on labour's products, which Marx theorized in terms of the notion of exploitation (see chapter 3).

In looking at market society primarily as a capitalist society, modern thought focuses on the formal deregulation whereby all factors of production are 'free' to compete on markets, seeking to maximize their profit or wages. At the same time, the condition of that formal freedom is a dispossession of the means of production, which creates profound market inequalities and compulsions: workers simply do not compete on the same terms as those who own capital; women historically do not have the same access to markets as men; slavery and indentured labour indicated the willingness of market society to ignore even the formal freedoms of liberal capitalism in the drive to profit. Hence, thought about as a new social order, market society presented a Janus face of formal freedom and efficient co-ordination, on the one hand, and systemic inequality and oppression, on the other.

Finally, commodification involved more than subordinating factors of production to market competition and the profit motive. The idea of a market society means that more things in general are exchanged through market processes and institutions. It is no doubt significant that the word 'commodity' only accrued its contemporary meaning of an *exchangeable* good' in the eighteenth century. Before that it simply meant a useful good: that is, it was defined by use value rather than exchange value (Rowling 1987: 7). This meaning is still retained in the use of 'commodity' to denote goods that are raw, generic or primary materials in production terms ('commodities markets' contain things like coffee, grains and cotton). It is in the modern period that the word 'commodity' inextricably ties useful things to market exchange. More specifically, commodification generally implies two kinds of dependency on markets: the production of things and services is profoundly governed by the need to sell things on the market; and the reproduction of everyday life and culture is governed by the need to buy things on markets. People increasingly meet their consumption needs and desires by buying commodities rather than making things themselves. This includes a range of necessities that might previously have been acquired through domestic production and skills (clothes, food, housing). It also involves the orientation of activities, entertainments, leisure and socialization around things that are bought.

It is important to recognize that modern goods can still be embedded in non-commodity relations. For example, people still give gifts and make things for their own immediate consumption. Buying commodities like groceries is the point of departure for the domestic labour of cooking a household meal for the obviously non-market, non-commodity consumption of household members. Household members may go to great lengths to decommodify things within the household. Goods may move into and out of commodity status, into different frameworks of ownership, exchange and valorization, a process that Appadurai (1986) described as 'the social life of things'. An object such as a wedding ring or heirloom passed down through the generations may be regarded as non-alienable from the personal relationships in which it is embedded, except in the most extreme case of need. Yet the notion of the social life of things equally implies that under capitalism *any* thing could at some point in its existence be sold or considered as a commodity. It would be hard to deny that a central pressure of modern life is the always *potential* commodification of any object, event or action. Anything – literally including one's mother – really could be sold, could find a price (indeed, Hardy's *The Mayor of Casterbridge* starts with a man selling his wife on market day). Marketization spreads through inventive ways of commodifying things that are not normally viewed as alienable (water, air), and by transforming into saleable objects social phenomena which were not previously framed in that manner (advice, love, care).

We can talk about some of the cultural consequences of these developments through the notion of 'market mediation'. Modern production and consumption are increasingly the production and consumption of commodities; therefore crucial aspects of social reproduction are mediated through market processes. For example, because most of the goods we consume are not only produced but also *designed* (given cultural form) by profit-seeking firms, we therefore carry out much of our everyday life using a material culture that is governed by market interests rather than directly by our own needs. This mediation may be associated with domination and alienation, in that the relationship between needs and goods is not direct but managed by market-oriented enterprises. On the other hand, as discussed in chapters 6 and 7, it can be argued that people creatively appropriate the products of capitalism: it is in the process of consumption that we take the enormous objective outpouring of capitalist production, mediated to us through market processes, and attempt to assimilate it within our everyday life on our own terms (see Miller 1987, 1995; Slater 1997a; Willis 1990). Whichever position is taken, market mediation has often been perceived as inexorable or irresistible, indeed as epitomizing the globalizing power of modern western capitalism. If anything can be bought or sold, then there is a constant movement from cultural or other social values to economic value. On this basis alone, market society has been widely understood as corroding other value systems.

Money and calculation

Significant marketization – the permeation of market exchange as a social principle – is associated with the spread of monetarization. Of course, market exchange may take the form of barter (direct exchange of goods); and large swathes of contemporary exchange activity – informal economy, black markets – may take the form of non-monetarized exchange, or use quasi- or unofficial moneys (see, for example, Ledeneva 1998). Nonetheless, we associate the extension of market relations as a mode of social order with various facilities that money instruments provide and which have been institutionalized over the modern period. Money, conventionally, may act as a medium of exchange, as a store of value, as a unit of account and as a means of payment. It therefore 'acts both as a lubricant of exchange and as an independent expression of value' (Leyshon and Thrift 1997: 5; see also Dodd 1994). Not all forms of money perform all of these roles equally well (this is one reason why there are always many co-existing forms of money); nor can we define 'money' as such purely in terms of abstract economic or market functions (see, for example, Zelizer 1997, 1998).

The relation between monetarization and marketization is highly complex and historically variable. For example, money and money calculation gradually enter into everyday life through the process of commodification, as people come to depend more on markets than domestic production for their consumption goods, and they become increasingly dependent on labour markets for money for subsistence. This process is extremely uneven: money as such may be reserved for special kinds of goods or events (buying luxuries from a peddler or at a fair), while the rest of everyday life involves domestic self-sufficiency and personalized exchanges. Historically. there has often been desperate resistance to money as an alien, colonizing force: for example, among certain peasant communities (Taussig 1980). As Zelizer (1997, 1998) argues, the acceptance of money into everyday life is highly complex and tied to negotiated meanings. For example, the early twentieth-century incursion of money into the home required a complex framing of the meaning of that money: the transfer of money from a husband's paycheque to a wife's household budget could be treated as a payment or as an entitlement or as a gift (1997: 42). Each of these would place a very different construction on the relationships involved and on their relation to the market.

In general, monetarization is bound up with two critical developments that are equally definitive of a market society: depersonalization, and the increase of calculation and quantification. Although, as Zelizer argues, money is compatible with more personal relationships, and is itself personalized in various ways within such relationships, nonetheless monetarization is connected to broader processes of depersonalization that are inseparable from marketization. The classic formulation of this is Tönnies' (1957) distinction between *Gemeinschaft* and *Gesellschaft*, between 'community' and 'society', in the sense of an order based not on organic personal connections but on contractual and corporate links. For example, the replacement of feudal personal obligations of labour and loyalty by money payments such as taxes represents a decisive move to an order based on private individuals entering into fixed and limited contracts. Monetary payment implies that an obligation (conceived of as a limited contract) is fulfilled and hence a relationship is terminated; whereas feudal obligations based on the person are in perpetuity. Simmel (1990 [1907], 1991 [1896]) placed such depersonalization at the centre of both modern gains and problems: money released individuals from institutions and obligations that 'included the entire person' (1991 [1896]: 18): 'By paying money the person no longer offers himself, but only something without any personal relationship to the individual' (p. 22). This increases individuals' sense of objectification and alienation. Yet at the same time it places them within networks of trade and interdependence that enhance a different sense of social connectedness, as well as a sense of individuality and personal independence:

> It is precisely these types of relationship which must produce a strong individualism, for what alienates people from one another and forces each one to rely only on himself is not isolation from others. Rather, it is the anonymity of others and the indifference to their individuality, a relationship to them without regard to who it is in any particular instance. (p. 21)

The impersonality of money exchange is also tied to the notion of formal freedom and to commodification. This aspect of marketization means that people can buy whatever they have the money to purchase. The contrast is with the traditional constraints of sumptuary law (often grounded in religious prohibition) whereby the goods one was allowed to consume were restricted to those appropriate to one's status in the social order. A member of a guild or lordly household would have to wear the uniform or livery attached to their station in life. More informally, goods that formed part of an aristocratic lifestyle were not simply unaffordable by lower orders; they were also *inappropriate*. The transition to a monetarized economy in which what one could own was no longer regulated by who one was provoked or reflected a crisis sense of status disorder. For example, the comic figure of the *nouveau riche*, central to eighteenth- and nineteenth-century literature, portrayed a world in which people could buy the markers of high status (clothes, land, art, lifestyle) purely on the basis of their market and money success without the innate breeding that traditionally gave entitlement. Finally, depersonalization is also associated with a new brutality in social relationships: exchange is detached from any other way of valuing the person; the fate of the person has no bearing on the transaction.

The second development that flows from monetarization is that exchange is governed entirely by rational calculation and quantification. The appearance of money prices allows the precise quantification of alternative courses of action, so that one can assess both the costs of inputs and the magnitude of possible gains. One can therefore compare the costs and benefits of one's options, however dissimilar they might be in qualitative terms. Calculation and quantification are centrally tied to the historical rise of money and markets. They are also linked to a more general identification of modernity with rationalization processes that extend to science, law, culture and all spheres of social life (see chapter 3). The spread of this kind of instrumental rationality produces a central problematic in modern thought. Calculation and quantification, on the one hand, are associated with increased efficiency and material well-being, and the more effective solution of social and technical problems, and hence with the idea of modern progress. At the same time, to the extent that these processes involve the calculation and quantification of people, their labour and their social relations, they represent a reduction of the person to an object of calculation, to means to various ends, and to domination by impersonal forces beyond their control.

Market society and the emergence of modern social thought

These complex developments were a key focus in the emergence of modern social thought. An advanced division of labour, processes of commodification and monetarization shaped a new social order that generated quite new social issues at the level of both individual life and the nature of society itself. We can summarize these issues in the following way:

1   What was the nature of the new social actor – the formally free individual – that apparently emerges in market society? In particular, how could one conceptualize the rationality, self-interest and sovereignty that seemed to structure its actions?
2   How could social order emerge from a system based on independent individuals? Was the market a sufficient mechanism for co-ordinating their actions? What were the properties and principles of this social order?
3   How rational was this social order itself? Did an economy or indeed society based on rational individual action produce progress and efficiency, or chaos, crisis and misery?
4   What new forms of inequality and power were characteristic of a market society?
5   What social values could survive the transition from the supposed fixity of traditional order to the fluidity and formal freedom of individual choice co-ordinated by money and prices? To what extent were the values and structures of market exchange spreading to the rest of social life? To what extent, in short, was economic life coming to dominate cultural, social and political life?

In what follows, we outline some of the basic positions that developed in social thought in response to these questions.

Early liberalism

In many respects, the earliest and most direct engagement with this new order as a market or commercial society was also the most consequential for the development of modern social thought: the liberal and utilitarian tradition that embraces Hobbes, Locke, Hume, Smith, Bentham and Mill. Liberalism takes individual liberty as a normative foundation of social life and looks for mechanisms – like the market and representative democracy – that will ensure order while not compromising freedoms. This tradition has been most influential in political and economic thought, as well as psychology. It also set out the positions against which much sociological and critical social theory defined itself (as discussed in chapter 3). Whereas the liberal-utilitarian tradition has been concerned with the forms of social order that are possible or desirable in a society based on the autonomous actions of independent individuals, critical traditions have argued that such an order is anarchic, irrational, oppressive or indeed simply impossible.

In the standard definition, liberalism is generally concerned with a political zero-sum game between citizens and states in which the liberty of the former is to be defended against the interferences of the latter. In fact, there are strong arguments for understanding these political concerns in terms of a modern engagement with markets rather than states. The most famous such argument is Macpherson's (1962) contention that a deep liberal continuity resides in the notion of 'possessive individualism', which – from its inception in Hobbes' works of the mid-seventeenth century (1968 [1651]) – generated a view of humanity and political society directly out of the experience of an increasingly commercial society. Rather than founding political rights in natural law or traditional authority, Hobbes saw these as arising from the interests of isolated individuals. The possessive individual is

essentially the proprietor of his own person or capacities, owing nothing to society for them. The individual was seen neither as a moral whole, nor as part of a larger social whole, but as an owner of himself. The relationship of ownership, having become for more and more men the critically important relation determining their actual freedom and actual prospect of realizing their full potentialities, was read back into the nature of the individual. . . . Society consists of relations of exchange between proprietors. Political society becomes a calculated device for the protection of this property and for the maintenance of an orderly relation of exchange. (Macpherson 1962: 3)

Hobbes' famously cynical characterization of the state of nature as a war 'of every man, against every man', in which life is 'solitary, poore, nasty, brutish, and short' (Hobbes 1968 [1651]: 185–6), is really the conclusion of a thought experiment in which he asks: what would happen if the life of men in a commercial society were not regulated and restrained by an incontestable, sovereign authority? The 'man' whom Hobbes extrapolates from market society is an 'automated machine' (Macpherson 1962: 31) whose movements are governed by certain appetites and aversions and by the possession of certain 'powers' (such as labour power or political power) which can be alienated – sold on the market. The next step in the argument – that men require a sovereign power over them, which they establish contractually by surrendering some of their own power – assumes rational individuals who recognize their own best interest in the proper regulation of the competitive market in power.

This connection between self-interested individuals, private property and political rights became well established in liberal thought. Above all, Locke (1960 [1690]) completes the move by grounding rights in property, based on his distinctive notion of labour. It is by combining one's labour with things that one gains ownership over them, and these property rights give the individual his (sic) stake in the social and political order. As in all social contract theory, Hobbes and Locke see political society arising from the identity of interests between possessive individuals, individuals with attributes that they can freely alienate in a rational calculation of their longer-term interests: they alienate sovereignty to a legislator or governor in the interests of order. This political exchange of powers with a sovereign contrasts with, and is necessitated by, the unstinting competition and conflict of desires that arises within the marketplace and all spheres of social aspiration. From the vantage point of market competition, the appointment of a sovereign or legislator to regulate the excesses of competitive individualism appears as a 'forced' or 'artificial' identity of interests. These terms come from Halévy's (1972 [1928]) classic work on philosophical radicalism, in which he distinguishes them from a belief in a 'natural identity of interests'. In this respect, Smith departs from earlier liberal thinkers in arguing that the 'hidden hand' of the market represents a natural meshing of interests that automatically creates social order (see chapter 2). This links with arguments for the necessarily harmonious nature of capitalism based on people's interdependence within an extensive division of labour (discussed above).

If Smith represents a belief in the natural order of markets, Jeremy Bentham – founder of utilitarianism, that philosophy which gave a psychological grounding to further extensions of liberal economic and political thought through its influence both on John Stuart Mill and on neoclassical economics – was through and through a legislator. Smith and Bentham had common concern with liberty, rationality and private interests, but the 'natural harmony of interests', or social order as a self-regulating outcome of interactions, was only one strategy for furthering them. Bentham produced the most insanely rigorous rationalist psychology. In his account, people choose their courses of action through a 'felicific calculus' in which they compare the relative quantities of pleasure or pain that might arise from that action. They can express such quantities in terms of 'utility', and this utility can itself be calculated in relation to market prices: how much utility will I obtain if I spend my £10 on the two second-hand CDs I can purchase at that price as opposed to the one paperback thriller I could get for the same money (see chapter 2)? On a societal level, exchange between individuals, in which one party hands over money and the other hands over goods, operates according to these kinds of calculation made by each individual: such exchanges are really the exchange 'of a pain with a pleasure, of the pain of parting with a useful object with the pleasure of acquiring a more useful object' (Halévy 1972 [1928]: 93). But the same applies to any aspect of social order, and indeed social order can be made to arise from precisely such exchanges of pleasures and pains, though this may well require the intervention of a legislator rather than arising naturally. For example, a law-abiding citizenry will exist only if the pain of punishment outweighs the pleasure of crime. The legislator must create conditions (such as prisons) which ensure that this is how the individual's felicific calculus will indeed work out. The social good is represented simply by 'the greatest good for the greatest number' of the population. In Bentham's world, individuals simply seek to maximize their exchanges of pleasures for pains. All of social value and order is reducible to a rationalist psychology in which humans have neither any intrinsic moral sense nor even an innate sociality such as that presumed in Smith's *Theory of Moral Sentiments* (1853 [1759]), in which moral behaviour is tied to empathy and social regard.

Despite such differences between Smith and Bentham, each treats market society as both rational and natural on the basis of a particular view of human nature in which individuals are defined by their pursuit of those things which would satisfy their desires. This view of the world was not only drawn from the emerging centrality of market behaviour, but made of market behaviour the model and mechanism for achieving order and ethical life throughout society.

Methodological individualism and the division of intellectual labour

Liberal-utilitarianism did not only contribute an influential perspective and political standpoint on market society. It also clearly established certain models for the very idea of studying societies and therefore helped to create the core structures of modern social thought. Two features are crucial and set the backdrop for all that is to follow: methodological individualism, and the division of intellectual labour between the various social science disciplines.

By methodological individualism we refer to the foundation of all liberal thought: the idea that the basic unit of social analysis is not 'society' but individuals, their desires and calculations. Just as the market, in this account, is merely the sum of all the individual actions that occur (resulting in things like prices, transactions, quantities of supply and demand), so too all that goes by the name of 'society', or social structure, can be reduced to individual actions. Society, in this account, is not a thing with its own properties. In more extreme formulations, as in the neoliberal view discussed in chapter 5, society has no reality at all: 'There is no such thing as society, there are individual men and women and there are families' (Thatcher, quoted in Heelas and Morris 1992: 2).

Of the many problems with this position, modern social thought has tended to focus on two major ones. First, as discussed further in chapter 3, it is argued not only that social institutions and structures have a real existence external to the individual (even if they depend on individual actions to reproduce them), but that it is impossible to conceive of any social order without them. The classic argument, largely deriving from Durkheim, is that even the most purely instrumental contract would not be honoured unless the parties to it were ethically and legally, as well as self-interestedly, committed to it. But this presupposes a view of society as an ethical community, not just a congregation of atomized individuals. Second, methodological individualism, by starting from these atomized actors, assumes that they are formally equal as social actors and therefore ignores real structural inequalities – inequalities that have nothing to do with the different desires, capacities or rationality of the individual. Differences of gender, race and class are not accidents of birth, or incidental to social order. Rather they are institutionalized in the social order itself, not least through different kinds of market power, and therefore constrain the opportunities and fate of individuals whatever their particular abilities.

The other major methodological legacy of liberal-utilitarianism arises from the way in which it conceptualizes individuals in terms of the *rational* pursuit of their self-interest. As we will explore in subsequent chapters, this is a highly normative view of social actors as calculative agents, as people whose actions are governed by seeking the most efficient means to achieve a given end. The study of such rationality became central to modern economics, the discipline which most clearly exemplified the liberal-utilitarian world view and which understood market behaviour as entirely comprehensible within this concept of rationality. A sharp division emerged between disciplines which produced a formal analysis of rational action and those which studied the substantive culture, values and structures that governed social action in general. To the extent that economics could construe other areas of social life in terms of rational choice (as in the case of neoliberalism) or could enlist other fields such as psychology, it moved on to the terrain of other disciplines. To the extent that it could not construe social actions as rational, it divided the social field with other disciplines such as sociology or anthropology.

Oppositions and objections

With its focus on individuals and their desires as the basis for social order and explanation, the liberal-utilitarian tradition could see the market both as exemplary of human society and as a mechanism for increasing reason, freedom and progress. And yet Hobbes was immediately vilified as a crude materialist. Benthamite utilitarianism was soon identified as a 'pig philosophy' (Ryan 1987: 14) that conceptually reduced humans – indeed, *aimed* to reduce them through governmental policies – to the basest materialism, and to reduce their most noble motives – moral, spiritual, altruistic – to selfish calculation. It was also immediately recognized as an extreme point in the long rise to modern dominance of commerce, industry and scientific materialism. If nothing else, the rosy liberal view was being expounded across a period of intense structural dislocation, inequality, war and oppression.

Alternative currents in modern social thought – probably the dominant ones in sociology and anthropology and the humanities – were equally structured around responses to an emergent market society. However, here the market appears not as the apotheosis of the individual, but rather as part of an inhuman structure in which the individual is subordinated to implacable forces of supply and demand, the rule of money and profit. The market displaces individuals, removes them from richer social and cultural relationships and reduces them to being impoverished calculators or – still worse – to being the calculated means to others' economic ends. One central conceptualization of this process can be summarized as 'alienation'. Under the kinds of market transition we have outlined, modern people are alienated from a vast range of social relations within which they can properly be themselves. In various formulations, critics have argued that people are alienated from organic or traditional forms of life that are more holistic, natural, stable or meaningful than market-governed societies; from each other through market competition, calculation and depersonalization; from their own activities through dispossession from the means of production and subordination to labour processes over which they have no control and with which they cannot identify; from the products of their effort through the ownership of capital by capitalists.

Some responses to these developments can be labelled as romantic or organicist, a belief that pre- or post-market societies allow a wholeness of both individual and society. Such perspectives can be either radical or conservative (or even reactionary, as in a desire for a return to a mythic premodern past). In each case, the argument is that social life must be governed by a collective sense of order or moral community rather than by atomized and self-governing individuals. Hence, for example, eighteenth-century attempts to resist marketization by asserting a moral economy in which prices were subject to traditional rights and to the needs of the community (rather than the merchant) are echoed in Luddite resistance to machines that would destroy the older relation of labour to craft, and in contemporary movements like communitarianism which argue that the radical dislocation of the individual promoted by neoliberalism can produce only personal anomie and social disorder: social life requires shared collective values and responsibilities as well as rationally self-interested individuals.

The assertion of collective social life over market co-ordination of atomized individuals found in organicist traditions is more conventionally formulated within modern social thought in structural terms. The paradigm case is the classical sociological tradition, which starts from the assumption that social structures have some reality and determining force above – and operating upon – the individual. Far from being the harmonious orchestration of individual intentions into social order, markets are part of a social order that dislocates individuals in various ways. Firstly, the disorder, irrationality and crises attendant on both the birth of market society and its operation are seen not simply as transitional costs into a harmonious order, but as structural problems whose resolution is far from obvious or even possible. Secondly, market society involves new forms of power, inequality and oppression that are not incidental or even amenable to reform, but rather arise from the very structural principles of that society. Thirdly, liberal traditions have assumed that individuals not only are rational, but also have a clear knowledge of their own needs and of the goods that might satisfy them; this extends to the realm of political choice, in which it is assumed that people know what is in their own interest. Structural analysis has tended to argue that market society can produce forms of mystification which prevent individuals from understanding themselves, their interests or the courses of action that might promote them. Finally, the formal rationality of market behaviour is associated not with the furtherance of individual empowerment, but rather with the subjection of the individual to social structural logics.

Conclusion

The emergence of market society, then, was bound up both with major social transformations and with the rise of specifically modern forms of thought. Put simply, the idea of market society attempts to come to terms with what was understood as a new social order, based on distinctly modern principles. The market itself exemplified that order, for good and ill, being the site for such emergent features as individualism, rationality, division of labour, commodification and monetarization; and a driving force spreading them throughout the social world. If market forms were crucial to broad intellectual perspectives on this changing social order, they were also to provide the focus for a more technical concern with the workings of the market as a specific institution. Chapter 2, therefore, considers the rise of economics as a mode of social thought which took the market as its distinctive object of study.

2

Markets and
Economic Order

Introduction

The previous chapter considered the market as a historical form; a type of exchange that developed in particular contexts and became integrated into a larger social and economic system. Markets were linked to the emergence of modern – and, more specifically, capitalist – modes of social and economic organization. This chapter has a more narrow concern with formal conceptions of the market, drawing on key perspectives from economic theory. It is organized around two themes: first, the market as a means of allocation and co-ordination; and second, the market as a site of social action. This is in line with our larger interest in the market as a principle of social order. Economic theories of the market, that is, have developed not only as reflections of empirical reality, or as expressions of mathematical law, but in response to enduring problems in modern social thought – notably regarding the conditions for collective order and the basis for social interaction.

We therefore understand economics as sharing in the wider aims and themes of social science. Our point is not to counterpose economic accounts of the market to perspectives that stem from another field called 'social theory', but to view economics as itself a species of social thought. Economic theories and models are inescapably social theories and models, even if the partition of economic science from other spheres of social inquiry has at times been very pronounced. This chapter does not exhaust economic approaches to the market (for valuable discussions see Hodgson 1988; Lane 1991); rather it considers how key perspectives on markets offer accounts of social order and agency. We start by outlining a basic model of the market, as a point of reference for the different perspectives that follow. The discussion goes on to consider arguments that markets are the most efficient basis of economic order. These begin with the founding story of modern economics – the classical political economy of Adam Smith – and his account of market exchange as securing 'harmony' between atomized private interests. Smith's concern with the natural order that emerges from markets develops into modern economic claims for the market as a technical instrument of co-ordination. There are two main arguments here: the first, as typified by neoclassical approaches, centres on the conditions under which markets 'clear' to produce an optimal allocation of resources; the second, developed within Austrian school economics, argues for the dynamic nature of market processes and the critical role of competition and information. The latter part of the chapter considers critiques of these core arguments in modern economics, focusing on issues of market failure, and problems concerning the model of individual agency set out by economic theories of rational choice.

Markets and economic theory

In arguing for the continuity of economics with other fields of social theory, it is nonetheless important to stress the remarkable clarity with which economists have defined their special domain of study. The economy, though often viewed as an arcane or expert field, is generally seen as a self-evident object of inquiry. It can be harder, in contrast, to describe what sociologists or anthropologists study. In point of fact, attempts by political economists in the late eighteenth and early nineteenth centuries to analyse a distinct economic realm provided one of the first occasions for thinking about the 'social' in a modern sense. That is, the study of an emergent market economy centred on the interactions of free individuals and the roots of spontaneous order that are at the foundation of modern social science.

While all social sciences are concerned in various ways with the study of human behaviour, economics marks out its concern with specific aspects of human behaviour under particular conditions. In a textbook definition, Lionel Robbins (1935: 15) isolates economics as 'the science which studies human behaviour as a relationship between ends and scarce means which have alternative uses'. The modern 'science' of economics is one concerned with how people make choices in conditions of scarcity. An economy, in simple terms, can be understood as a network of interaction between agents, as they singly or collectively make choices about how to allocate their scarce means in pursuit of their ends. It might be noted that a market *per se* does not at this stage figure in the self-definition of economics. Modern economics begins with the necessity for people (as individuals or in groups) to make choices, rather than with assumptions about the allocative mechanisms they use to do so. An economics of markets, then, represents one – although very dominant – approach to this problem of allocation. Market forms enter the picture as individuals seek to satisfy their wants through particular kinds of interaction (competitive exchange), rather than through others (such as collective planning, self-sufficiency or centralized distribution).

Put simply, a market consists of the buyers and sellers of a particular good or service. It comprises three core elements: supply (the goods that sellers bring to market); demand (the goods that buyers wish to and are able to purchase); and price (the value at which goods are exchanged between buyers and sellers). These three formal components are interdependent. Supply does not refer simply to the quantity of goods available, but to the decisions of sellers in offering these goods for sale at given prices. Demand, in turn, is more obviously expressive of a kind of social action – the call of prospective buyers for particular types and quantities of goods at a given price. Price, thirdly, ultimately represents an agreement between buyer and seller. What are sometimes called the 'laws of supply and demand' – the way in which price works to bring supply and demand into balance – are in essence modes of human action and interaction. Let us elaborate this basic model a little further.

1   *Markets are integrated systems of exchange.* The market reduces to a central element: the exchange between buyer and seller. Markets integrate these many single transactions into a network of exchange – in principle, each transaction affects all others. In a context of scarcity (of time, resources, money), each transaction occurs at the cost of other options, actors, goods or satisfactions. It is through this complex system of exchange that economic resources are allocated, settling the basic economic questions of what is to be produced, how it is to be produced, and for whom it is to be produced.

2   *Actors pursue private interests within the market.* Economic models of the market rest on a specific kind of interaction. While markets involve a type of social exchange, the market relation (and the market as a whole) is impersonal. In principle, actors operate within markets on the basis of self-interest, they encounter each other as strangers, and the exchange relation lasts only as long as each

transaction. Buyers do not discriminate between different sellers other than on the basis of price, and vice versa.

3 Competing private interests are reconciled through agreements on price. The interests of different market actors are aligned through agreements on price – an agreed price indicates that a state of equivalence has been achieved between the interests of the buyer and those of the seller. Price in this sense acts as a neutral 'mechanism' to bring supply and demand into balance within specific exchanges, and to establish equilibrium across markets.

4 Markets are co-ordinated by price. In this basic model, the market is not an institution as such – it does not possess formal stability, structures of organization, rules or conventions of conduct. Rather it represents an extended series of exchanges, mediated and co-ordinated by the price mechanism. Price signals work to co-ordinate a dispersed range of economic activities between a diversity of individuals. The market in this way can be seen as a self-regulating or self-ordering system, rather than one subject to external controls.

5 Market behaviour is calculative. Measures of price function as the primary form of information that actors use to make their market decisions (see Hayek 1945). The reliance on price produces particular kinds of calculative behaviour on the part of market actors. Given conditions of scarcity, limited means must be deployed prudently so as to realize one's ends in an optimal manner. In market contexts, this mode of 'formal rationality' (as Weber referred to it) is oriented to price. A calculative rationality is therefore typical of market actors and of market relations in general.

We enlarge on these basic propositions over the discussion that follows. At this point, they outline an ideal-type market, one closely aligned with neoclassical approaches – what Stiglitz (1994) calls the 'standard theory' – in modern economics. This model is based on a state of perfect competition, such that the market tends towards equilibrium. It assumes that markets contain goods that are homogeneous (of the same kind and identical in quality), and that there are sufficient numbers of buyers and sellers to prevent any one actor from significantly affecting prices. Furthermore, both buyers and sellers possess complete knowledge of goods and their costs so that they can compare the different options that are available to them. Prices are established in a perfectly competitive market through the free interplay of supply and demand. Markets attain equilibrium at the point where price adjusts to bring supply and demand into balance (where sufficient quantity of a good is offered on the market to meet the demand for it at a given price). This conceptual version of a simple free market is rarely approximated in reality; however, it provides a benchmark for the study of more complex market forms. Economic analysis is concerned with a vast range of market conditions, from highly ordered markets in specific locations – such as local cattle markets presided over by an auctioneer – to extremely complicated and diffuse markets – such as those dealing in financial futures or derivatives. In these different settings, the model of perfect competition offers a technical analytic device, rather than a tight descriptive fit.

Apart from empirical questions concerning different market forms, however, the simple market model opens on to an extended set of questions of both a technical and a critical nature. Do market exchanges produce general prosperity or systematic inequality? Does the market model offer a normative or an objective account of economic relations? What realms of exchange and which human decisions are included in a market model of calculation? How does an individual come to behave rationally in a market context? Do people really *think* like this? It is around questions of this kind that economic analysis of markets bears heavily on wider social and political concerns. Such questons have been posed in various ways within different traditions of modern economic thought.

Markets and social order: Adam Smith's political economy

In an important sense, 'modern economics can be said to have begun with the discovery of the market' in the work of Adam Smith (Wilson and Skinner 1976: 113). Smith's *An Inquiry into the Nature and Causes of the Wealth of Nations* (1991 [1776]) provides a story of origins both for modern market society and for a distinctly economic manner of understanding it. At the same time, his work fits into an early modern concern with questions of social order. Smith can be placed within a tradition of thought that includes Hobbes, Locke, Montesquieu, Steuart, Rousseau and other figures associated with the Scottish Enlightenment, such as Millar and Ferguson. As we saw in chapter 1, such thinkers were engaged with the problem of how social order could be secured in a rapidly changing society. Their concern was not only with the problem of political authority over the private activities of citizens, but with the potential conflict between individual interests in the absence of traditional social and political structures. Such an interest in the relation between private interests and public order was compounded by the growth of exchange relations during the eighteenth century, and this provided a central problematic within Smith's political economy.

Smith's innovation was to construe problems of social order principally in economic terms: the basis of order, put simply, lay in economic interaction. Economic theories of the market originate in Smith's attempt to reconcile public good with individual interest – a problem that for Smith was moral and economic at the same time. His political economy in this sense responded to social questions even as it laid the foundation for a market economics. *The Wealth of Nations*, if often viewed as a before-the-event manifesto for market capitalism, was rooted in the problems of eighteenth-century political thought. Winch (1978) argues that reading Smith as an advocate of liberal capitalism depends on a *post facto* perspective on his work. Meuret, too, suggests that 'Smith's system could have remained an appealing construction' within political theory if industrial capitalism had not developed in ways 'which came to verify Smith's account (in that industrial capitalism, in its forms and effects, is closer to Smith's economy than to merchant capitalism)' (Meuret 1988: 246–7). While we lose much of the sense of Smith if we lose his continuities with earlier thinkers, his work does mark an important theoretical shift. Smith's political economy involved a rethinking of the problem of social order that turned from political and legal structures towards questions of economy. Specifically, he was to find the sources of social solidarity in the same conditions that promoted the 'wealth of nations'. As a movement away from earlier liberal theories that were largely addressed to the political role of the state, Smith saw the civil sphere of exchange as the primary domain of social order. Political economy in this way analysed a social system in which the mode of exchange was also and at the same time the mode of integration and order.

Smith begins by positing production as the source of all wealth – the prosperity of nations, he argued, relied on the productivity of labour, not on the activities of merchants. Productivity was greatly enhanced by a division of labour, where each person produced that to which they were best suited, relying on the work of others to provide for the rest of their needs. It was Smith who coined the maxim that you should never make for yourself what you can buy for less (what economists would call the principle of 'comparative advantage'). The farmer looked to the tailor to supply his clothes, just as the tailor turned to the cobbler for his shoes – just as many of us buy our bread from the supermarket on the way home from the office. The necessity to look to the work of others for the greater part of our own needs results in a system where each individual 'lives by exchanging, or becomes in some measure a merchant, and the society itself grows to be what is properly a commercial society' (Smith 1991 (1776): 20). In Smith's vision of an expansive 'commercial society', the principle of exchange is the basis of both economic and social order. While his own account draws on a folksy pre-industrial tale of farmers and cobblers, the Smithian division of labour was to form a centrepiece of both modern economic theory (as in Ricardo's argument for free trade on the principle of comparative advantage) and modern sociology (where a complex division of labour underpinned Durkheim's conception of organic solidarity). The argument in *The Wealth of Nations* rests on a simple premise: that individuals' private economic activity conduces to the general good. An advanced division of labour gives rise to a dense system of economic interdependence, such that the pursuit of private interests in a market setting leads to mutual advantage – as Smith so succinctly put it, the gain from trade is a matter of saying, 'Give me that which I want, and you shall have this which you want' (Smith 1991 [1776]: 13).

In advancing a claim for the mutual gains from trade, Smith drew on the eighteenth-century physiocratic belief that a 'harmony of interests' ordered human affairs. While seemingly guided only by self-interest, market behaviour is in fact co-ordinated as if by an 'invisible hand' to bring general benefit to all. Smith in this way twinned the physiocratic concept of natural order with a contemporary philosophical emphasis on 'interest' as shaping individual action (Hirschman 1977). His work involved a specifically economic understanding of the interests that guided individual agency. Such a conception is well expressed in his famous construction that 'It is not from the benevolence of the butcher, the brewer or the baker, that we expect our dinner, but from their regard to their own interest. We address ourselves, not to their humanity, but to their self-love, and never talk to them of our own necessities but of their advantage' (Smith 1991 [1776]: 13). The art of association in a commercial society, then, is based on the beneficial effects of self-interest. Smith's trick is to show how individual interests are not hostile to moral order and the general good, but provide their precondition in a social sphere governed by market exchange.

There is a further level on which to consider Smith's commitment to a general 'harmony of interests'. The economic order he describes is based not simply on the integration of many individual interests into a larger public; Smith also looked to a harmony of interests between different social orders and classes. Both conservative and romantic critics saw the emergent market order in the eighteenth century as involving inevitable conflicts of interest between economic classes (see Clarke 1982). Smith, however, aimed to show that exchange produced general social benefits as well as personal advantage, outlining the terms of a *détente* between different classes in market society. Specifically, he held that a common interest in economic growth was shared by the labouring classes and the emergent class of capitalist proprietors. Those involved in productive markets, whether as owners of capital or as those who sold their labour power, had a mutual interest in increased productivity and trade. What might appear as antagonistic exchange relations in a capitalist market in fact disguised a fundamental harmony of interests between the different economic actors who found their livelihoods there. While Smith's argument is typically eighteenth-century, such a claim for the general benefits of free market growth was revisited in the 1970s and 1980s, when a version of Smith's ideas was revived (notably in Britain and the United States) in support of a neoliberal 'trickle-down' theory of economic growth – a position for which Smith provided a moral as much as an economic pedigree (see Galbraith 1992: 98–105; and see chapter 5).

Smith's harmony of class interests existed not simply as a philosophical postulate, but was worked out in his theory of price. The creation of price is crucial to economic conceptions of markets, and was a source of fundamental debate in the foundation of the discipline. In analysing how prices are formed, Smith made a distinction between a commodity's 'value in use' (its utility) and its 'value in exchange' (its purchasing power in respect of other goods). This distinction was to preoccupy the very different work of Marx and the theorists of marginal utility (see below). Smith himself concentrated on the second category, 'value in exchange', which he further divided into two elements – natural price and market price. In line with his larger materialist perspective, Smith based a good's natural price on its costs of production. Price, that is, stems from the costs of the resources (of labour, land and capital) deployed in production: it therefore equals the costs of wages + rent + profits. Each product's natural price reflects the lowest possible price at which it can be sold without a loss, taking these costs into account; while its market price is the price at which it actually sells.

For Smith, in free competitive conditions the market price of a good tends toward the natural price. In this manner, market operations produce general and mutual advantage among buyers and sellers – all are paid what they are due, and pay others no more than they should. This key assumption in Smith's work, and the labour theory of value on which it was based, was the subject of intense debate throughout the nineteenth century and into the twentieth. Its implications go beyond guaranteeing a 'fair' market exchange. A cost of production model – where price is based on the interplay of wages, rent and profit – is at the same time a model of economic distribution between the classes of labour, property and capital (see Clarke 1982). Such a happy solution to problems of market distribution was to come under severe criticism from Ricardian socialists and from Marx, who argued that the costs of production equation ignored the uneven way that wages, rents and profits are themselves set in markets – and in markets that fail to price labour at its real productive value (see our discussion in chapter 3). Smith's theory of 'natural price', in these critical accounts, is no more than a quasi-technical apology for capitalist class relations, securing an economic settlement between hostile class interests. As technical as the arguments might appear, such debates have important moral and political dimensions in tying the terms of economic exchange to the larger social order of a market and a class society. In this context, Smith's accomplishment was to ground a vision of normative social order in the 'natural' workings of the economy.

From social order to market equilibrium: marginalist economics

In its concern with the economic basis of social order, Smith's political economy addressed earlier philosophical problems, and these did not disappear from the subsequent development of economic thought. Thinkers such as Ricardo, Senior, Bentham and Mill in the early to mid-nineteenth century were equally interested in how economic knowledge could inform the social and political questions of the day. However, while certain political impulses in Smith's work endured, methods of analysis greatly changed. The English political economist David Ricardo is an important figure to note here, and not simply as a successful stockbroker who became an economist, rather than (as has been the pattern in more recent times) the other way around. Ricardo's *Principles of Political Economy and Taxation* (1817) sought to develop Smith's political economy along scientific lines. This move is significant not only in marking a 'scientific turn' in economic thought, but because of how such a turn produced the market as an object of analysis. If the 'invisible hand' that seemed to guide market exchange was a passing metaphorical conceit in Smith's work, in Ricardo we find a more distinct conception of the market as a system or mechanism. While Smith understood the order established by market exchanges as an expansive 'system of natural liberty' (1991 [1776]: 9), Ricardo was more narrowly concerned with the technical order of the market itself. In particular, he sought to analyse the conditions for general equilibrium in markets, and stressed their self-regulating nature as economic systems *sui generis*. Accordingly, Ricardo saw threats to economic stability as coming from outside the market order; being caused by such factors as war, force of nature, or political intervention. In a market regulated through competition and the play of supply and demand, internal crises of overproduction and underconsumption were held to be impossible. Via Ricardo's political economy, then, the concern with social and moral order that animated Adam Smith's work translates into a more formal concern with the *inherent* order of markets.

This focus on market equilibrium was central to the development of modern economics. As a discipline, economics can be traced to the rise of 'marginal utility theory' in the 1870s. Arguably 'the first really novel big idea to emerge in economics since Ricardo' (Blaug 1985: 584), this body of thought originated with such figures as Jevons, Menger and Walras, and was later refined by economists including Alfred Marshall in Britain, Vilfredo Pareto in Switzerland, and John Bates Clark and Frank Knight in the United States. While none of these could claim the enduring public renown of an Adam Smith, their analyses formed the basis of a neoclassical 'normal economics' as this was practised throughout much of the twentieth century. Indeed, the relative obscurity of a Jevons or Menger beyond the field of economics indicates how, following the 'marginalist revolution' (Swedberg 1994: 259), economics developed as an increasingly formalist discipline that spoke less directly to a wider public sphere (see McCloskey 1994). In marking out economics as a distinct discipline, marginalism established the market as *the* primary economic institution. Richard Swedberg (1994: 259) suggests that 'though criticism can be directed at the marginalist revolution, it must be acknowledged that one of its greatest accomplishments was to conceive of the market as the central mechanism of allocation in the economy. This idea no doubt reflected the change that had gradually come about in the West: the economy was increasingly centered around markets.'

This disciplinary development involved two key shifts. First, it signalled a movement away from political economy's explicit concern with problems of social and political order, focusing instead on market exchange as the basic object of economic inquiry. Second, it saw the adoption of a mathematical approach to economic knowledge, notably in the analysis of how economic choices were made in market settings. In these respects, marginalist economics addresses problems of market order and market action as technical questions. It is from this point that modern economics can be defined as the study of choice under conditions of scarcity. However, if marginalist economics set itself a more specialized and a more technical project than that of classical political economy, it was based on a similar claim for markets as the most effective means of allocation and co-ordination. Market exchange represented the *sine qua non* of economic activity, providing the most efficient answers to the core economic questions: what is to be produced, how is it to be produced, and for whom is it to be produced?

In this way, markets provide the starting-point and centre of the economic system; the entire production and distribution process might be understood as a series of markets in labour, raw materials, land, finance capital, technology, goods and services. Market economies are co-ordinated through the decisions of many individual firms and households as they interact in a range of markets. The marginalist approach to this complex market system, however, is based on a simpler model. Marginalist accounts of the market centre on a concept of 'general exchange equilibrium', a situation where supply matches demand perfectly. Such a state is also captured in the notion of 'market clearance'. Walras explained the concept of market clearing using the analogy of the *prix crié* – the price called out by the auctioneer – to describe the way supply and demand are brought into alignment at the right price. This neat metaphor captures the central idea of marginalism: the way real markets work (or don't) can be explained using formal market models. Actual market processes can be measured against the axioms of perfect competition and general equilibrium. Social action in markets can be expressed as technical – and predictable – variables of supply and demand.

Marginalist economics in this sense represents a highly technical approach to markets, based on a conception of 'the market' as an abstract form. While there are clear antecedents for the marginalist concern with market equilibrium in Smith's approach to economic order, the moral and political dimensions of political economy are less apparent. Indeed, the technical turn that economic thought took from the late nineteenth century made it possible for economics to claim the status of a neutral science. Marginalist economists and their neoclassical inheritors have frequently stressed the value-free nature of their analysis – as in Lionel Robbins' claim that there was 'no penumbra of approbation round the concept of equilibrium, equilibrium is just equilibrium' (Robbins 1935: 143). The efficiency of the market as a mode of allocation, that is, should be seen as a *technical* rather than as a moral or political question.

Market calculation and social action

While earlier political economists linked market order to a wider social order, marginalist economics addressed market order as a more strictly technical question. Under what conditions did markets 'clear', or achieve equilibrium between supply and demand? At the same time, the marginalist approach to markets involved a distinct conception of social action in markets. The primacy of price in co-ordinating markets depended on a particular kind of calculative rationality among market actors. A technical approach to market processes was therefore twinned with a technical approach to market agents – captured most famously in Pareto's figure of *homo economicus* as a type of human 'calculating machine' (McCloskey 1994: 48). This model allows economists to analyse how individuals allocate their resources so as to maximize their economic utility. While this marks the increasing formalization of economic theory, it owed much to contemporary movements in philosophy. The marginalist emphasis on individuals' calculation of their economic utility has clear affinities with the liberal philosophies of utilitarianism and hedonism we discussed in chapter 1. These latter doctrines locate notions of the good in the individual maximization of pleasure – understood in terms of benefit, satisfaction, happiness or simply the absence of pain. In addition to these links to liberal philosophy, the new economics – with its emphasis on individual utilities and choices – appeared particularly well suited to the analysis of an emergent consumer society wherein consumption was becoming a primary economic activity (see Slater 1997a).

Marginal utility theory rests on a simple proposition about human action: individuals exchange goods so as to maximize the sum of their own utility. Economic behaviour is governed by the desire to maximize utility (or, in hedonist terms, pleasure) and to minimize disutility (or pain). Whereas our desires tend to be unlimited, however, the resources we have to satisfy them are not: people's pursuit of their utility is therefore constrained by the scarcity of their means. Within the constraints of scarcity (of goods, time, resources), the individual must make choices between available ends. Economics, then, analyses the kind of formal rationality that people use to allocate their scarce resources to maximize their desired ends. Such a definition proceeds on the following assumptions:

1 Individuals possess wants, which can be ranked in order of preference.
2 Conditions of scarcity apply, such that there are limited resources with which to satisfy individual wants.
3 In this context of scarcity, individuals make choices in order to maximize their own benefit.

We noted at the start of the chapter that economics as the study of choice under conditions of scarcity is not limited (in principle or in practice) to the study of markets. However, the model of individual utility maximization is especially well suited to market contexts because each has a critical orientation to price. In the model outlined above, economic choice is, fundamentally, a calculative process. When I go into the café on my way to work with £1 in my pocket, I can choose between a camomile tea and a newspaper, or a double espresso. In making my choice, the economist assumes, I calculate the utility of these goods in relation to price. Note that utility, here, is a formal and a relative means of expressing the different kinds of satisfaction that I derive from these items. 'Utility' doesn't refer to the peculiar pleasure of a strong shot of caffeine, the virtues of herbal tea, or my interest in reading the sports pages. Rather, it refers in a quite abstract sense to the capacity of each good to satisfy my private desires. It allows me to trade off between items that are in themselves not strictly comparable.

Say I choose to spend my £1 on camomile tea and a newspaper. If I am assumed to be maximizing, we can deduce that this combination represents the greater utility to me. In other words, private wants and subjective values are inferred from the revealed preference of objective consumer demand: that is, the actual choices that individuals are observed to make in their market behaviour. Marginal utility theory, in this move, makes a clear distinction between value and price. Whereas classical political economy had struggled to establish the relation between the material value of goods and the prices they commanded in markets, marginalist economics largely dispenses with this project. Value is not a material or objective factor, fixed by the costs of production and reflected in a good's 'natural' price. Rather it is a subjective concept, relative to different consumers of that good. The classical effort to ground prices in values was, in this view, an ill-conceived attempt to explain economic phenomena (prices) on the basis of a non-economic notion (value). In crude terms, goods in a market are worth as much as someone is willing to pay for them. Economics could say nothing about value, but supplied the technical means for analysing how prices are arrived at.

Thinking at the margin

This orientation towards price produces a particular kind of rational and calculative behaviour on the part of market actors. Centrally, the model of rational calculation is one based on how people 'think at the margin'. Economic decisions, that is, frequently involve trading off between marginal costs and benefits. Marginal calculations are applied within economics to a number of spheres of activity, from labour productivity to rates of taxation. These different applications, however, reduce to a basic model of marginal utility. Think about economic choices as representing a kind of 'auction'. Say I go to market wanting to buy a second-hand car. My first bid is £500. As the bidding goes up, I offer £600, then £750. When the price reaches £800, however, I'm no longer prepared to bid further because the car is now overpriced in relation to the utility I expect to enjoy from owning it. My key calculation takes place at the margin between £750 and £800 – at which point I exit the market. Another way to think about these calculations is in terms of the marginal utility of income. For a person on a low income – say, someone whose income is based on state unemployment benefit – the marginal utility of each extra pound of income is greater than it would be for a person with an income of £100,000: it is, as it were, *worth more* to them. For someone on a lower income, the marginal utility of extra earnings might merit working (or disutility) to obtain it, as compared to a high-earner who 'wouldn't get out of bed' for less than £500 a day. In this sense, the marginal utility of the good relates to the final unit of that good that one consumes. To someone on an income of £60 a week, the marginal utility of the final £1 will be relatively high. In contrast, for someone whose income is nearly £2,000 a week, the marginal utility of the last £1 will be relatively low. Marginal utility tends to diminish as one consumes more of a good – the first piece of chocolate cake tastes better than the fifth. In general, as the supply of a good increases, its utility decreases to a point, as Jevons had it, of satisfaction or 'satiety'.

This notion of thinking at the margin, however, does not fully explain the process of choice. The cost of a good or service to an individual is also determined by what they must give up in order to get it. In this sense, the price of a double espresso may be £1, but its cost to me also includes the camomile tea and newspaper that I chose to forgo. This is the opportunity cost (sometimes called the marginal disutility) of acquiring the good. The calculation I make about the coffee involves weighing up the benefits of a caffeine fix against its money price *and* its opportunity cost. A theory of disutility was originally applied not only to the activities of consumers, but also to the supply and price of different factors of production. For example, marginalists would see the wage (the price of labour) as partly set by the disutility involved in the worker's giving up their free time – an enduring hangover from Adam Smith's view that work represented an unwanted burden on individual liberty. Similarly, the profits that accrue to investors (the price of capital) reflect the disutility of having to defer their immediate consumption by investing their money, as well as the disutility of having to risk loss. This notion, as developed by Senior, was pilloried by Marx in *Grundrisse* for its suggestion that 'the capitalist too is making a sacrifice, the sacrifice of absti- nence, for instead of directly consuming his produce, he is enriching himself'. Marx, for his part, was quite certain that in fact 'Senior's miser takes pleasure in his abstinence' (Marx 1977: 368–9).

We might note that the theory of utility can only explain the formation of price given the demand for particular products (water, camomile tea, espresso coffee). It cannot explain the demand for these products in themselves. In this sense, utility theory is not a theory of 'usefulness'; it does not explain why people subjectively value certain goods, only how value comes to be expressed as price. The subjective reasons why I might prefer tea to coffee are, in this economic model, unknowable. All that can certainly be known about my preferences is what is expressed or revealed through the act of choice. The utility of a good is relative to the preference of each individual consumer of that good. Such individual preferences are privately formed outside the exchange context, are radically subjec- tive, and in these terms do not admit of comparisons between individuals. The concept of utility is a highly formal one that abstracts the diversity and contingency of human needs and wants into a logic of maximization.

Marginal utility theory, in its analysis of individual calculation and choice, developed a rigorously formalist methodology. Nothing could be known of the formation of private preferences, in terms either of personal taste or of the exogenous factors that might be taken to influence this; only objective outcomes regarding market choice were empirically observable – the behaviours of individuals as they mani- fest their 'revealed preferences'. Such a methodology is positivist in the sense that it deals strictly with the external features of human action. It is also behaviourist in its understanding of human action –

in this case, activity within the market – in terms of a set of responses (demand) to stimuli (movements in price), which were observable, calculable and predictable.

In this context, economics encounters a common problem for the social sciences – an occupational hazard, as it were, of studying human agents. It has to do with the relationship between formal methodologies for studying human action, and normative versions of human nature or motivation. In its origins with influential early marginalists such as William Stanley Jevons and Vilfredo Pareto, the idea that individuals made choices through calculations of utility was not simply a persuasive analytic device. Jevons was committed to the Benthamite view of a utilitarian calculus of pleasure and pain, while Pareto thought his model of *homo economicus* accorded well with human psychology. Using calculations of price to order your preferences and allocate your resources was not simply an efficient way to act in markets; it was an expression of one's rational human nature. Such a conception was held to operate independently of any specific social and historical context. People acted, in markets and in general, according to an individual calculus of pleasure and pain that drove them to maximize their subjective utilities.

The marginalist revolution, then, as it placed markets at the centre of economic analysis, was also crucial in promoting a certain version of the market actor. In this respect, it developed highly formal perspectives on markets as both systems of order and sites of agency. The basic precepts of marginalism – concerning market equilibrium and individual choice – provided the foundation for neoclassical economics as this emerged as a dominant paradigm in the twentieth century. They also sparked critical and enduring debates across the discipline. The latter part of this discussion looks to some key critiques, focusing on these dual questions of order and agency.

Competition and market process: Austrian perspectives

While marginal utility theory formed the basis of the neoclassical mainstream in twentieth-century economics, its origins were in three distinct schools – a British school associated with Jevons and Marshall; a Swiss school, based at the University of Lausanne and associated with Walras and Pareto; and an Austrian school, associated with thinkers such as Carl Menger, Ludwig von Mises and Friedrich von Hayek. This latter strand of economic thought developed perspectives on market processes that marked it out in critical ways from the growing neoclassical orthodoxy. Both Austrian and neoclassical approaches argue for the market as the most efficient means of economic allocation and co-ordination. However, whereas neoclassical perspectives originate in Walras' notion of market clearing or equilibrium – the way supply and demand interact to allocate resources in an optimal way – Austrian economists emphasize the dynamic effects of competition and innovation in markets. Against a neoclassical concern with market *equilibrium*, then, we might set the Austrian concern with market *processes* (see Kirzner 1973).

In the neoclassical equilibrium model, a fixed amount of goods and services is allocated among competing demands and price functions as a mechanism to bring these supply and demand factors neatly into alignment. This supply–demand model assumes that perfect information exists in market settings – that is, markets are transparent systems of exchange in respect of the range, price, quantity and quality of goods on offer. It is as if buyers, on entering a market, know what goods are on offer and at what range of prices, while sellers know the type, quantity and price of all their competitors' goods. In a perfect market, the price mechanism directs production and distribution of goods without the necessity of control or intervention. Alternative buyers and sellers are always available, information is perfect and each transaction is over once the exchange is complete.

Austrian approaches conceive the market not in terms of such formal tendencies to equilibrium, but in terms of dynamic and contingent processes of competition. Market processes are context-dependent, unpredictable and – because information is imperfect – uncertain. Friedrich von Hayek, a key exponent of the Austrian view in the twentieth century, asserted that economics should concern itself not with stationary models, but with 'an explanation of the economic process as it proceeds through time' (Hayek 1941: 173). Neoclassical approaches, in contrast, tend to view time merely as an ordering variable; one that prevents everything in the market happening at once. Market exchanges here are momentary transactions, which themselves have no relevant history or relation to the future. Such transactions occur within a market setting where only the present disposition of things is relevant. While any market exchange is assumed to affect all other exchanges, this happens in the context of an endless present – a kind of stasis implied by the central notion of equilibrium.

In this connection, Israel Kirzner (1973) argued that models of equilibrium were incoherent in marking the *end* (rather than the optimization) of the market process: perfect competition in fact meant no competition at all, as there was no incentive for any actor to alter the situation. In assuming perfect competition and perfect information as conditions for market equilibrium, neoclassical models ignored the way both competition and information were generated by the market process over time. As actors engage in market processes, that is, they enhance their information of what is going on (at the very least, I know how much I paid for my last double espresso), and draw on this knowledge in making subsequent decisions. This, for Kirzner, is an intrinsically competitive process, as market actors gain greater knowledge of who and what they are up against in trying to buy and sell. Price is the crucial information signal in the Austrian market. A price acts in this sense as a 'tip' or a 'comment' – a source of *knowledge* about market processes (Hayek 1945). The Austrian economists, particularly Hayek, greatly enhanced and socialized the analysis of markets by treating price explicitly as an information signal or system of shared meaning between market actors, rather than as a neutral mechanism that brought supply and demand into alignment. With this move, markets may be seen as rich information networks – even as a kind of 'conversation' between buyers and sellers (McCloskey 1994). Indeed, certain theorists have taken this concept so far as to suggest that the economist's task of explanation is as much interpretive or hermeneutic as it is mathematical (see Lavoie 1990).

The Austrian interest in the dynamic and open nature of market processes, however, does not dispense with questions of the market as a mode of order. To the contrary: Austrian versions of the competitive market process suggest a complex, spontaneous order, but not one that can easily be controlled. Neither neoclassical economists nor interfering political planners, in Hayek's view, for instance, can replicate the virtuous order of the market. Hayek subscribed to the liberal belief that free market exchanges conduce to overall order and a harmony of interests. However, he located this effect not in an abstract model of equilibrium, but in dynamic processes that could not easily be modelled. Market order did not reduce to the careful models of the neoclassicals – it is dynamic, complex and highly variable, even if ultimately conducive to social and economic harmony. This was not a narrowly economic argument. As an economic liberal, Hayek saw the market as the central institution in a free society, allowing individuals to pursue such ends as they saw fit and to reckon how best to provide for their own needs. The market nexus, moreover, was the means by which diverse individuals were brought into relation with each other: 'What today connects the life of any European or American with what happens in Australia, Japan or Zaïre are repercussions transmitted by the network of market relations' (Hayek 1991: 299). Neither did this represent the triumph of economic values and ends over all others. Hayek held that ultimately there were no economic ends as such; economic action always served ends that were non-economic in character because needs and desires are exogenous (or external) to the market setting. Economic activity, that is, involves allocating scarce means between competing ends that are, in themselves, non-economic (back in the café, my calculation is an economic matter; the fact that I want espresso coffee is not). Hayek returns to Smith's belief that the free pursuit of many individual interests produced spontaneous market order as both an economic and a social good. And as with Smith's analogy of the hidden hand, Hayek suggests that market order is the product of many individual actions, but not of any single design.

Market disorder

If neoclassical theory implies a static model of the market, and Austrian economic theory rests on a dynamic notion of market process, each is committed to markets as efficient and, in principle, self-regulating modes of co-ordination. This conception is at the base of their larger claims for markets as effective systems of economic order. However, there are important critiques within contemporary economics of forms of market *disorder*; the kinds of market failure that undercut the efficiency and the equity of economic allocation. Concepts of market failure put into question two crucial principles of market efficiency: competition and information. They also point to the wider *social inefficiency* of market processes, in respect of the external costs that attach to various economic activities. Forms of market failure, then, can broadly be understood in terms of imperfect competition, inadequate information and externalities.

These are not simply technical arguments about the formal operation of markets. Rather, they bear on larger questions about the social effects and the political regulation of market processes. As we discuss further in chapter 5, such arguments have been critical to debates over the degree of government intervention in market economies. Austrian economics, in particular that of Hayek, developed important claims for the efficiency of markets over economic planning as a basis for resource allocation. Planners, in this view, could never replicate the efficient manner in which price competition and information signals worked to co-ordinate economic processes. In an important riposte to these older arguments, Joseph Stiglitz (1994) returns to this terrain in response to the evident 'triumph' of free market models over socialist alternatives in the last decades of the twentieth century. Here, Stiglitz objects to the idea that neoclassical models somehow provide an argument or explanation for the success of liberal capitalism. In practice, he notes, successful economies are not based on a system of free markets, but usually combine mixed economies with large governments (p. 4). This gambit opens on to a critical account of market failure, and of neoliberal market rhetoric as a protocol for economic government.

The problem is that market processes rarely clear to produce either formal equilibrium or efficient resource allocation. The dominant paradigm in contemporary economics – what is termed the competitive, neoclassical, Smithian or Walrasian market model – is based on the interaction of large numbers of firms and consumers, all seeking to maximize their utility in a system of competitive markets (p. 5). Such a model is muddied by substantive problems of imperfect competition and information. As noted earlier, the model of perfect competition assumes there are sufficient numbers of buyers and sellers in a market to prevent forms of collusion or monopoly from distorting prices. Such a model is rarely, if ever, realized in actual market settings. Whether in the case of US airlines in the 1970s, or the British sugar market in the 1990s, where there is a limited number of suppliers, firms effectively control the market and are able to avoid real competition over price. The assumption of free competition within the standard model is deeply shaky, given the interest of firms to see off or collude with their competitors so as to maximize their own value. This quite 'rational' tendency to seek monopoly control has long been subject to anti-trust or competition laws. Examples of market monopoly stretch from John D. Rockefeller's Standard Oil to Bill Gates' Microsoft Corporation, which by 2000 could boast that 90 per cent of the world's personal computers ran on its software. Microsoft's attempts to use this dominance in operating systems to establish similar dominance in another market, that of Internet browsers, led to anti-trust charges in the US courts on the grounds that these activities were anti-competitive, and as such detrimental to the interests of both consumers and rival firms. The point here is that effective economic order is not secured along the lines of the 'standard theory', but via regulatory measures to institute and protect competitive markets. But the necessity for state intervention rarely appears as an assumption within market models of competition – however widely accepted it is in modern market practice.

Issues of imperfect competition bear on the second key form of market failure – inadequate information. Austrian approaches identify problems of information as a fundamental flaw in neoclassical market theory. Imperfect competition both produces and is a product of asymmetries in information. Here Stiglitz finds much to agree with in Austrian perspectives on information and innovation, but he questions the 'mythic' primacy of price as both a market relation and a source of information. A vast number of key economic relations, in particular those within firms, are not governed by price (see also Williamson 1985). Firms and consumers, what is more, use diverse forms of information other than price when making economic decisions, from inventories to corporate reputation to the economic 'demonstration effect' that is more commonly called fashion or 'keeping up with the Joneses'. For Stiglitz, problems of information are especially acute in relation to the risks of long-term investment and finance. Economic risk – uncertainty about future outcomes – represents a key information problem in markets. Price signals do not easily answer this kind of problem.

Once issues of imperfect competition and inadequate information are introduced, the efficiency of markets can no longer be assumed. The standard model, therefore, may offer a version of an abstract market order, but it cannot in itself offer directives for governing a real market economy. In this sense, neoliberal claims for the restructuring of advanced capitalist societies cannot be sustained purely on the basis of neoclassical models of the market (see chapter 5). Stiglitz agrees that competition, information and decentralization are crucial to economic success: while standard models of market efficiency *assume* these factors, markets themselves do not necessarily *produce* them. Governments, consequently, have a chief role to play in securing competitive and efficient markets, preventing cartels and monopolies, promoting consumer information, and so on.

Government actors also play a critical role in respect of the third key problem of market failure we have identified – that of externalities. This term refers to the costs and benefits of economic activities that do not figure within market prices. When a firm's production process pollutes a local water supply, this represents an external cost that is not directly borne by the firm or its consumers. Similarly, when I listen for free to the concert that others are paying to attend in my local park, this external benefit (assuming, of course, that I enjoy it) is not reflected in the ticket price. While there is probably rather little that can be done about my free-riding in this case, a primary form of government intervention in markets is to address issues of externality, whether through 'polluter pays' taxes or charges, or by providing collective goods (from defence to roads) where it is hard to limit the benefits of a good or service to those willing to pay directly for it. As we discuss further in chapter 5, these government interventions suggest that economic order is as much a legal and political artefact as it is a property of market forces. As principles of social and economic order, that is, markets must also be seen as problems of political order.

Social action and market calculation: critiques of economic agency

These critical arguments are directed towards the market as a model of social and economic order. We might also look to economic arguments that question a market model of agency. As noted earlier, the figure of the maximizing, self-interested actor that stands at the centre of neoclassical economics is one based on narrowly formalist or behaviourist premises. In this light, Weber argued, the market agent posited by modern economics offers an ideal-type of formal rationality, useful as an analytic measure of empirical economic behaviour (Weber 1949). The danger, for Weber and others, is that this figure might be taken as a reflection of human psychology, or as an ethical norm for human behaviour. Although the individualist focus of economic theory is sympathetic to that of Weberian sociology (see Clarke 1982), its 'undersocialized' view of the human agent constitutes one of the central points of argument between economic models and the 'oversocialized' conception of the individual offered by disciplines such as anthropology and sociology (Wrong 1961; see also chapter 4). It also has been subject to serious critique within economic theory itself.

It is open to question, then, how well a model of what has been called (after Pareto) 'economic man' functions as an ideal-type of economic behaviour. Sen (1977) traces economic models of the individual to liberal theories of social contract, and argues that the economic version of the individual that appears in neoclassical theory loses much of the complexity of these earlier discourses. Economic theory drops the ethical and empirical problems found in ideas of a social contract, particularly concerning the relation between individual interests and a general good. Rather, it serves to 'mathematize' what had been an essentially ethical and political set of questions about the nature of individual behaviour and how this fits into a collective order. Within liberal economics from Smith onwards, as we have seen, collective economic good is understood in terms of the mutual advantage of individuals in a market society, and is dependent on each pursuing his or her private interests. However, as Sen notes, between the individual and the collective lies a multitude of corporate interests – of the family, the firm, the friendship group, the community, the economic class – which ultimately are irreducible to a model of individual advantage.

The behavioural and atomistic focus of economic theories of utility in this sense is based on a rather rudimentary understanding of the relation between the individual and the collective. Sen's account seeks both to reveal the limited behaviourism of neoclassical models and to restore an ethical component to the understanding of individual rationality. He points to the circular nature of economic reasoning from preferences to choices. In analyses of economic decision making, preferences explain behaviour, which in turn is understood as an expression of individual preference. The reasoning goes like this: if someone buys a tomato, the economist accounts for this by saying, 'She wanted a tomato.' But how do they know she wanted a tomato? 'Because she bought one.' Such a tautological argument, for one thing, offers only a weak causal explanation of social action. More importantly, Sen wants to disrupt the easy linkage of individual interests to individual choices. Subjective interests cannot simply be read off from objective behaviour. An individual's choices might also be seen as an expression of commitment – to a cause, set of principles, person or group – which is not identical to their private interest. Where Sen uses a concept of 'commitment', we might just as easily think of solidarity, conviction or love.

For Sen, the kinds of choice made in a context of collective interests, such as those of the family, friendship or community, are based on a rationality of commitment (care, love, comradeship, etc). They are expressive of 'ethical preferences', which are distinguished from the narrowly 'subjective preferences' of economic theory. This is a simple point: one's individual choices do not always stem from one's subjective wants. People are able to and do take others into account when making decisions, and these decisions are at least partly governed by social rules, structures and conventions. Moral reasoning, as well as norms and incentives, provides motivations for action just as individual interests do. In response to the formal rationality of economic theory – where the economic actor appears as a kind of 'rational fool' in single-minded pursuit of his or her private utility – Sen argues that individual rationality is based on different calculations of utility together with forms of moral reflection. Certain desires may then be judged preferable to certain others on ethical grounds. Our imaginary consumer might have bought an organic tomato because she was boycotting genetically modified goods.

As the example of consumer boycott shows, the realm of ethical preferences is not limited to non-economic matters and relations. It also extends to more clearly economic choices, and can redefine what is meant by 'economic rationality' in these contexts. Millions of people, for example, choose to take jobs in voluntary sector organizations, even though such work is generally more poorly paid than equivalent work in the for-profit sector. This 'salary sacrifice' represents a trade-off between potentially higher wages and the ethical and job satisfaction of working for a cause to which one is committed, doing socially useful work or serving particular communities: 'you do it', as it is said (often ruefully), 'for love'. The utility to the worker, that is, is bound up with ethical or social values apart from the wage. And, of course, millions more people do voluntary work for no wage at all. Economic calculations, if they sometimes proceed on the basis of strict maximization, are also frequently cut through by other preferences, whose basis lies in the domains of ethics, affective relations, social norms or desire. One might extend Sen's account, then, by noting that any institution, system of social relations or form of knowledge that produces values – such as families, religious institutions, communities, subcultures and political movements – is also productive of utilities. It is not simply that individuals sublimate their subjective preferences in favour of an ethical alternative – putting what you should do before what you want – but that love, faith, duty, solidarity and honour may be pursued as utilities in their own right, as may such affective impulses as envy, rage, guilt and revenge. Perceptions of utility, that is, are formed and organized within larger systems of meaning and social order (see also O'Neill 1998).

This critical conception of utility, ironically, feeds back into an expanded neoclassical analysis of rational choice. Gary Becker's 'economic approach to human behaviour' (see Becker 1976) applies an economic model of choice to a diverse range of social phenomena, from drug taking and racism to love and marriage. His central thesis is simple: people's decisions in diverse social spheres can be analysed using economic models of rational choice. Individual behaviour – in families, at work, in love – can be read as efforts to maximize different forms of utility. Such behaviour is organized within markets that are both explicit, as in the labour market, and implicit, as in the 'market' in potential marital partners (Becker 1991). In these market contexts, individuals make choices (they can't, after all, marry everyone) so as to increase the benefit to themselves. Individual utilities do not have to be rational to fit with Becker's model (they could be ethical, whimsical or eccentric in any kind of way), but the choices people make in pursuit of these ends play out in rational terms of maximization. To return, one last time, to our early morning café scene: I buy the camomile tea and the newspaper. Let's say I really wanted to drink coffee, but the newspaper that day is making a donation to charity for every copy sold. On balance, that proves more important to me. Or let's say I take the newspaper because there is a colleague in the café whom I don't want to sit and talk to. Either way – 'altruistic' or 'selfish' – this choice realizes the greater utility to me. The calculation is economic, the want is not. Becker advances a large claim for the analytic value of this economic model of choice outside of 'real' market contexts. The analysis of rational choice is not confined to obviously economic issues, but extends to such non-material aspects of life as romance, leisure, fertility and divorce (Becker 1991). Moreover, Becker sees his analysis as relevant to both market and non-market societies. Rational choice models are especially well suited to economic choices in market settings, but are not limited to these contexts.

If Becker offers a total theory of utility, questions remain concerning the formal rationality of individual action. Economic theories do concede that individual rationalities, and the actions that arise from them, are shaped by specific contexts and constraints. Rationality tends to be 'bounded', in that actors lack perfect information about the risks of certain courses of action, or the range of opportunities that are available to them. However, the problem is not only that people often lack relevant information, but that they make 'irrational' decisions even when they are well informed. Amitai Etzioni (1988) argues that individual rationality frequently fails to produce optimal outcomes. Forms of private rationality tend to include such calculative strategies as 'procrastination', 'hedging one's bets' and 'trial and error'. The outcome of such processes is less a case of maximizing utilities than of 'muddling through'. Etzioni joins this account of the limitations of individual rationality with a case for the greater efficiency (even in markets) of collective rationalities. The group's cognitive efforts can make up for the calculative inadequacies of any individual in respect of knowing both what they want and how to pursue it. It is this principle that underlies the everyday practice of taking someone else shopping or house hunting or to an auction with you – two heads in these contexts being seen as better (and cooler) than one. The model of individual utility maximization, as it turns out, tends to be rather more rational than the human actors who clumsily act it out.

Conclusion

Central traditions in modern economic thought have offered approaches to market order and market action via technical models of co-ordination and rationality. The issues here are, to be sure, as much methodological as they are ethical. As Oliver Williamson (1985: 391) points out, economic models do not purport to represent 'an accurate view of human nature', given their neglect of 'kindness, sympathy, solidarity and the like'. Rather, they are designed so as to produce empirically refutable propositions. This methodological standpoint has been crucial to the formation of modern economics as a distinct social science discipline, particularly in its leanings to mathematization, modelling and prediction. However, it is valid to ask what kinds of knowledge one might want economics to produce as a social science. Is it enough to deal in 'toy economies' or ideal-types of rational choice? The claims of falsification stand in contrast to other arguments that economic models should aim for 'realistic' accounts of human behaviour (see Mäki, Gustaffsson and Knudsen 1993: 7–8). The two positions are easily confused. Critiques of neoclassical economics, for example, are arguably based on a misconception that a methodological premise regarding utility maximization is in fact an assumption about the way that people 'really are'.

There are two responses to make here. The first is to note that models of rational choice – especially as these have been extended to increasing domains of economic and social action – do not themselves subscribe to a methodology of falsification. If all action is assumed to be maximizing, then the assumption of maximization is itself non-falsifiable. The hypothesis falls into the trap of *si omnia nullia* – as a theory of everything, it ends up accounting for very little. It becomes difficult to think of an example of social action that *could not* be read as maximizing (see Boland 1996). It is also arguable, second, that speculation about how people 'really are' – or how they should be – is rarely far removed from economic analysis. Making a distinction between positive and normative statements in this context is not always straightforward. Hayek, for example, has this to say:

> the misconception of the individualism of Adam Smith and his group is the common belief that they have invented the bogey of the 'economic man' and that their conclusions are vitiated by their assumption of a strictly rational behaviour or generally by a false rationalistic psychology. They were, of course, very far from assuming anything of

the kind. It would be nearer the truth to say that in their view man was by nature lazy, improvident and wasteful, and that it was only by the force of circumstances that he could be made to behave economically or carefully to adjust his means to his end. (1976: 26)

Hayek's statement displaces the problem from one of 'how best can we understand the nature of the individual?' to 'what are the conditions under which an individual (whatever the truth of their natures) might be brought to behave rationally?' Although this question arises in the framework of economic theory, it became a special concern for sociology. In the next chapter, we set questions of rational action and rational order in the context of classical sociological theory, as major thinkers examined the rationality of modern market society and the nature of the individuals who populated it.

3

Rationality, the Individual and Social Order

Introduction

As the last two chapters have indicated, the liberal-utilitarian traditions of social thought that dominated economic theory promoted both a model of individual behaviour based on the rational pursuit of self-interest, and a model of society – exemplified in market mechanisms – in which efficiently orchestrated individual actions produced social order. And yet the history of modern social thought, particularly in sociology and anthropology, has been structured by doubts about precisely these models. Can a stable social order really emerge from the rational, self-serving actions of private individuals alone? And to the extent that it can, in what sense is it really 'rational'? For most social theorists, particularly of the classical tradition, the reality of market society was quite different from the normative models: both society and even markets themselves required social values and commitments that had to go beyond individual calculation of self-interest if they were to hold together. To the extent that these were lacking, market society appeared to be brutal, crisis-ridden and irrational. At the same time, where markets, capitalism and rationalization were apparently successful in compelling modern social actors to behave according to economic and utilitarian models, the result did not seem to be reason and freedom for the individual. To the contrary, when reduced to atomized actors, real individuals experienced themselves as alienated, as anomic and as the objects of calculation rather than as calculating subjects.

In this chapter, then, we will be looking at the main lines of classical sociological theory – Marx, Weber, Durkheim, Simmel and Parsons. In each case, the transition to market society is seen as posing the central problems of social thought rather than their solution. This is evident both at the level of social order, which, when grounded in the economic alone, breeds crisis and irrationality, and at the level of the individual, where the dominance of a reductive version of the person is the measure of modern moral dislocation.

Marx

Where liberal social and economic thought envisages a natural harmonization of conflicting interests through market mechanisms, Marx sees systemic and ineradicable contradictions between social interests. These systemic contradictions not only make capitalism technically crisis-prone, but also mark it as a fundamentally immoral and exploitative social order. In both respects, it can be regarded as profoundly irrational. The market plays a complicated role in this picture. Marx crucially defines the capitalist mode of production in terms of markets, and indeed begins *Capital* with a discussion of the commodity form, the great mystery at the centre of modern order. Capitalism is distinguished from other modes of production in that the central principle of economic life is production for the market: people do not produce specific goods for their immediate consumption, but rather produce goods solely for profitable sale in the marketplace, in order to realize through exchange the surplus value that has been extracted from labour in their production. Hence, capitalist society is structured by the mediation of markets, by the fact that the ever-expanding accumulation of capital always depends on the capitalist's ability to convert goods into money through market exchange.

Nonetheless, Marx regards the market as 'epiphenomenal': it is not itself the basic social reality or principle that accounts for modern social order, but is rather the effect of deeper causes. Marx constantly warns his readers *not* to study the market in itself, and treats the market as a sphere of mystification and irrationality. Indeed those who, like the political economists, place markets centrally in their models of social co-ordination are at best unscientific, at worst engaged in ideological manoeuvres. This is because neither the structure of the market nor the quantities of supply and demand circulating within it are explicable in terms of the individual preferences, decisions or behaviours that show up in the market itself. Rather, markets and market behaviours are determined by structural constraints and processes that lie outside them. Adhering to the labour theory of value, Marx argues that although values must be realized in exchange, exchange processes cannot create values. Above all, value arises not from the subjective valuations of buyers and sellers (as in neoclassical economics), but through the amount of labour expended in production. Prices might deviate from these values as a result of temporary competitive forces, but ultimately, and above all across the capitalist marketplace as a whole, markets operate within the constraints of the values generated in production. Economists who are exclusively focused on the market are therefore engaging in a kind of fetishism, worshipping it as if it were a real source of power.

It is not just the quantity of value in the market that is determined outside the market, through labour in production. Value created in production is distributed according to capitalist social relations of production in which the determining feature is whether one is an owner of means of production and therefore has a share in profit rather than wages. Those who do not possess means of production – the workers – must sell their labour to those who do; in alienating their labour as a commodity, they receive as wages only a portion of the value they create, the rest being appropriated by their employers as surplus value or, ultimately, profit. The employers' profits and competitive success depend upon the intensity with which wages can be reduced and surplus value increased: the 'rate of exploitation'. This division between profits and wages is not a simple matter of contest or competition, nor can it be overcome by co-operation. Rather it is a structural feature of capitalism; indeed a structural *contradiction* that results in fundamentally opposed and irreconcilable interests: whereas workers further their interests by using their limited powers to increase their wages, the survival of capitalist enterprises depends upon increasing the gap between wages and total value produced. Marx uses the term 'rate of exploitation' in a technical sense to measure this process, but it also has a clear moral-political sense – however free and equal market exchange might appear, the market power of any individual depends on their position within a structurally unequal system. This is not because capitalists are greedy (though of course they are), but because a decline in their rate of profit makes their businesses unattractive as investments (capital flees to sectors with higher rates of return) or requires them to sell their goods at uncompetitive prices. Nor can the fundamental injustice and inequality of market society be reformed through good will or amelioration at the level of the market: it is systemic and could be overcome only through the revolutionary overthrow of capitalism itself.

Moreover, markets are driven by forces outside themselves in another sense, one that is reflected in the very form of the commodity as it appears in the market. A commodity is both a use value (a particular object with specific properties that might satisfy needs) and an exchange value (something that can be valued in terms of an abstract monetary price in exchange). At the most general societal level, the production of all the things required for the reproduction of a society relies on the distribution of all available social labour to all required branches of production in correct proportion to what is socially needed. People do specific forms of work on specific materials (concrete labour) in order to produce specific things with properties that satisfy needs (use values). This is 'socially necessary labour', and is fairly self-evident in a society where people produce directly for their needs: a fifteenth-century household could allocate its collective labour and other resources to make a range of specific goods it deemed necessary. This transparent relationship between production and consumption, which Marx believes to characterize non-capitalist societies, is split and mystified by the market. Instead of producing use values directly in relation to their needs, people – whether as capitalists, or as workers whose labour has been bought and subsumed by capitalists – produce goods that can be sold in the market. While these goods must have use value for other people (else they could not be sold), the producers regard them solely as exchange values: their value lies not in their concrete physical properties, but in the abstract quantity of money for which they can be exchanged. Within such a system, the values and goods that appear in the market are entirely to be explained by the capitalist's drive to expand exchange value, rather than to meet needs, produce the material basis of a good society, promote culture or anything else of a substantive nature.

Hence, markets are determined by structures outside themselves – above all, the social relations of production. In this respect, Marx extends the central concerns of classical political economy with the derivation of income from different forms of ownership, the division between profit, rent and wages, and the distribution of wealth via social classes as opposed to individual choices. Marx was also therefore concerned with social structures as objective and determining realities, and not as reducible to individual acts. Finally, this means that Marx is concerned with how these objective determinants operate regardless of the consciousness of either workers or capitalists – 'behind their backs' – and therefore a gap may arise between the appearance and the reality of market society. In particular, the concepts of 'alienation' and 'commodity fetishism' are used to argue that markets generate a systematically false view of the social, one in which commodities have apparently supernatural powers to generate and sustain value in their relation to each other through exchange, rather than in their relation to the human labour that produced them, or in their real and functional properties in use (use value). This misperception and consequent fetishism is called to account for ideology and for the *inability* of modern social subjects – *contra* liberalism – even to perceive their real social interests accurately, let alone pursue them rationally. Hence – as in many Marxian-derived accounts of consumer culture (for example, Marcuse 1964; Williams 1980; Williamson 1978) – market society is characterized by people identifying their interests with an increasing standard of living measured in greater power to purchase consumer goods in the marketplace. Rather than actually increasing well-being, this sinks people yet further into class-based relations of exploitation and alienation, which are no longer even perceived or challenged: people will sacrifice control over their individual labour in order to be able to buy a few more consumer goodies in the marketplace. Moreover, a focus on the market even distorts our understanding of class. From a Marxist point of view, market-based analyses of inequality (such as Weber's account of the relation between life chances and market position) can only see the fragmented appearance of multitudinous market positions, thus missing the fundamental class structure derived from two clear opposing positions within the relations of production.

Marx's analysis of the market in terms of essence and appearance is complemented by a concern with the formal as opposed to 'real' values of market society. For Marx, the central values of liberalism, such as individuality, rationality and freedom, are connected to the formal appearances of market relations, but are belied by its real underlying compulsions. Markets are based on the formal assumption of equality and freedom – although individuals enter the market in possession of different quantities of means, they have equal rights and freedoms to enter into contracts with each other. 'Equality before the law' means that any legal contract, voluntarily entered into, is binding and must be enforced regardless of the social status of those who entered into it. Moreover, if the sources of market inequalities are assumed to be 'accidents' of individual ability, nature or chance rather than structural disadvantages, then income inequality is justifiable, so long as people are granted the legal or formal equality that allows them to realize whatever individual capacities they happen to have. This, as we shall see, was the basis of Durkheim's meritocratic prescription for a renewed moral legitimacy within the modern order – that individual differences must be socially accepted as justified only if they were based on differences of ability rather than of opportunity.

Bauman (1990: 208–13) expresses these themes very clearly in relation to consumer culture. Modern consumerism, he suggests, is about the ability to construct identity through the untrammelled exercise of individual choice – consumer culture 'suggests the equality of consumers, in their capacity as free choosers who themselves determine their social standing' (p. 210). On the one hand, this seems obviously ideological, belied by real inequalities of wealth and power. On the other hand, the market historically wraps these inequalities in egalitarian assumptions that may indeed have real force, particularly legal force. Above all, the market destabilizes status systems (see also Turner 1988):

> The market thrives on inequality of income and wealth, but it does not recognize ranks. It devalues all vehicles of inequality but the price-tags. Goods must be accessible to everybody who can afford to pay their price. Life-styles – *all* life-styles – are up for grabs. The purchasing ability is the only entitlement the market would recognize. It is for this reason that in a market-dominated consumer society the resistance to all other, ascribed inequality grows to unprecedented proportion. . . . The overwhelming power of market-supported criteria of social differentiation seemingly invalidates all its competitors: there should be no goods that money cannot buy. (Bauman 1990: 211)

Thus, the idea of clubs or public facilities that debar women or people of colour on the basis of their sex or race as opposed to their ability to pay (though the two are so patently linked in our sexist and racist societies) is anathema to liberal market ideology. Indeed, capitalist development has generally been characterized by the slow extension of formal rights against a background of real disadvantage. Whether we are to regard this extension as primarily the advancement of purchasing powers over political ones, of commercialization over the social, is another story. Marx's concern is generally to present these formal qualities of market relations as baselines for critique: the aim is to judge market society by its own promises of freedom and equality, and to measure its ability to deliver on these promises. At the same time, these promises are understood as themselves socially effective or functional in the maintenance of power. Marx regards formal market freedom and equality as 'bourgeois', in that they can be enjoyed and used only by those who have real economic power (the bourgeoisie), and therefore help to maintain their sectoral interests. At the same time, they are presented as universal values, as representing the general interest – a claim that could be given substance only once market relations are no longer based on class (itself an impossibility within the Marxist framework).

The market, for Marx, is therefore a place of mystification. It obscures the structural contradictions that are constitutive of capitalism. And yet it is also in the marketplace that capitalist societies register their contradictions in the form of economic crises. In technical terms, Marx's micro-economics – his model of what happens within the market, all other things being equal – is not significantly different from that of any other political economist. However, although in Marx's account market behaviour is rational at the level of the individual, market outcomes can be highly irrational from a technical point of view and counterproductive from the point of view of capitalist reproduction. Because markets mediate between production and consumption, their co-ordination over space and time is always fragile and contingent, if not actually accidental. As it involves production of commodities *for* the market, the limits of capitalist production are determined by what the market will absorb, by what people can and will buy. However, these quantities, as we have seen, are determined not by the market but by the social relations of production, which determine both the content and scale of need in a given historical society. On the one hand, Marx relates the general level of social need to the reproduction of labour power and therefore to a standard of consumption that arises from class struggle and the balance of class forces within the relations of production (see, for example, Rowthorn 1980). On the other hand, such demand becomes effective demand – money-backed demand – only to the extent that labour receives a portion of the value it produces. This is determined by the rate of exploitation and analysed under the laws of surplus value: capitalist relations of production are such that the workers, as a class, *never* receive the full value of their labour, a value which instead is divided between them and the capitalist owners of the means of production. This is a *systemic* feature of capitalism. Hence, the workers as a class can never purchase and consume all that they have produced. In seeing this overproduction/underconsumption problem as structurally endemic to capitalism, Marx is also rejecting the widespread assumption of Say's optimistic law by mainstream economists from Smith until Keynes, an argument to the effect that there is always and automatically present in the market sufficient effective demand to purchase all the goods that have been supplied to it. This is argued (by Say at least) on the basis that the value paid out in wages as a cost is equal to the value of the goods produced. The doom-saying deniers of this 'law' include Malthus, Marx and most influentially Keynes, all of whom understood that substantial amounts of value are not paid out as wages, but rather go by way of profits into savings and investment. Therefore, this value is not made effective as demand and there is always the possibility there will be insufficient effective demand for what is produced.

This is apparent to Marx, who is surveying the scene at a structural level. At the level of individuals and firms, 'at the level of competition', the view is quite different. On the one hand, firms are driven to expand the forces of production in a generally open-ended manner: in their drive to accumulate exchange value, they are constantly innovating production technologies and organization, discovering or inventing new use values (including new raw materials) and intensifying both efficiency and exploitation. In this drive, firms are limited by their capital and technical expertise rather than by consumer demand *per se*. Indeed, if they do not continually develop the forces of production, their competitors will reap efficiency gains and therefore market advantages (lower prices, better goods, new use values) and drive them out of business. On the other hand, with each efficiency gain in the forces of production achieved by each obsessively driven firm, struggles within the relations of production tend to drive up the level of exploitation and therefore drive down the level of market demand. As Marx put it, each firm sees its own workers as workers (whose wages are to be reduced) and everybody else's workers as consumers (whose purchasing power must be expanding in line with the expansion of production). The fact that this is a fundamental and systematic crisis tendency that is *constitutive* of the capitalist social order as well as of its ultimate demise is registered in trade cycles and crises. Although the expansion of production and the restriction of purchasing power through exploitative production relations are part of one and the same process, they are developed in the market as separate forces. That is to say, capitalists constantly push production beyond the limits of commodity exchange in the pursuit of surplus value, but they experience this as an external constraint that comes – as a surprise to them – when they find that they are simply unable to sell all their goods because there is insufficient purchasing power in the market. As chains of production elongate through a more sophisticated division of labour, this market mediation becomes ever more opaque and extended over time. Hence, in one of Marx's most detailed descriptions of a trade crisis in *Capital*, firms producing capital goods persist in expanding their capacity long in anticipation of the needs of consumer goods firms, whose failure is not signalled to them until after consumer demand has already dried up in the marketplace.

This technical example from Marx illustrates a sense of the relation of markets to social order that is a million miles away from Smith and a natural harmony of interests. For Marx, it is possible to conceive of the social order as both systematic and law-like and yet incipiently crisis-prone and self-defeating – and to do so at the level of the market itself as a mechanism of socio-economic integration and reproduction. The market is not simply a place of rational or genteel competition (*doux commerce*), or even of desperate conflict, but far more than that, it is a place of *contradiction*, and indeed of contradictions that are properly apprehended only as manifestations of deeper, more fundamental and essentially contradictory 'principles' (relations of production based on exploitation). Both Marx's famous dictum that capitalism goes on behind of the backs of the capitalists, and his general concern with the difference between objective class interests and subjective (mis)perceptions of social place, have a dual function in this context. In one sense, they go to argue that the competitive forces within which social actors must operate are indeed objective and external to them: there *is* such a thing as society, or what a sociologist might now call a social structure, which is not necessarily meaningfully understood in terms of – let alone *by* – individual actors. At the same time, there is a disjuncture between the rationality of the actor and of the system, rather than mechanisms that routinely convert actions into rational collective outcomes. Technical rationality at the level of individual social action – all of that efficient, calculative, methodical pursuit of self-interest – may be revealed as entirely and dangerously irrational at a collective or systemic level. Smith's point was that the imposition of any rationality on to the actor will disrupt the natural harmonization of interests that emerges from their local rational action; Marx's point is that the irrational social conditions within which they pursue that self-interest – however rationally – will yield irrational results.

For Marx, then, the market is deemed to be systematically crisis-ridden, mystifying and based on exploitation. Contrary to liberalism and liberal economics, it also marks a fundamental debasement rather than liberation or empowerment of the individual, indeed – especially for workers – the entire loss of any real individuality (see Marx 1959 [1844]). Above all, Marx associates the authentic individual with humanity's 'species-being': that is to say, their fundamental nature as human beings. This he defines in terms of *praxis* or creative labour, through which people are able to transform the object world around them in relation to their needs, imagination and intellectual capacities (forces of production). Under capitalist relations of production, humans are alienated from themselves and their fellows through the reduction of praxis to labour as an abstract quantity of labour power, sold in the market (literally 'alienated') as a commodity. Under these conditions, a worker's labour – the very source of his or her real self – is sold to those who own the means of production, who subordinate it to their own ends and to production processes over which the worker has little or no control. This is done under conditions of exploitation, whereby the worker does not even receive in return the full value produced by their labour. Workers' labour is subsumed within a division of labour in which they carry out specialist tasks; they therefore cannot identify with the entire labour process and hence cannot identify its product as the result of their own praxis. They are, moreover, alienated from their co-workers as atomized individuals. Finally, the product of their labour does not appear to them as their own because they confront it only in the marketplace, as something that appears as if from nowhere, at a price they cannot afford, and under the aspect of consumption, a social moment separated from production by the mediation of markets. Thus, capitalist relations of production and market mediation tear apart the very process – praxis – by which individuals become themselves and are able to recognize themselves as human.

If this were not bad enough, Marx also understands the debasement of the individual within market society in terms of needs and consumption. His utopic notion of praxis is a question not simply of work, but of a complex dialectic between needs and creative transformation. As humankind expands its power to create new use values, its needs expand too. For example, in forging new modes of communication such as the Internet, populations perceive new possibilities and hence develop needs for new kinds of sociality, pleasures, knowledges and political powers. They can become more complex, realize more potentialities within themselves and become, to use Marx's formulation of proper humanity, 'rich in needs'. Under capitalist social relations, mediated by markets, however, this dialectic is deformed. On the one hand, workers suffering under an ever-increasing rate of exploitation and impoverishment are reduced below the level of basic human needs to that of animal needs for food, air and light. On the other hand, the needs of those with sufficient money to satisfy them are regarded by capitalists merely as means to the end of selling things. That is to say, in an early formulation of consumer culture, Marx argues that from the point of view of realizing exchange value, needs are seen not as the basis for developing a rich individuality, but rather as the basis for another kind of exploitation: capitalists pander to the basest and most luxurious tastes of increasingly jaded consumers in order to create opportunities for profit. At the root of both kinds of debasement – of worker and bourgeois – however, lies an even more fundamental one: the real need in a market society is not a need for particular use values that are defined in terms of the development of a specific individuality. Rather, under market conditions, the only real need is for the most abstract commodity – money – which becomes the measure of all other things. The individual becomes enslaved to the laws of motion of money, which subsumes all use value and hence individuality.

Weber

For Marx, the irrationality of the market is largely to be explained in terms of deeper contradictions within the forces and relations of production. For Weber, the market is one example – albeit one of the most important – of the dominance of one narrow form of rationality over all others within the modern world. Moreover, Weber is not greatly concerned with either economic or social disorder in a market society – by and large, to him, it seems to work. Rather, Weber is concerned with the generally tragic position in which the modern individual is left by the very success of market society. Market rationality is part of a process of social rationalization, which leaves the individual with less and less meaning and freedom. Weber's position is all the more remarkable given that it was based on a methodological individualism that he largely shared with liberal and neoclassical economic traditions.

In much of the social science tradition, 'rationality' and 'rationalization' have a dual meaning. On the one hand, being rational involves the ability to give reasons for one's actions that are logically consistent and coherent with respect to a particular standpoint. If I say that I would give my life to protect free speech, this might appear irrational from the point of view of a cost–benefit analysis based on individual self-interest, but more than rational – exemplary – if my actions are to be governed by such values as integrity, panache or citizenship. On the other hand, rationality is often associated with one single set of values that are concerned with selecting the 'best' means to a given end – efficiency, calculability, quantification, control and prediction. Weber's central concern is how this one notion of rationality – instrumental rationality – comes to be seen in the modern context not as one mode of operating sensibly but as the only one that is deemed sensible at all. Conversely, how do all other modes of behaviour, those which are oriented to values other than efficiency, come to be seen as 'primitive' or irrational? The social science concern is to analyse the restrictive notion of reason that appears to have triumphed in modern times within a broader and more historical view of reason.

In Weber's work, goal-rational action – instrumental rationality – is seen as one ideal-type of action in a schema that also includes habitual, traditional and value rational action (Weber 1978), yet it has increasingly come to dominate modern society. Market exchange appears as both its paradigm and its promoter. In market exchange, the pursuit of interests is conducted without hindrance from tradition, taboo, status and other substantive obligations, all of which appear 'irrational' from the point of view of choosing the most efficient means to achieve a given end. That is to say, market exchange, like modern rationality overall, is impersonal and unsentimental, applying a logic of calculation regardless of who or what is involved in any particular transaction, or what end is in view. Moreover, monetarized market exchange exemplifies the central defining feature of modern rationality: all possible courses of action and their outcomes can be quantified in terms of a single measure of costs and gains.

We can disaggregate Weber's analysis of instrumental rationality into several features that are market-related (see Brubaker 1984). First, as just indicated, monetarization is bound up with quantification. Money prices are not 'mere tokens' of utility, but are rather 'the product of conflicts of interest and compromises' (Weber 1947: 211) arising from market competition between economic actors. Therefore, money 'is essentially significant as a means of quantitative expression of estimated opportunities and risks met in the pursuit of competitive advantages' (p. 211). Every salient aspect of a situation can be expressed in monetary terms arising from market competition and corporate planning (pp. 186–91), and thus different courses of action can be precisely compared in terms of both costs and outputs. Weber is clear that the formal rationality of a money economy, and hence of modern social order, is dependent on 'far-reaching market freedom' (p. 211). Furthermore, he very clearly understands these themes in terms of conventional marginalist accounts of opportunity cost and the optimization of utilities by individual competitive calculators.

Second, rationalization depends on control over the production process within both economic and bureaucratic enterprises, the subordination of all elements of a process – including labour – to planning, thus increasing the calculability of all input and output costs (pp. 275–8). This is partly bound up with the increase of technical and scientific knowledges that can rationalize the flow of materials and labour through production (for example, Taylorism). Within such knowledges, all factors are treated as means to the end of efficient production, including humans, who by rights should be regarded as subjects, not objects, and from the viewpoint of substantive rather than formal values. In this regard, Weber, much like Marx, sets great store by the separation of workers from ownership of the means of production – a deprivation which, by rendering them entirely dependent on labour markets for their livelihood, makes them powerless to control the production processes within which their labour is used. This allows for an intensification of the technical and social division of labour, which increases economic efficiency and output while at the same time increasing alienation and powerlessness.

Third, Weber argues that a central condition of calculability is a stable and therefore predictable social environment. This condition is met in great measure through the evolution of 'legal formalism' (Brubaker 1984: 16–20), in which legal concepts such as contract and ownership are given clear and enforceable definition that is – through bureaucratized institutions – applied impersonally. That is to say, in principle the enforcement of a contract depends not on the whim of an arbitrary ruler or on personal obligations or kinship ties between magistrate and petitioner, but rather on the application of general principles to specific cases. Not only does this render the law rational, but also it allows market transactions to be calculated against the backdrop of predictable legal outcomes should the contracting parties not meet their obligations. This point is shared with Marx and, we shall see, Durkheim and Polanyi: free markets require both formal state structures and informal understandings that structure and enforce market transactions.

Finally, it is crucial to note that Weber is not only addressing objective conditions of both markets and goal rationality; he is equally concerned that market exchange promotes a subjective orientation to calculation while also benefiting from other cultural sources of methodical and formal control (such as the Protestant ethic). Goal rationality involves an 'intellectualization' or disenchantment of the world, such that we orient our thinking in terms of empirical and causal accounts of the world, rather than religious or traditional ones in which the world appears as inherently meaningful or as governed by supernatural forces. In line with this instrumental mode of thought, markets promote a crudely materialistic orientation in which things are ascribed value only insofar as they can act as means to ends; they can have no intrinsic value.

In contrast to Marx or Durkheim's accounts of capitalist or utilitarian society, Weber's rationalized modernity *works*; indeed, it works efficiently, exercising ever more detailed bureaucratic and commercial power over individuals. Moreover, the impersonality and calculability of means–ends rationality that characterizes market exchange is also the basis for rationalizing all key sectors of modern social structure, and is associated with modern progress in science, governance and even aesthetics. Indeed, as Weber continuously points out, any aspect of social life seems capable of being rationalized in terms of its own internal standpoint and goals. What is the problem then? First, and at the very centre of Weber's thought, is the distinction between formal and substantive rationality. Formal rationality refers simply to the calculation of *means*: market society makes calculation central to social action. Substantive rationality refers to the *ends* of actions and particularly to the ultimate values that underpin our commitment to various goals. In the case of economic action, whereas formal rationality refers to the extent of quantitative calculation, substantive rationality denotes the extent to which actual needs of a particular sort are met (Weber 1947: 185). In terms of the market, this distinction maps easily on to the economist's distinction between price and value, or the Marxist's distinction between exchange value and use value, or abstract and concrete labour. Indeed, the utilitarian 'felicific calculus' or the marginal utility calculations of the optimizing individual exemplify this distinction: actors abstract from their particular wants and assess the amount of 'satisfaction' or 'utility' they might secure from different expenditures of resources. This calculation depends on an ability to quantify different courses of action (which money prices accomplish very well); but it can be applied to any particular situation. One need not know the substantive nature of an individual's goals or desires in order to know whether he or she is behaving rationally; the individual's rationality is a matter of his or her formal ability to translate desires into numbers that reflect their relative urgency and cost.

Weber claims to be value neutral in the sense that his concept of rationality is empirical rather than evaluative. In his account, a 'more rational social order' is one that empirically exhibits the characteristics of greater impersonality, calculability and means–ends orientation rather than one that is in some broader moral sense a 'better' social order. That is to say, 'The formal rationality of the modern social order is a matter of fact; whether or not this social order is substantively rational, in contrast, depends on one's point of view – that is, on the ends, values or beliefs one takes as a standard of rationality' (Brubaker 1984: 37). And the substantive point of view from which one might assess a social order, for Weber, is necessarily a matter of moral decision rather than scientific judgement. This is because Weber – at a methodological level – adheres to the positivist distinction between facts and values, in which substantive values cannot be established as true through observation of the world (see Weber 1949, 1991b). At a sociological and historical level, he argues, the disenchantment of the modern world has reached such a state that there are no longer any unquestioned substantive values left that command our belief.

Nonetheless, while Weber as scientist must refrain from judging the social order, he can certainly make a fateful observation: the empirical fact that calculation has become the basis of modern social order produces profound ethical dilemmas for its citizens. First, there is a confusion of ends and means: efficient calculation and maximizing choice are no longer simply ways of doing things, but rather become the proper goal of society in themselves. For example, modern economic debate is dominated by the 'cult of GNP', in which economic growth is treated as an end in itself, abandoning all discussion of *what* is wanted or why. Similarly, neoliberalism treats marketization as promoting an efficiency that is good in itself. Such a critique is developed by the Frankfurt School and animates the work of Habermas: the deification of formal rationality as an end in itself means either that substantive values are left to the private and arbitrary world of individual choice, or that the very questions of the goals of social life or the meaning of individual life are simply never raised. Instead there is merely a disciplined drive to accumulate more goods that have little qualitative significance (Slater 1997b; Soper 1981, 1990). Second, the formal–substantive split is linked to a technocratic mentality within the division of labour whereby individuals allow themselves to be efficiently integrated within processes whose ends or consequences (nuclear bombs, pollution, exploitation of workers in other countries) they never question (Habermas 1970). Finally, figures like Marcuse (1972) and Kolakowski (1972) have argued that the formal/substantive distinction is misleading in the sense that the so-called formal criteria of efficiency or calculability actually are themselves substantive values that are chosen and command belief just like any other values. They have no greater factual character than values such as honour, *caritas*, equality or any of the others that Weber treats as substantive and arbitrary. By focusing on the ever-increasing formal rationality of modern capitalism, Weber ignores its substantial irrationality: that it fails to deliver on any of the substantive values that lie at its core. Whether or not Marcuse's argument is correct, it is probably unfair to state this as a criticism of Weber, who actually seems to be arguing something very similar (Mommsen 1989): formal and substantive rationality are in a constant state of tension with each other, in the sense that basic conditions of capitalist rationalization (for example, 'formally free labour' that is sold on labour markets) are patently irrational with respect to achieving core social values of the modern world (real equality, freedom from exploitation, solidarity).

The same problems of formal rationality can be taken up at the level of the individual, for the split between formal and substantive rationality structures the central existential dilemmas of the modern subject. To the extent that modern market society intensifies that split, it intensifies – to tragic lengths – those dilemmas. However formally rational an individual actor may be, it can only be rational with respect to attaining a goal. But any such goal must itself be a matter of arbitrary choice: one cannot rationally choose between competing values. Hence, values take on the form of something like mere consumer choice – whether I rigorously aim at constructing a just society or at efficiently selling lots of chocolate bars at a profit is a matter that cannot be pursued beyond the notion of individual 'preferences', 'wants', 'desires' and 'choices'. The formal rationalization of modern life undermines modern individuals in at least three ways (Brubaker 1984: 103–6). First, the disenchantment of the world empties the world of intrinsic meanings (as opposed to causal connections and empirical consequences), making it ever more difficult to define the meaning of life, to formulate any ultimate ends that inspire sustained conviction. Second, rationalization reduces freedom, as argued by Marx, by separating individuals from the means of production and thereby reducing them, despite formal freedom, to labour power that can be sold and, once sold, is subordinated to rational production processes beyond the individual's control. It also reduces freedom through the extension of bureaucratic control over all aspects of social life. Third, the dominance of instrumental rationality 'threatens to subvert individual autonomy from within' (p. 104): a purely formally rational calculator of marginal utilities, unbound by tradition or values other than his or her own wants, appears to be utterly free, but in fact this kind of individual is merely driven by given wants, by unchosen impulses (however rationally pursued).

Weber proposes an alternative moral conception of the individual, attempting to counter this atomized individualism with moral individualism that might ground ethical subjects in the modern world (see also Featherstone 1995; Hennis 1987). He describes this conception as an 'ethic of the personality': the moral dignity of the person resides in their ability to rationalize *themselves* rigorously in relation to the goals and values they have embraced (however arbitrary these substantive value choices must be). The truly autonomous person is one who unifies him- or herself around whichever values they have chosen, systematically devoting themselves to values that take on the character of fate. This moral individualism is therefore also described as an ethic of responsibility, in that it involves people treating their value commitments as 'vocations' in relation to which they rationally work upon themselves (Weber 1991a, 1991b). This is an ethic of both self-creation and yet subordination of the self to something higher, an ethic that both accepts and seeks to transcend the tragic position of the individual in a utilitarian market society.

Hence, rather as we shall find with Durkheim, modern society both creates the individual and at the same time destroys that individual through the lack of binding value commitments that might promote the ethical integrity of the person (personality) or of the social order (solidarity). The market is a strategic site for both the creation and destruction of the modern individual. It presumes the autonomy of subjects who calculate courses of action in relation to their private desires and then enter into contracts to realize them. At the same time, their very ability to do so arises from social conditions that destabilize the broader value commitments that would allow for a true autonomy and sociality. Nowhere in modern social thought are these dilemmas more clearly spelled out than in the painful final pages of *The Protestant Ethic and the Spirit of Capitalism*. The emergence of capitalism depended upon the subjective re-ordering of individuals around an ethic of methodical duty, a formal rationality that spoke directly to a substantive ethic of salvation. All this changes once capitalism is established, for 'the Puritan wanted to work in a calling; we are forced to do so' (Weber 1958: 181). Asceticism played its part in constructing an order that is now 'bound to the technical and economic conditions of machine production which to-day determine the lives of all the individuals who are born into this mechanism . . . with irresistible force'. The 'care for external goods' has become 'an iron cage' ending in a 'dissolution into pure utilitarianism' (p. 183):

> Where the fulfilment of the calling cannot directly be related to the highest spiritual and cultural values, or when, on the other hand, it need not be felt simply as economic compulsion, the individual generally abandons the attempt to justify it at all. In the field of its highest development, in the United States, the pursuit of wealth, stripped of its

religious and ethical meaning, tends to become associated with purely
mundane passions, which often actually give it the character of sport.
(p. 182)

We might counterpose Weber here to his contemporary Georg
Simmel. Simmel takes up many of the same themes as Weber –
individuation, rationalization, monetarization as a basis of the intellectualization of contemporary life, and loss of individuality through
the power of objectified social processes. He placed these themes
even more explicitly within an analysis of market society, especially
through his concern with money as a socially transformative and
mediating force. This concern can be placed within his overall sociological method. Simmel defines forms of 'sociation', or interaction,
as the primary figure of analysis, rather than either individuals or
social structures. Exchange, as a form of sociation, 'is one of the
functions that creates an inner bond between men – a society, in
place of a mere collection of individuals' (quoted in Turner 1986:
96). Such an orientation places him firmly within the classical sociological concern with the ethical individual, as opposed to the utilitarian concern with the atomized one. Moreover, for Simmel
exchange processes, like all forms of sociation, are not mere artefacts of individual interactions, but are objectified in social structures and material cultures that take on a logic of their own,
separate from particular interactions. Hence, Simmel is concerned
with processes of reification, a term which he bequeaths to Lukács,
Benjamin, Adorno and many other figures, and which he (unlike
they) construes as 'the tragedy of culture', rather than as a direct
consequence of capitalist and market relations (see chapter 6). Thus
'money is the reification of exchange among people, the embodiment of pure function' (quoted in Turner 1986: 96). Historically,
money becomes increasingly abstract and symbolic, a measure of
value which is not tied to particular goods or a particular substance (such as gold), but rather – being utterly without its own
value – can express the value of anything else. Hence 'Money per-
mits an objectification of subjective value, in a universalistic form'
(Holton 1992: 207). That is to say, Simmel starts from a subjective
theory of value (value is tied to individuals' evaluations of their
preferences, resources and possible satisfactions), but treats money
as the means by which private evaluations are objectified in the
social world.

At the same time, the possibility of objectifying these exchange
relations depends on more than individual rationality and isolated
individual transactions. Rather than stable social order being a result

of individual interactions, those interactions already require the existence of a stable social order. For example:

> the general stability and reliability of cultural interaction influences all the external aspects of money. Only in a stable and closely organised society that assures mutual protection and provides safeguards against a variety of elemental dangers, both external and psychological, is it possible for such a delicate and easily destroyed material as paper to become the representative of the highest money value. (Simmel, quoted in Turner 1986: 96)

Simmel sees the permeation and objectification of this one form of sociation, monetarized exchange, as a dialectically mixed blessing. First, it presupposes and yet massively intensifies the 'intellectualization' of modern life and consciousness. This term includes the features of methodicalness, calculativeness, quantification and goal rational action that Weber also puts centrally in his work. However, Simmel gives centre stage to the impersonality of exchange that is a result of monetarization. This impersonality is in many respects a historical achievement, a real gain: for example, replacement of feudal obligations with monetary payments such as tax frees individuals from personal bondage. As in Marx and Weber, this depersonalization is corrosive of traditional order, dissolving old bonds and their legitimating frameworks and increasing social and legal freedom for the individual. Simmel also links it to personal autonomy in terms of the development of the individual, and the individual's ability to make choices and to calculate the satisfaction of their needs, especially in the context of industrial production. Confronted in the marketplace as well as in urban life with the massive array of things produced by the modern world, the individual becomes capable of increasing refinement in their needs and perceptions, able to make ever more precise and sophisticated discriminations. Here Simmel comes very close to Marx: market societies produce both massive alienation and also the potential for the development of the individual who is 'rich in needs'.

The question, for Simmel, is one of assimilation: how can individuals reincorporate within their subjective experience the massive objective culture produced by modern capitalism? For Simmel, like Weber, the problem is that while depersonalization through money calculation allows greater individual freedom, it also subjects modern life to ever more regulation and control, partly through quantification. This includes a concern with 'the preponderance that the technical side of life has obtained over its inner side, over its personal values', resulting in a domination of objective over subjective culture such that technical and formal rationality become ends in themselves. As a consequence, we are left with the 'specifically modern feelings, that life has no meaning, that we are driven hither and thither in a mechanism built out of mere preliminary stages and means, that the final and absolute wherein consists the reward of living, ever escapes our grasp' (cited in Frisby 1988: 43). At the same time, the very profusion of things, the scale of objective culture that confronts the individual in modern life, in the marketplace and the city, is profoundly disorienting, seemingly beyond the ability of individuals to assimilate into their personalities. For example, Simmel maps out modern experience in terms of an oscillation between, on the one hand, a condition of 'neurasthenia' (an anxious overstimulation, in which one is overwhelmed by the sensorium of modernity) and, on the other hand, a defensive reaction – 'the blasé attitude' – in which individuals distance themselves from all this excitement by taking refuge in a state of mind in which all these different sensations look very much the same (Simmel 1950). Here, again, the intensification of individualism in market society appears destructive of the individual as an integral, ethical subject.

Durkheim

Although all the classical social theorists were concerned with the fate of the individual within modern social order, Durkheim produced the most frontal assault both on the concept of the liberal-utilitarian individual and on its adequacy for either understanding or producing social order. Indeed, Durkheim was such an effective opponent of utilitarianism because he did not offer an alternative psychology, but rather – true to his methodology of explaining the social by way of social facts – he produced an account of the modern individual as itself a social product. Moreover, the modern individual was the product of society as a moral order, not simply as an economic system. If the modern individual emerges from utilitarian society as atomized and asocial, this is not because individuals are naturally so, but because they have been produced – socially – in a pathological form that must be overcome.

From the point of view of Durkheim and later economic sociologists (for example, Parsons and Smelser 1956), utilitarianism is an implausible basis not only for society but even for the market itself. The very idea of orderly exchange based on contracts voluntarily entered into by individuals presupposes a moral order: few contracts would be honoured in a society based purely on self-interested calculation, or they would require a higher level of policing and enforcement of exchange than is actually found in liberal market societies. There is the old conundrum of the Chicago-trained economist who, away at a conference and eating alone in a restaurant in a city to which he will never return, nonetheless leaves the waiter a tip. His motivation evidently lies in his membership of an ethical community rather than in his self-interested calculations. As Durkheim put it, there is an irreducible 'non-contractual element in contract', the background assumption of a moral authority that renders the contract binding. This non-contractual element normally takes the form of juridical regulation and state authority, but even these are to some extent merely objectified evidence of deeper moral bonds that are themselves necessary to legitimate any official, institutional sanctions.

In a complete reversal of liberal-utilitarian principles, this moral order is regarded by Durkheim as the logical and historical presupposition of exchange rather than as its consequence. Neither market exchange nor social order results from individuals entering into contracts; rather, individuals, contracts and exchanges make sense only against the background of a social order. 'Yet if the division of labour produces solidarity, it is not only because it makes each individual an agent of exchange, to use the language of the economists. It is because it creates between men a whole system of rights and duties joining them in a lasting way to one another' (Durkheim 1984 [1933]: 337–8). Indeed, Durkheim's most influential arguments revolved around the division of labour, precisely the modern development from which Enlightenment thought derived the idea of society as based on isolated individuals entering into interdependent contracts based on self-interested exchange. Durkheim starts from a model of mechanical solidarity based on the similarity of members characterized by a uniform *conscience collective*. The modern division of labour arises from a process of 'sharing out of functions that up till then were common to all' (p. 218). Hence, modern order arises from a process of differentiating a collectivity, not of aggregating individuals. Moreover, as part of the process of differentiation, the emerging division of labour requires constant communication between the 'specializing parts' so that they can divide up tasks properly. Hence, 'the division of labour can therefore only occur within the framework of an already existing society. By this we do not just simply mean that individuals must cling materially to one another, but moral ties must also exist between them' (p. 218).

Durkheim also argues on the basis of time and continuity:

exchange should not be understood in terms of the simultaneous and instantaneous exchanges that clear neoclassical markets. Rather, it should be understood in terms of the more enduring interconnections that characterize the organic solidarity of a society based on a division of labour:

> even where society is most completely dependent on the division of labour, it is not reduced to a collection of juxtaposed atoms, among which it can establish only external, temporary contracts. On the contrary, the members are united by ties that extend deeper and further than the brief periods of exchanges. Each of their functions is performed in a fixed way, dependent upon others, and forms a solidary system with them. . . . Because we fulfil a specific domestic or social function, we are involved in a complex of obligations from which we have no right to free ourselves. (Thompson 1985: 50)

Durkheim, then, ultimately bases his belief that ethical solidarity will emerge in modern society on an organic model of the social. However, he does not argue that the division of labour automatically produces new forms of solidarity: indeed, he understood the crisis-torn society in which he lived precisely as a crisis of solidarity. In this picture, utilitarian self-interest appears as a kind of pathology that emerges in a transitional period in which western societies are caught between the older moral basis of mechanical solidarity (largely religious and collectivist world views) and a new organic one that is yet to emerge. In the first instance, the division of labour is indeed a massively individualizing force, one that differentiates people in terms of unique roles and perspectives within the social organism. At the same time, it removes them from traditional communal structures and representations that previously provided the ethical basis of social order. How can society persist in holding together under these conditions?

Obviously, given Durkheim's premises, the market alone cannot provide social order, but rather requires order itself. Yet this will have to be a form of order that is in tune with market relations and the extended division of labour. As Holton (1992: 189) puts it, in a modern individualized world, the emergent moral basis of solidarity, 'if it is to have any binding force at all, must be expressed in terms of individual action, and in particular in terms of the obligations upon individuals'. Individualism is necessarily the modern idiom of social cohesion: what are required are forces that will promote a moral individualism rather than stopping – as does utilitarianism – at the atomized, desocialized individual. Hence, Durkheim looks to an emergent 'cult of the individual', arguing that society can foster certain values that are incipient within the division of labour: above all, a high valuation of mutual interdependence, coupled with a respect for other individuals and a concern for their freedom and equality. Again, these values are put forward by Durkheim not as basic rights or as properties of the self-interested individual, but rather as social norms or beliefs that fill the functions vacated by the old *conscience collective*. From this perspective, morality and self-interest are not mutually exclusive options; nor are they identical, as in utilitarianism. As Holton puts it, for Durkheim morality is not a denial of the self, but 'the tying of self to moral obligation' (p. 191). This bears some similarity to Weber's solution to the problem of modernity in the form of an ethics of personality and responsibility that simultaneously recognizes the necessity of individual choice and also the subordination of the individual to higher values.

In Durkheim's work, moral bonds are also necessary to market exchange for the purpose of securing legitimation: we do not honour or legally enforce market contracts when they are not seen to meet certain ethical preconditions that are ultimately justified in terms of the individual. For example, where exchange is forced, based on (unacceptable) inequalities of wealth or power, and where this results in a clearly disproportionate exchange of value (where one party receives the 'lion's share'), then the contract may not be accepted as binding, for 'we have come to require not only that they should be by consent, but that they respect the rights of the contracting parties' (Thompson 1985: 155). Similarly, we have come to set great store by equality of opportunity. We can accept widely disparate market outcomes, but they are legitimate only on a particular moral basis – that they can be traced to inequalities of ability rather than to inherited advantages. Finally, Durkheim links the transitional lack of solidaristic bases in modern market society to the breakdown of individuals as well as of social order: the concept of anomie, linked to the suicidal destruction of the individual whom market society also creates, characterizes individuals who do not know their social place, do not know the rules and cannot rely on stable structures. Moral deregulation means that individuals do not know where they stand, as evidenced by insatiable appetites that can be moderated only by 'society' as the sole moral power greater than the individual. Yet utilitarianism does not recognize society; in this sense, 'the amoral character of economic life amounts to a public danger' (Durkheim 1987 [1897]: 254).

Durkheim's stress on the moral presuppositions of exchange is compatible with an analysis of both conflict within the sphere of competition and conflict over the legitimacy of the system as a whole.

A real weakness arises – as Clarke (1982: 121, 127) points out – when he goes beyond arguing the 'need for moral and political regulation of social relations' and tries 'to specify the content of that morality or the means by which that content was elaborated socially'. For example, Durkheim advocated the establishment of professional associations that would reach across the divides between classes or between producers and consumers to make visible the values that naturally arise from their interdependence within a division of labour. Yet this seems hardly convincing in relation to the structural scale and depth of social division in capitalist societies. We might be similarly unconvinced by contemporary advocates of communitarianism, such as Etzioni, followed by political figures such as Clinton and Blair. Reacting to the late, crude Benthamite neoliberalism of their own day, this line of thought argues that 'the repair that was needed was one that would bring back a sense of the moral worth of the individual, and combine it again with a sense of the moral value of community' (Macpherson 1962: 2, writing of John Stuart Mill's similar concerns over a century earlier). Taking Etzioni (1988) as figurehead, we might say that communitarianism attempts to replace both the reductive psychology and the methodological individualism of utilitarianism and economic liberalism. On the one hand, Etzioni argues (as we have seen Sen argue in chapter 2) that individuals cannot be reduced to the monotone utility of self-defined pleasures; they also seek morality itself as a utility. Indeed, Etzioni proposes that there is an inherent moral sense at work in human action. On the other hand, Etzioni argues that society should be seen neither as reducible to individual actions nor as an end in itself: he proposes 'I&We' thinking in which, embedded in responsive communities, 'people are viewed as pursuing goals they acquire from their communities, and inner moral and emotive developments' (Etzioni 1988: 10). In practice, communitarianism has garnered both radical right-wingers and neoconservatives as well as progressives seeking to construct a post-Marxist centre-left capable of embracing market forces while repairing the socially anomic results of neoliberal marketization. Proponents of all stripes tend to seek new sources of ethical order in abstract or traditional concepts: family and socialization, community, tradition, religion, innate moral sense and so on. These appear to be rather empty; references not to real entities, but rather to somewhat nostalgic representations of where they think we used to find our moral anchorage. Moreover, much like Durkheim's stress on corporatism, communitarianism has been rife with the language of co-operation and partnership, languages that ignore the sectoral and class interests that are endemic to market societies.

Durkheim and Etzioni are far from alone: much of modern social thought starts from a perception of the cultural deficits of capitalist and utilitarian modernity, arguing that to the extent that market society has introduced utilitarian calculations into everyday life, it has actually undermined itself, eating away at the normative and solidaristic foundations it requires for its own stability. This kind of argumentation has taken many forms. Whereas Durkheim argues that market society cannot look to past (for example, religious) sources of solidarity as a basis for modern stability, others, such as Schumpeter, have argued that market society actually depends on traditional culture and morality to ensure essential market preconditions, such as discipline, acknowledgement of obligations and honouring of contracts, a work ethic and so on. And yet the effects of market self-interest and capitalist 'creative destruction', in which 'all that is sacred is profaned', corrode precisely these ethical and solidaristic sources. Weber offered several different versions of this argument, most famously his account of how the religious bases of the Protestant work ethic are undermined by their own material success. In Bell's (1979) influential variant of this argument, the fundamental 'cultural contradictions of capitalism' comprise a split between the Protestant ethic that supports work discipline and a hedonistic ethic that – promoted by advertising and the need for ever-increasing sales and consumption – reinterprets individualism not in terms of sober self-reliance, but rather in terms of maximum self-development, experience, pleasure and gratification. Consumer culture is symptomatic of the resulting contradiction. It directly undermines both the work ethic and the collective values and socialization processes on which it depends. This kind of argument persists less apocalyptically in current concerns with 'reflexive modernization' in the work of, for example, Giddens (1991), Lash and Urry (1994) and Featherstone (1991, 1995). They argue that modernity does indeed promote a radical individualism in which everyone is required to construct, choose, monitor, maintain and market a 'self-identity'. In such accounts, the market is a mixed blessing, one that certainly acts as a destabilizing force that intensifies the pluralization and instability of life-worlds (largely by proliferating the number that we are exposed to or have to negotiate), while at the same time providing vast new resources for producing our selves and new modes of stabilizing these selves (for example, through the notion of lifestyles). Moreover, such theorizations – for example, Giddens, much in the Durkheimian vein – do not view the individual in individualistic terms. It may well be that the cult of the individual, as a solidaristic basis for a market society, has emerged not from the old modernist ideals of freedom, equality and rights, as Durkheim expected, but from the putatively 'postmodernist' ones of desire, playful and ironic identity formation, and provisional and fragmented (rather than enduring) forms of sociality (see chapters 6 and 7).

Talcott Parsons and economic sociology

We will round off this discussion of rationality and solidarity in market society by exploring the work of Talcott Parsons, who – as Holton and Turner (1986) and Holton (1992) make clear – translates these concerns into a project of economic sociology proper. Parsons pursues the big question bequeathed by liberal-utilitarianism and marketization: to the extent that society comprises a multitude of individuals pursuing their independent goals (and, following Weber, under conditions of irresolvable value conflict), how could society conceivably hold together? A large part of Parsons' solution revolves around the notion of culture, which he generally formulated as a kind of social glue. In his early work, conceived in Weberian terms as a theory of social action, Parsons is concerned with the construction of goal-oriented action as subjectively meaningful. As this still cannot solve the problem of social integration under conditions of value conflict, Parsons focuses more and more on 'the concept of the social system as a functional complex of institutions within which cultural values are made binding for action. Sociological analysis (for Parsons) is concerned with cultural tradition to the extent that it has been incorporated in binding social norms or institutionalized values, that is, to the extent that it has attained normative force for orienting action' (McCarthy 1984: 216). This formulation shares Durkheim's functional and organicist tendencies: social integration is understood in terms of how the individual is socialized into systemically defined roles that have objective implications for the ways in which social processes and institutions are able to function.

Parsons argues that the economy is therefore always embedded within a social order, although in a markedly different manner from Polanyi's account, as discussed in chapter 4. Parsons and Smelser (1956) argue that no social institutions or formations can be purely economic; rather 'the economic' approximates to one of four universal functions that all social systems must carry out: the function of Adaptation (the others are Goal-attainment, Integration and Latent pattern-maintenance). Real-world institutions like markets or enterprises may appear to be almost exclusively focused on one of these functions (on adaptation, in the case of markets), but this is never really quite the case. Market institutions must also deal with issues of pattern-maintenance (culture), of goal-attainment (political direction and regulation) and of integration (establishing stable normative frameworks). The function of integration, for example, covers the clearly Durkheimian territory of establishing rules of the economic game that bind people into orderly social roles and relations while in the heat of economic competition, notably the institution of contract and the conduct of 'entrepreneurship' (see Holton 1992: 259–62).

Hence, Parsons' systems theory places market exchange within the context of the maintenance of social order through systemic integration, while at the same time conceptualizing it as intrinsically political, cultural and normative, as well as 'rational' in the neoclassical mould. As in Durkheim, culture and normativity enter into all aspects of social activity. Nonetheless, Parsons and Smelser's framework is not quite the radical departure it first looked. First, 'the economic' is defined in conventional formalist mode (responses to situations of scarce resources through alternative strategies). As Godelier argues (1986: 184), this renders Parsons' work an apologia for the market as the world's most rational system. Second, in Parsons' work the economic relates to the other subsystems largely as externalities: 'economic structures and processes constituted the parametric constraints for other bodies of theoretical and empirical investigation and vice versa' (Martinelli and Smelser 1990: 25–6). Hence, Parsons' agenda included investigation into exchange between subsystems (for example, working for money for consumer goods represents an exchange between subsystem L [latent pattern-management] in the form of the family and A [adaptation], the economy). It also included analysis of the ways in which other subsystems determine the parameters of economic activity – for example, the way tastes are 'structured by the exigencies and activities of the other subsystems' (Martinelli and Smelser 1990: 27); and research into the ways in which non-economic forces structure economic exchange through the institutionalization of normative systems (law, property, contract). The non-economic appears merely as the exogenous environment of rational economic behaviour, much as in any neoclassicism. Finally, as Habermas (1987) argued, Parsons never really departed from the liberal problematic in which monadic individuals pursuing their self-interests have to be brought together somehow, anyhow, in order to account for the fact that societies seem to keep on keeping on. Like Durkheim, Parsons ultimately does this by simply reversing the terms of liberalism (society now creates the individual), producing an 'oversocialized' concept of the modern individual, one who simply fills functionally defined social roles.

In sum, figures like Durkheim and Parsons see market rationality, particularly in its utilitarian guise, as limited, reductive and productive of anomic individuals and social disintegration; but they also see distinct and cheerful possibilities of social *re*integration, of adding 'a cultural dimension' that will resocialize economic actors, economic thought and sources of social conflict. Both do this by reasserting organic and functionalist accounts of the social that are also to be adopted by social actors who might come to see themselves in terms of functionally interdependent roles within legitimated social orders. This optimistic addition of 'a cultural dimension' or an ethical subject may be facile and wish-fulfilling in the case of communitarianism, but could also be argued to provide the shaky foundations of some brands of economic sociology (see the critique in Callon 1998a).

Conclusion

As Holton and Turner (1989: 14) note, sociology is often reckoned to be methodologically and theoretically hostile to both individualism and liberalism (see also Abercrombie, Hill and Turner 1986). And yet, Holton and Turner argue, this is not strictly true: in fact, 'the whole tradition of classical sociology, far from being opposed to individualism *per se*, presented a well-established critique of economic utilitarian and hedonistic individualism while supporting an ethical or social notion of individualism'. Classical sociology consistently attacked economic individualism, but for precisely the same reasons that its founding fathers all placed concepts of 'moral individualism' (Abercrombie, Hill and Turner 1986: 26) at the very centre of their projects. Figures like Mill or Weber placed the cultivation of the individual personality centrally as a calling or life plan around which an ethical status was constructed (Featherstone 1995; Löwith 1982 [1932]; Whimster and Lash 1987); Marx strove for the non-alienated individual who is 'rich in needs'; while Durkheim sought the roots of a new cult of the individual in the very division of labour that ostensibly condemned both ethical individual and social order to anomic disarray.

That is to say, for classical social theory the individual who emerged both from modern capitalism and from the ideas of its liberal proponents was in some sense not a true individual. In the very process of constructing rational pursuers of self-interest, the modern order was detaching individuals from those 'sources of the self' (Taylor 1989) which made for both a normative order and a moral individual. By and large, classical sociology located such

sources of the self in over-arching moral frameworks that transcended the individual, and in substantive values that transcended
the formal rationality of modern economic action. These values
might be sought in the legacies of the premodern world, in the
contemporary life of the community or in the socialist hereafter of
capitalism. But what sociology consistently argued is that there had
better be such a thing as society, otherwise neither social order nor
even economic order could persist. As we shall see in the next
chapter, a variety of positions in economic sociology and economic
anthropology have started precisely from the argument that economic order, including market order, is *always* embedded in such a
thing as 'society'.

4

Markets and Social Structures

Introduction

In their respective analyses of modern market society, economics and sociology take up critical common themes, each addressing the rationality of market order and individual action. However, the history of the social sciences has been marked by the pronounced separation of different areas of inquiry: as Durkheim (1984 [1933]: 304) remarked, 'the jurist, the psychologist, the anthropologist, the economist, the statistician, the linguist, the historian – all these go about their investigations as if the various orders of facts that they are studying formed so many independent worlds. Yet in reality these facts interlock with one another at every point.' Such divisions in part were the outcome of turf wars that took place in the late nineteenth and early twentieth centuries, as the proponents of various social sciences sought to establish their intellectual claims together with their legitimate academic status (see Kadish and Tribe 1993). These disciplinary manoeuvres produced an intellectual division of labour that would allow the neoclassical economist Paul Samuelson to 'separate economics from sociology upon the basis of rational and irrational behaviour, where these terms are defined in the penumbra of utility theory' (Samuelson 1955: 90). Rationality was defined in terms of the rational calculation said to be evident in markets, and this definition served as the dividing line between the interests of economics and those of sociology. While economists occupied themselves with rational, maximizing behaviour in markets, the study of 'irrational' (affective, rule-governed, ritual, deviant, customary) behaviour was left to sociologists and anthropologists. Both the narrow definition of rationality and this division of intellectual labour have come under challenge from perspectives in economic sociology and anthropology.

While there are disagreements among economists as to the nature and functioning of markets, there is an orthodox consensus that markets operate in a distinct sphere with a significant (and desirable) degree of autonomy from political and social structures. The strong version of this economic approach views the market as a form *sui generis*, which works according to intrinsic rules and generates its own categories of inquiry. A crucial tension within conceptions of the market arises, then, along the disciplinary boundaries of economics with related social sciences such as anthropology and sociology. The latter put into question economic assumptions about the market's autonomy from other structures of social life. Rather than understanding the market as a purely economic mechanism, these alternative approaches view markets as social institutions, and market relations as continuous with an extended range of social interaction.

Within these more 'social' approaches to the study of economic life, an argument has developed that the marginalist shift in modern economic thought had the effect of abstracting – or 'disembedding' – markets from their social context. Economic action in this account is enmeshed in 'non-economic' networks, institutions and relations (Polanyi 1992: 34). This body of analysis argues for a basic connection between economic and social processes, viewing market relations as embedded in wider social structures, networks and meanings (Granovetter 1985; Polanyi 1992; Zukin and DiMaggio 1990). Moreover, market relations are not based simply on one-off exchanges and impersonal interactions, but harden into more stable social forms as 'economic institutions are constructed by mobilization of resources through social networks' (Granovetter and Swedberg 1992: 18). In turn, the numerous organizational structures through which market exchanges are ordered – firms, banks, finance houses, factory-floors, shopping centres, auction rooms, telephone networks, corner shops, news-stands and so on – are instrumental in creating and maintaining social relations. Economic action is irreducibly social action, and economic institutions are social forms.

A 'disembedded' model of the market might be challenged in two ways. It can be criticized, first, as an account of how markets emerge in distinction to alternative modes of exchange and allocation. Second, it is open to question whether the modern market economy is in some way 'more' disembedded than forms of economic organization in other societies. The discussion in this chapter is grounded in a key critique of formalist conceptions of the market, that of Karl Polanyi. We begin with Polanyi's historicist approach to market exchange, and outline his arguments concerning the 'embedded' and 'instituted' character of economic forms. These twin concepts – markets as *embedded* and *instituted* – provide a frame for the discussion that follows. Polanyi's concept of economic embeddedness underpins our discussion of anthropological accounts that locate market exchange in more general processes of social exchange, and situate market behaviour in relation to wider cultural norms and patterns of association. The discussion goes on to consider the instituted nature of markets: here Polanyi's argument is linked to more recent accounts within economic sociology and institutional economics of how markets are instituted through legal and organizational means, as well as through informal rules and routines. Questions regarding the relationship between markets and social structures open on to issues of law and politics, institutional design and technical strategies of market *making*. In this connection, we examine Michel Callon's innovative attempt to rethink markets as social artefacts that are instituted via purposive strategies and technologies of calculation.

Markets and embeddedness: Polanyi

A primary impetus for the development of a new economic sociology in the 1980s came from the reappraisal of Karl Polanyi's earlier work in economic history and anthropology (see Granovetter and Swedberg 1992). Polanyi's ideas offered a sustained challenge to the 'economistic fallacy' of liberal economic thinking, in which market relations and market behaviour in specific historical settings come to be viewed as universal models of human conduct. Both his study of the emergence of liberal political economy in Britain and his work on economic organization in premodern societies point to the conventional and historical nature of market forms (Polanyi 1957 [1944], 1977, 1992; Polanyi, Arensberg and Pearson 1957). Taken together, Polanyi's works function as a critique of formalist approaches to the market, and as an alternative approach that grounds economic arrangements in their historical and cultural settings.

Polanyi's argument turns on a simple distinction between two versions of the 'economic'. On one hand, *substantive* economics concerns the provisioning of human needs through economic action and interaction. On the other, *formal* economics is based on the model of means–end rationality implied by 'economizing' behaviour in conditions of scarcity, and typical of market calculation (Polanyi 1957 [1944], 1992). The concept of economy, that is, refers broadly to a material realm of subsistence and, in a more limited sense, to a mode of rational conduct. In Polanyi's account, modern market society is distinctive in bringing these two senses of the economic together. In modern contexts, the market comes to represent '*the* economic institution' (Polanyi 1992: 47), rather than one form of substantive provisioning among others. As market exchange becomes central to modern forms of economic organization, market rationality dominates modern ways of thinking about economic action and motivation.

In this way, market society is characterized by the 'disembedding' of market behaviour from a wider context of social relations, norms and institutions. Economic behaviour is isolated as a discrete type of social action, governed by the formal rationality of the market and based on impersonal exchanges between buyer and seller. Whether given 'by virtue of the laws of nature or by virtue of the laws of the game' (Polanyi 1992: 31), market processes are understood to operate according to an internal logic that marks out the economy as a distinct sphere. Polanyi interrogates this formal conception of the economy on two levels. First, he examines market exchange as a specific form of economic interaction that emerges under particular historical and institutional conditions, rather than as an abstract or technical logic in itself (Polanyi 1977; Polanyi, Arensberg and Pearson 1957). In tandem with this argument, Polanyi uses reciprocity and redistribution – as non-market modes of economic interaction and allocation – to examine how economic processes are embedded in broader social structures.

Polanyi identifies three different means of allocation – reciprocity, redistribution and market exchange – which each depend on appropriate social conditions and organizational forms. Reciprocity, for example, is based on relations of symmetry between social actors, while redistribution relies on centralized political and economic structures. By the same token, the kinds of calculative exchange described by formal economics can take place only within the institutional setting of the market. Here, Polanyi challenges formal approaches to market order which begin with the isolated act of exchange between a single buyer and seller. Different types of exchange – as different means of allocating resources – *make sense* only in terms of the economic order in which they operate. Exchange oriented to price, Polanyi argued, has no meaning outside the larger market system:

> random actions of barter between individuals, if they occur at all, are incapable of producing the integrating element of price . . . the organizing factor springs not from the individual but from the collective actions of persons in structured situations. Exchange, as a form of integration, is dependent on the presence of a market system, an institutional pattern which, contrary to assumptions, does not originate in random acts of exchange. (Polanyi 1977: 37)

This account inverts the economic model in which the basic unit of market theory is the single exchange, mediated by price. For Polanyi, the concept of price becomes possible only within a *collective* context of structured exchange. Specific transactions, that is, take on market qualities only within the already institutionalized setting of the market. The market model of exchange, he argues, assumes a wider context of prices, competition and market culture for which the isolated exchange itself is supposed to provide the basis.

Polanyi's own account of market exchange is based on a dual understanding of the market – as a sociospatial artefact and as a mechanism or 'gadget'. This recalls the distinction we traced in chapter 1 between the market as a place and the market as an abstract exchange process. The market as a physical place, Polanyi contends, greatly preceded the historical development of the market as a supply–demand–price mechanism. He identifies a number of elements of which markets, in this original sense, may be composed. These include functional elements such as a geographical site and a set of goods; rules of custom or law; a supply crowd and demand crowd; principles of competition; and rates of exchange. Different kinds of exchange can possess a number of such market elements without constituting a 'market' as this would be understood in a formal economic sense. Similarly, these exchanges may be co-ordinated in a variety of ways – for example, trade may be governed by social custom, rather than by the 'hidden hand' of the price mechanism. It is only in those settings where these market elements are co-ordinated through the price mechanism that the formal market of modern economic theory may be said to exist. Polanyi therefore sees exchange as a diverse system of interaction that may involve market elements, but which only in certain historical and institutional settings (a system of private property, money, price and particular norms and knowledges) takes on the formal character of a supply–demand–price market.

Polanyi's arguments, it should be noted, rest on a sharp distinction between modern and 'premodern' modes of economic organization. His insights regarding modern market society arise in large part from the contrast with other economic systems. Here he draws heavily on Malinowki's classic anthropological studies of social and economic organization among the Trobriand Islanders of the Western Pacific (Malinowski 1922). The substantive economic system of the Trobriand people, in Malinowski's account, was based on a non-reciprocal system where a man assisted his sister's family, and in turn was assisted by his own wife's brother. Apart from this kinship system of economic provisioning, Malinowski noted more than eighty different types of (non-market) exchange within Trobriand society. Polanyi's primary interest in Malinowski's work, however, lies with the latter's account of the Trobriand *kula* system of gift exchange. Under the *kula* system, gift and counter-gift were exchanged at different points in time, between designated status positions, and in a ceremonial context which precluded notions of equivalency.

Exchanges within the *kula* and kinship systems were linked to issues of family and civic honour, rather than to economic self-interest. As in the lavish destruction of the Kwakiutl potlatch described by Franz Boas, gift giving was a matter of honour and status (Boas 1974; see also Bunzel 1938). This represents a rather different version of the economic self to that conceived within theoretical economics, and one which rather tells against any universal psychology of the market. The point of kinship and ceremonial exchanges, from these anthropological perspectives, was to enact certain social identities, to tighten collective bonds and to minimize conflict, as well as to distribute material resources. Indeed, the distribution of material resources in such a society is inseparable from what might be seen as 'merely' cultural or symbolic exchange. 'The economic' – as defined in modern thought – had little independent existence. While there was barter among the Trobriand Islanders, this took place in a restricted way, stood outside ceremonial forms and involved no definite relations between transactees. Insofar as this *gimwali* system of barter lined up with a formalist conception of the market, it played only a limited role in the economic life of Trobriand society. The circulation of goods, rather, was embedded in non-economic relations, rituals and institutions: there existed no distinct 'economic' realm in a formal or structural sense.

In drawing on these ethnographic arguments, Polanyi challenged the formalist conventions of the then-dominant economic anthropology, associated with such figures as Firth or Herskovits, that applied neoclassical models to 'premodern' economies. In turn, Polanyi's work was to influence a self-consciously 'substantivist' approach within anthropology to the study of economic life (see Dalton 1961; see also Sahlins 1974, 1976). The relationship between economic anthropology and formal economic theory had not been an especially easy one. There was seen, on both sides, to be a basic incompatibility between the methods of economic science and those of anthropology. The leading marginalist economist Frank Knight, for example, offered a review of Herskovits' (1940) *The Economic Life of Primitive Peoples*, in which he clearly demarcated the deductive methodology of theoretical economics from the inductive methods of descriptive ethnography (Knight 1941). And while the British anthropologist Raymond Firth has been seen as a classic exponent of formalist approaches in anthropology (Marcus 1990), he expressed worries as to the degree of abstraction in theoretical economics, and its consequent usefulness for anthropologists. A deductive science, based on testing propositions logically derived from a set of assumptions about human behaviour, was somewhat contrary to the empiricist and observational foundations of anthropology. Certainly Firth joined the critical questioning of formalist approaches following the arguments of Polanyi and others – revising his own work on Polynesia and going so far as to question the meaning and actuality of 'the economy' in this context – even if he continued to argue for the existence of a distinct economic sphere in certain 'primitive' contexts (see Firth 1965 [1939]).

Polanyi's reading of economic anthropology anticipates more recent critical arguments that western market models are cultural constructs of limited general application, rather than reflections of an abstract rationality (Gudeman 1986; Marcus 1990; Sahlins 1976). For his own part, Polanyi rejected the differentiation of the 'savage mind' as an explanation for the absence or marginality of markets in premodern societies. The presence of market or non-market forms of economic organization was to be explained in terms of cultural difference, rather than through the differentiation of 'rational' from 'pre-rational' psychologies. Similarly, Polanyi dismissed the relevance of 'primitive individualism', or a Marxian notion of 'primitive communism', to cultural contexts where modern liberal conceptions of property did not exist. In these cases it might as well be said, following the argument of Margaret Mead, that people 'belonged' to certain pieces of land, as that pieces of land 'belonged' to certain people (Polanyi 1977: 51). Substantive economic systems that did not centre on the market form could not be analysed using a set of categories, such as property, price, equivalence and utility, derived from modern market theory. Questions of allocation, distribution and consumption, rather, were in these contexts decided within kinship, familial or communal structures. Ernest Gellner (1988: 44) makes the argument this way: 'a man buying something from a village neighbour in a tribal community is dealing not only with a seller, but also with a kinsman, collaborator, ally or rival, potential supplier of a bride for his son, fellow juryman, ritual participant, fellow defender of the village, fellow council member.'

Social order and generalized exchange

The import of anthropological theories of exchange, however, is not limited to observations about the supposed sociability of the 'tribal community'. Exchange can be conceived not only in terms of specific social relations (in a village or anywhere else), but in relation to a stronger and more basic sense of the 'social'. Mauss' work on the gift (Mauss 1990), and later work by Lévi-Strauss and Sahlins, used an expanded notion of *generalized exchange* to explain the basis for social solidarity. Social order is only possible, in this view, given general conditions for exchange which exist prior to and outside of any specific interaction. Such an idea is indebted to Durkheim's arguments, as we saw in the previous chapter, regarding the pre-contractual basis of social life (Durkheim 1984 [1933]). We have noted how critical the rise of contract was to the constitution of modern social relations; however, Durkheim argued that forms of contract (finite, impersonal, specific) rest on a more fundamental sociality. The pre-contractual elements of social life include, in the simplest terms, the obligation to take part in social interaction, and to observe certain rules in doing so. We can engage in specific exchanges or contracts with other social actors only if we share a basic understanding of the terms of social exchange. This shared understanding allows us to hold expectations about others' behaviour and to act on the basis of trust in contexts where we cannot control or guarantee the other's actions (see Seligman 1997: 81–2).

There are, then, elementary 'rules of engagement' for any mode of social exchange. Mauss' notion of generalized exchange reappears in Lévi-Strauss' distinction between general and specific exchange (see Leach 1970), and in Sahlins' conceptions of generalized and balanced reciprocity (Sahlins 1974). While these represent rather different anthropological perspectives, all serve to distinguish between direct exchanges and the general system of reciprocity that underpins them. Mundane examples of the way this reciprocity is played out in everyday social life would include doing a favour for a friend, paying for your partner's meal and giving directions to a stranger on the street. Such acts assume general relations of reciprocity which 'all even out in the end'. In a larger sense, relations of generalized exchange can be seen to support all social exchanges, including those economic ones conducted on a strictly calculative basis. Commercial transactions depend on the notion that people share an understanding of the terms of the exchange. Whatever regulations and contracts might govern particular transactions, they rest on a basic and collective notion of what exchange entails – and, moreover, on the fundamental necessity for social interaction and interdependence. As Durkheim (1984 [1933]: 158) would have it, even 'in a contract not everything is contractual'.

Social and economic life, then, exists only on the basis of generalized exchange, of the circulation of 'symbolic credit' among many social actors (Seligman 1997: 82). This kind of symbolic credit – a sort of good economic karma – is presumably at work when our neoclassical economist leaves the tip in that restaurant he will never visit again. The *kula* system of the Trobriand Islanders represents an unusually explicit version of generalized exchange, as all other transactions (including barter) take place within and rely on the social peace secured via the *kula* system. While both Lévi-Strauss and Sahlins distinguish between generalized reciprocity and the direct exchange associated with markets, market relations also rest upon such an underlying framework. Other theorists have pointed to the importance of symbolic credit for the development of market economies, particularly given the historical role of middlemen in mediating between buyers and sellers (Plattner 1989; see Seligman 1997: 82). Confidence in these developing trading patterns depended on the ability to form expectations about the economic behaviour of others, based on the iteration and institutionalization of market exchange. Anthropological perspectives on generalized exchange, then, go beyond seeing economic activity as embedded in prior social relations (and, therefore, being potentially 'disembedded' in a market context). Rather, economic and social relations, including instrumental market exchanges, are linked into the very foundations of human association and social solidarity.

In summary, there are two key insights to be drawn from these anthropological perspectives. First, they point to the practical role of 'non-economic' factors – social ties, cultural norms – in processes of material allocation. Second, they situate specific forms of exchange, including markets, in a context of generalized exchange that provides the basis for social interaction, reciprocity and collective action. Each of these insights puts into question a model of the market as a strictly 'economic' form, disembedded from a wider social and cultural setting. Indeed, a rather simple division between formal and substantive economics constitutes the major problem with Polanyi's thesis. Mark Granovetter (1985) has suggested that there tends to be a greater degree of formal rationality in non-market economies, while market economies are more fully embedded in social networks, than Polanyi's strict separation allows. Economic embeddedness, then, cannot simply be taken to distinguish non-market (or 'premodern') from market (or 'modern') societies. *Contra* Polanyi, economic modernization indicates a change in the forms and degree of social embeddedness, rather than a wholesale 'disembedding' of market relations from a wider social context. Different economic rationalities and relations, furthermore, are given to overlap in a range of economic settings. Hart's work on the Frafra minority in urban Ghana, for example, considers how this group mediates the contract-based market economy of the city with customary forms of kinship exchange, via trust networks of horizontal association (Hart 1988). In his work on social capital, James Coleman (1988) famously uses the case of the wholesale diamond market in New York to typify a setting where social networks, relations of trust, cultural norms and informal sanctions facilitate and regulate economic exchange. The close networks of Jewish diamond-traders in Brooklyn, he suggests, offer a kind of security for their trade, doing away with the need for costly and complex forms of contract and insurance. Such networks then are not simply social, but neither are they strictly economic in character (see Tonkiss 2000).

In a different way, non-market exchanges can involve quite tight degrees of formal calculation. While gift exchange has usually been seen as symbolic rather than economic, it might be argued that its 'non-economic' character rests on certain calculations about equivalence, utility and value. Recent anthropological work on gift giving has considered the calculative rationality that this can involve – how much should one spend on a particular gift, for example? Or how soon should one reciprocate with a gift in return? (See Bourdieu 1989; Miller 1998b.) These examples suggest that economic action is embedded in social relations and structures in complex and contingent ways. Zukin and DiMaggio (1990) seek to unpack the concept of embeddedness, arguing that we should examine the different levels on which economic arrangements are socially embedded: culturally, structurally, cognitively and politically. Economic processes – including market processes – are embedded in cultural norms and practices (from destroying a surplus to leaving a tip), institutional structures (from kinship relations to joint-stock companies), internalized rules and knowledges (from timing a gift to paying in a shop), and legal and political frameworks (from village hierarchies to laws of contract). Such arguments challenge a simplistic version of embeddedness that derives from an earlier period of anthropology in which premodern societies were seen as simple, undifferentiated or unitary cultures. As a consequence, 'the economic' could be seen as a natural or integral aspect of social life, part of the organic relationship between culture and nature that is common to human societies. Rather, in all societies economic forms must be instituted, regulated and reproduced via a range of social networks, ideas and practices. It is not clear, in this context, why potlatch should be seen as somehow 'more social' or 'more embedded' than contract – each represent specific ways in which economic relations are socially produced. As Polanyi (1992: 34) has it, 'The study of the shifting place occupied by the economy in society is therefore no other than the study of the manner in which the economic process is instituted at different times and places.'

Embeddedness and advanced market economies

The relationship between forms of social and economic interaction has recently entered arguments about economic success in advanced market economies. The notion that economic exchange is embedded in social relations and institutions has been taken up in accounts that see these social factors as a key influence on economic growth. Robert Putnam (1993: 152–62) suggests that levels of civic association within different Italian regions can help to explain – and even to predict – their respective levels of economic development. In a multination study, Fukuyama (1995) offers an analysis of the kinds of 'social capital' – the collective trust, social networks and cultural values – that conduce to economic prosperity. If it is now a commonplace of economic anthropology and sociology that forms of economic organization are embedded in systems of cultural relations, such work is distinctive in using this thesis as a basis for assessing relative performance in an international capitalist context. Social factors, that is, are seen not simply as an inevitable component of economic processes, but as helping to determine economic outcomes. Fukuyama argues that certain 'arts of association', and in particular generalized relations of social and economic trust, underpin different societies' chances of economic success. The shared values that constitute society as a moral community, that is, promote collective good in an economic as well as a broader cultural sense. A large part of Fukuyama's argument is that those societies that show a propensity for 'spontaneous sociability' (p. 27), such as the United States and Japan (whatever this pair's other differences), also tend to economic prosperity. Fukuyama locates these kinds of association beyond the domain of rational expectations and maximizing exchange. Neoclassical economic theory, he argues – in spite of its extended explanatory powers – is unable to account for the social ties that go beyond instrumental exchange in markets but nonetheless shape economic outcomes; it must therefore be supplemented by an analysis of economic cultures.

Much of this is to revisit Adam Smith's argument that both social and economic good are founded in people's propensity to 'truck, barter and exchange' – here appearing as Fukuyama's concept of 'spontaneous sociability'. For each thinker, a civic sphere of exchange is home to both the market relations and social ties that mutually underpin economic growth and social order. In Fukuyama's account the United States and Japan – with their vivacious parent–teacher associations and flower-arranging groups (p. 53) – can be contrasted to those cultures where social and economic relations are more highly regulated either by the state (France is a culprit here) or family (so-called 'Chinese societies'). To be sure, this kind of argument echoes the mantra of embeddedness, and even the World Bank has in recent years addressed different economies at least partly in terms of local legal, political and cultural structures.

At the same time, there is something curious about the way these ideas sit with contemporary market processes. For example, changes in industrial organization in late modern societies raise a new set of questions about the extent to which economic activity might be seen as embedded in the networks of social life. Complex transformations in market economies since the 1960s – often indicated by the shorthand of 'flexible accumulation' or 'globalization' – have worked to uncouple economic relations and processes from local social spaces. These changes include the widespread shift from productive to service industries as key sectors in advanced capitalist economies; movement of manufacturing away from urban centres together with decline in plant sizes; globalization of finance, capital and commodity markets; growth in transnational corporations and the dispersal of production processes; labour 'flexibility' and insecurity; and the increasing mediation of work by information technology. The rapid growth of new communications technology and the dispersal of economic activity represent what Lash and Urry (1994) call a 'speeding-up and stretching-out' of exchange processes that take place more and more quickly over greater distances (see chapter 7). If economic institutions are constructed through social networks, in a late capitalist context such networks loop over extended spaces and are increasingly electronic in medium.

While some of these changes are associated with the rise of new economic regions and elite corporate networks, they also point to the disembedding of numerous people's economic lives from local institutions and structures. In particular, changes in production and labour processes suggest that the modern forms of sociality and solidarity connected to work – based on proximity on the shop-floor or in the office, as well as in relations between firms and localities – are being transformed. It might be argued that these shifts represent a change in the form of economic embeddedness, rather than in its degree. However, the extension of social and economic networks across space tends to be at the cost – or at least 'thinning' – of more local networks. While Fukuyama's parent-teacher association might survive, the trade union ties might not. We saw in chapter 1 how modern marketization depends on the ability of certain actors to stand outside local economic relations and to insert their activities into 'abstract' or 'placeless' market processes. There is a real tension here between the rhetoric of local-ity that is the flip side of globalization theory – social capital, local economic development, endogenous growth and the rest – and the economic need to 'act global'. The form and degree of local eco-nomic embeddedness in this sense can determine individuals' and firms' access to global markets.

The market economy as an instituted process

Polanyi's thesis that the economy is embedded in social relations has become a central principle within economic anthropology and soci-ology, but this emphasis has tended to displace an equally valuable concept – that of economic 'institutedness' (Polanyi 1992: 33). While the notion of embeddedness runs the risk of naturalizing market relations as part of an organic social whole, the notion of markets as instituted processes suggests that they must be articulated through definite social institutions and legal and political strategies. The choice is not simply between the formal rationality of economic theory and the socially embedded character of 'real-life economics' (Ekins and Max-Neef 1992). Rather, these analyses need to be augmented by an account of the legal and political constitution of markets. In what follows, we consider different perspectives on the ways in which markets are instituted. These perspectives arise at the border between economics and sociology – in particular, within economic sociology and institutional economics. Our larger interest in the market as a principle of order, then, opens on to a concern with how market processes themselves are ordered through institu-tional means.

Polanyi rejects the classical liberal notion that market society arises organically out of a human predilection for exchange. Rather, he argues, markets must be instituted – and frequently legislated – in order to inculcate exactly such rational economic behaviour. The classic example is the English Poor Law Reform of 1834, which sought to create an industrial labour market (Polanyi 1957 [1944]; see also Dobbin 1994 on the role of US anti-trust law in creating and protecting markets). While theoretical economics takes a model of perfect competition as its starting-point for the study of markets, very few actual markets approximate this ideal. Within a model of perfect competition, the market system is a container for an extended network of exchange, lacking its own institutional properties. Market exchanges are momentary and impersonal: buyers and sellers do not need or wish to establish personal relations, nor is negotiation or complaint necessary, given the optimizing effects of the price mechanism. This model precludes any notion of market exchanges occurring over time, or in the institutional setting of relations between firms or agents. Indeed (and as Adam Smith feared), the smoke-filled back-room might be as good a model of the modern market as the anonymous exchange along a supply curve.

We can think about the institution of markets both in relation to the role of law and policy in shaping markets, and in terms of market institutions themselves. Law, first, is critically important in securing and regulating market relations through forms of contract. Legal contracts establish and maintain market agreements that liberal economic theory sees as essentially voluntary. The point here is not that legal interventions modify or constrain market behaviour, but that they work positively to *create* stable market conditions – to prevent monopolies forming and to promote competition, to debar insider trading and to ensure that transparent exchanges take place. Laws of contract are constitutive of market processes as much as they are constraints upon them. Similarly, employment and industrial relations law shapes market relations in formative ways. In regulating the relation between employers and workers, these areas of law produce labour markets as, in part, legal constructs. Interventions in the domains of contract and employment law, industrial relations and labour market policy, mediate the social power of property interests with the claims of those without property. Liberal economic theory assumes the existence of private property as the basis for market activity (see Bethell 1998), but property rights must be established within legal frameworks – from the Enclosure Acts of eighteenth- and nineteenth-century Britain, to current conventions of conveyancing – that are not *prior* to market forms, but through which market relations are constructed and ordered (see Thompson 1975; Turner 1984).

These legal measures point to the way that markets are structured by relations of social power. State intervention in market processes, to take a further instance, has been especially pronounced in relation to issues of gender – at times in preserving male privilege within labour and property markets; at other times in correcting the market effects that place women and children at greatest risk of poverty. A gendered division of labour in the household has long been reflected in the gendered division of paid labour in the market, where women have historically earned less pay for work of comparable worth, and where strong labour demarcation has protected a realm of male employment from encroachment by women workers. In these domains, the law, in the shape of equal pay and equal opportunities legislation, has been used to correct uncompetitive, inequitable and formally 'irrational' labour market processes. In these different senses, economic action is taken and economic agreements are made in a legal and policy domain that is distinct from, yet helps to institute, the market as an order of exchange.

If legal strategies can be seen as shaping market processes from 'outside' the market itself, the concept of economic institutedness also bears on the way market relations are structured within organizations. A range of economic thinkers have argued for the need to develop more complex theories and models of market institutions (see Hodgson 1988). Within the 'standard theory', corporate actors such as the firm or joint-stock company are logically no more than collections of maximizing individuals. The assumption is that the firm acts as a compound individual, and forms coherent interests that clearly may be articulated and pursued in market settings (see North 1993: 258). This is to see the firm as an entity whose actions are rationalized from a fixed centre of calculation, and whose maximizing objectives are unitary and clear. Corporate interests represent the common interest of members who contract voluntarily into the larger body as a kind of 'corporate personality' (Hirst 1994: 144). The interest of the firm, simply, is to maximize profits, and this logic of maximization can be used to explain the operation of firms in market settings. To a large degree, this model is supported by the way that corporations are constituted in law. The modern joint-stock company, for example, exists as a legal entity that 'owns itself' (Thompson 1986: 184). Shareholders do not own the company's assets, only a share in any profits that are generated; furthermore, the primary legal responsibility of management is to work in the interests of the firm itself – to keep it afloat and operating within the law. This takes legal precedence over any responsibility to shareholders. The notion of the firm as a unitary agent with distinct interests is in this sense shared between law and economics.

Alternative approaches to economic institutions seek to analyse these in terms of more complex structures, relations and rationalities. One of the most influential strands of argument lies in the field of new institutional economics. This body of thought can be traced to the work of Ronald Coase, who introduced the concept of 'social costs' as a basis for explaining the function and operations of the firm (Coase 1937, 1960, 1984). Coase's crucial argument was that there are 'social costs' involved in economic transactions, and these social costs are separate from the direct costs of production. The costs accruing to firms and other market actors, that is, involve the social costs of transacting in markets, as well as the direct costs of production. These social or 'transaction costs' include the time and money costs of searching for information in markets, and the costs of making, maintaining and enforcing contracts. The key point in Coase's argument is that such costs have a major influence on how firms are organized and how economic ownership is structured. The hierarchical organization of large firms is to be explained in terms of enhanced market efficiency: these structures reduce uncertainty, promote co-ordination of functions, regulate the conduct of individuals, and economize on the costs of enacting a large number of contracts with different suppliers and services. A firm employs its workers on a permanent basis, for example, so as to 'capture' information in the form of workers' expertise, and to reduce its social costs by avoiding the necessity of contracting repeatedly with many (in principle unknown) agents.

We can see here certain affinities with Polanyi's arguments concerning the institution of market relations. While Polanyi's account forms part of a critique of neoclassical economics, however, the theory of social or transaction costs remains wedded to core neoclassical precepts. This is particularly true of the work of Oliver Williamson, one of the most prominent theorists within the new institutional economics (Williamson 1975, 1985). Williamson's work is critical of the highly abstract nature of the orthodox conception of the firm. However, he sees transaction cost economics as 'complementary to, rather than a substitute for, conventional analysis' (Williamson 1975: 1). As within received neoclassical theory, Williamson's approach to economic organizations assumes that the latter are unified calculative agents whose decisions and organization can be explained in terms of maximization. Corporate structures emerge in competitive contexts so as to produce more efficient economic outcomes. Both corporate hierarchies and relational networks, in this context, can serve to minimize transaction costs: either by co-ordinating functions internally (within firms) or by maintaining relational contracts (in stable networks) that avoid frequent one-off exchanges with numerous external agents (see Williamson 1985; cf. Richardson 1972). While forms of corporate organization such as management hierarchies or vertical and horizontal integration may appear to sidestep market processes, in this account they remain driven by a calculative logic of maximization in the market.

Both Coase and Williamson remain firmly within a neoclassical framework, explaining economic institutions in terms of how these maximize efficiency by reducing social costs. Alternative strands of institutional economics, associated with thinkers such as Douglass North and Geoffrey Hodgson, set aside the primary focus on market efficiency as the explanation for different organizational forms (see Hodgson 1988, 1994; North 1981, 1990, 1993). This body of work owes much to the 'old' institutionalism represented most notably by Veblen, whose work itself was developed in challenge to neoclassical assumptions (see Veblen 1953 [1899]). These more recent accounts share a number of features. First, they are distinctive in emphasizing the role of power relations in shaping economic organizations. Firms in this sense are seen not as unified agents – or 'corporate personalities' – but as sites of competing interest and uneven power. Second, they conceive economic processes as dynamic and often contingent, rather than merely a question of rational maximization (North 1981). While these approaches commonly take up an evolutionary perspective on the development of institutions, they do so in terms of analysing the effects – including the unintentional effects – of historical change in the economy, rather than in terms of an unfolding logic of maximization (see Hodgson 1994). Third, and of greatest interest to us here, these alternative approaches involve an extended definition of what an 'institution' is. Institutions, that is, refer not simply to formal economic organizations and structures, but also to the rules, routines and norms through which economic activity and market exchange are ordered.

Such an understanding of economic institutions is consonant with a sociological account of institutions in terms of routinized manners of behaviour and interaction, as well as the implicit or explicit rules that govern them. As in a sociological model, an emphasis on the rule-governed nature of economic action assumes that people internalize these rules and base their expectations of others' behaviour upon them. It is shared expectations, as well as the more explicit rules encoded in economic organizations and legal statutes, that ensure stability in market transactions. Moreover, personal ties and informal networks work in tandem with corporate structures and relational contracts to co-ordinate economic action. Such an account might be compared with that of an economic sociologist such as Mark Granovetter, who argues that both formal and informal relations shape economic processes, including relations within and between firms (see Granovetter 1973, 1985). Granovetter (1973) argues for the 'strength of weak ties' – the value of extended, informal or instrumental networks – in promoting economic exchange and development. The institutional framework for economic exchange in this sense extends from the regulation of contracts between transnational corporations to the many little exchanges of everyday life. When I buy a newspaper in the morning, for example, it is with the implicit expectation that the newsagent and I share the same understanding of the terms of exchange. These kinds of mundane rule are basic to the manner in which our economic lives are routinely governed. They recall the terms of 'symbolic credit' or of 'generalized exchange', the underlying conditions for any social and economic interaction, that we discussed earlier in this chapter.

This perspective returns us to Polanyi's question of how to locate markets within different forms of social and economic exchange. Although markets apparently or ideally involve impersonal relations between rational agents (whether persons or organizations), they seem to merge into or depend on other kinds of exchange relations. Whereas market exchanges are co-ordinated through price, and market relations are 'informal', for instance, corporate hierarchies co-ordinate actions through formal structures of authority that enable organizations to operate more efficiently in an extended market setting. It might be argued, however – following thinkers such as North, Hodgson and Granovetter – that firms or hierarchies involve both formal and informal relations, stressing the role of different kinds of *network* in co-ordinating economic action and relations, including through more personalized obligations such as trust (see Granovetter 1985).

One can think of these different forms of co-ordination as alternative models, or indeed as successive stages of economic co-ordination. For example, it might be that the intensely competitive market-oriented firms of the nineteenth century transformed through increased scale of operations into the large multidivisional and vertically integrated firms of the twentieth. These brought a multitude of suppliers, manufacturers and retailers (formerly co-ordinated through price) into one organizational structure. Recent capitalist developments include 'down-sizing', in which these increasingly expensive, inefficient and unresponsive hierarchies are broken up, not into entirely independent rivals, but rather into subcontracted operations that are networked into close, long-term and co-operative relations with a dominant producer (see Hirst and Zeitlin 1989). On the other hand, it seems equally clear that markets, hierarchies and networks – and their principles of co-ordination (price, authority, trust) – exist at the same time and in close interrelation. In even the most market-oriented society, the majority of movements of goods between people will be accounted for by the division of labour within production processes *inside* firms, and will be governed by largely technical rather than competitive relations (see Stiglitz 1994). At the same time, relations between firms and even between firms and consumers will involve issues of trust, loyalty, custom or even personal connection that transcend or contradict the impersonality of 'pure' market relations. In other words, market society inheres not in the 'triumph' of one model of a disembedded market, but in the complex relations between different principles of co-ordination and exchange as these are reproduced through socio-economic networks and institutions.

Instituting the market as a space of calculation: Callon

A distinctive attempt to extend the concept of the market as an instituted process can be found in the work of Michel Callon (1998b). Callon's starting-point is to accept the standard definition of markets in terms of formal or disembedded rationality. Market behaviour is conceived in terms of agents pursuing their own interests by calculating in optimizing ways and resolving their divergent interests in relation to price. However, in line with both Foucauldian perspectives and actor network theory, he aims to account for such markets without assuming that agents are, by nature or inclination, given to calculate and optimize. While properly rejecting imported psychological assumptions (economists and others simply assume that individuals or collective agents have the mental capacity to calculate), Callon is also quite dismissive of notions of 'cultural influences', of versions of embeddedness that focus on the values, norms and beliefs that orient individuals towards market-style calculation. Callon argues that this is too weak an explanation and one that does not explain why particular cultural forces may be more or less effective in different times and places. Moreover, such notions retain a dualism between social agents, on the one hand, and the external value systems into which they are socialized, on the other. Rational calculation, he argues, is neither a universal property of human psychology nor a product of 'culture'. Rather, Callon looks to the practical market arrangements through which actors come to calculate.

Callon examines how markets are constructed, or 'formatted', through the operations of a range of social actors, including economists, lawyers and marketing professionals. In this context, markets are instituted as spaces in which 'all action is analysed in terms of combinations, associations, relationships and strategies of positioning. The agent is calculative because action can only be calculative' (p. 12). He offers as paradigmatic a case study of the transformation of the table strawberry market in the Sologne region of France (pp. 20–2). Dealing in this commodity was moved to a new warehouse that constituted a 'space of calculability' (p. 20) and conformed to neoclassical models of perfect competition. Such a model is not realized in terms of an abstract logic of equilibrium, or a native impulse for maximization, but is instituted via a range of 'equipment and devices': the way goods are displayed, measured and placed within procedures for relating quantities and prices. This is no accident: the actions of the local councillor who designed the market were 'largely inspired by his university training in economics and his knowledge of neoclassical theory' (p. 22). This theoretical training, in Callon's account,

> served as a frame of reference to institute each element of the market (presentation on the market of batches which account for only a small portion of supply; classification of strawberries in terms of criteria which are independent of the identity of their producers; unity of time and place which makes the market perfectly transparent; and, finally, the freedom of wholesalers and producers alike who are not obliged to buy or sell). (p. 22)

Callon sees the relation between embeddedness and disembeddedness in terms not of opposition, but of interlinked and reversible processes. Hence, for example, in order for an object to become a commodity and object of calculation, it must be 'disentangled' – 'decontextualised, dissociated and detached' (p. 19) – from its social ties, so that it can be alienated and sold, or alternatively those entanglements need to be 'internalised', brought within the frame of market calculation. Social investments in disentanglement indicate movement towards a market regime, towards an enlarged space of calculability, but this movement is not straightforward. When goods are disentangled from other social ties and placed in a space where they can be measured, assessed, alienated and so on, Callon describes them as 'framed': they are placed within a frame of calculation. However, not everything can be framed at once: there is an overflow or – in economic parlance – there are externalities. For example, a firm that produces chemicals may pollute nearby rivers or the water-table. These environmental effects may not show up as a cost to the producer (unless the government requires the firm to pay for cleaning it up) and therefore do not enter into the frame of calculation. Through local protests or through national policy, on the other hand, market structures might be reframed to incorporate this externality, disentangling it from wider social environments in order to isolate it as a measurable effect attached to various calculable options and strategies.

And yet, Callon argues, disentanglement or disembedding is not such a pure and simple abstraction: the very process of disentanglement actually entangles things in new contexts. For example, objects do not exist only as calculable commodities, but rather exist in many different contexts and therefore need to be thought of as intermediaries that constantly lead one out of the market into other ('embedded') contexts. In order to reframe local pollution as a cost to the producer, protesters may well place 'the environment' not only within a context of calculability, but also within discourses of 'restoration' and 'conservation', of 'the natural' or 'the beautiful', and so on. For Callon the very possibility of disembedded market behaviour relies on the institution of various practices, knowledges and spaces; however, the disembedding that results is neither pure nor permanent, but the object of continuous framing and reframing by a wide array of social agents.

Social relations in an economic frame: the case of gender

Callon's case study of the table strawberry trade provides a pristine kind of 'market laboratory' in which to examine how market activities are instituted through various technologies of calculation. However, his approach can be extended to more complex instances of how social factors are brought into – or left out of – the frame of market activity. Feminist theorists, to take a critical example, have argued for the traditionally non-economic space of the home to be 'framed' in market terms – that is, to be included in accounts of economic organization – and for economic analysis to take in unpaid domestic labour as well as women's distinctive experiences and patterns of paid employment (Ferber and Nelson 1993; Oakley 1974). These arguments represent a struggle to re-frame market analysis in light of issues of gender difference and power. A social factor such as gender, then, might be seen as constitutive of the form and functioning of markets – rather than simply acting as an exogenous variable that shapes subjective preferences off the economic stage.

From its origins in liberal political economy, mainstream economics has taken the maximizing market actor to be a male individual whose economic interests both include and obviate those of women. As Folbre and Hartmann (1988: 187) note, 'The most famous quotation from *The Wealth of Nations* reads: "It is not from the benevolence of the butcher, the brewer, or the baker that we expect our dinner but from their regard to their self interest" . . . But Smith never pointed out that these purveyors do not in fact make dinner.' In a similar manner to standard accounts of the firm, the family or household is reduced to a single market actor, whose corporate interest is taken to represent the common interests of its members. In this sense, the family acts as a unitary calculating agent in various market settings. Another way of putting this is to say that economists in effect treat each household as if it consisted of a single person, and do not take into account hostile or harmonious relations between its members (a criticism made by Becker 1991: 20). Ascribing economic choices to the household as a unit, moreover, ignores the operation and organization of power within the family, particularly in terms of men's and women's respective control over household resources (Ferber and Nelson 1993: 6). A number of critics, including feminist critics, have identified an apparent contradiction in economic reasoning here (for example, England 1993). That is, the (typically male) economic actor comes to lead a dual life within the public and private spheres. In the market, it is expected that he acts selfishly in rational pursuit of his interests. He is not, however, self-interested in respect of his family – in this context, the market actor becomes a benign head of household, who provides for his family and whose decisions are taken to reflect their general interests.

Such an understanding occludes the fact that household forms vary across time and space, are modified over individuals' life-courses, and are sites of unequal and often contested power relations. Abstracted as a single unit of consumption, the household is not seen in terms of the diverse, changing and even competing interests of its members; nor is it considered how these different interests are resolved across lines of gender, age and power into the expressed preferences of consumer demand. Issues of social reproduction shape market behaviour in interesting ways. Certain researchers have argued that male workers, socialized into a set of normative expectations about the value of work and its links to masculine identity, behave in a less utilitarian manner within labour markets than do women, who often behave in this context more like a rational 'economic man'. The trade-off between paid employment and unpaid work at home means whether women choose to pursue work, and of what kind, often becomes a tightly economic calculation (Bielby and Bielby 1988; see also Ferber and Nelson 1993). In Callon's sense, we might say that the economic decisions of many women with children are more tightly 'framed' in narrow calculative terms. For example, 'Welfare to Work' strategies in the United Kingdom and the United States have drawn on arguments concerning lone parents' desire to work (both as a route out of structural poverty, and in terms of self-esteem and social usefulness), but have used cuts in benefits provision to secure the marginal economic utility of paid over unpaid work, so as more firmly to inculcate such a desire. Other studies, however, have shown that a complex and variable network of factors shape women's economic choices. Childcare, if rather primary, is not the sole issue determining women's labour market activity. Other caring responsibilities, the structure of the benefit system, pay incentives and job opportunities will all shape women's decisions, as do their relationships with their partners and/or extended families (Duncan and Edwards 1997; Wheelock 1990).

It might be said, then, that these different social factors are brought at different times into the frame of economic choice and calculation. England and Kilbourne (1990), in contrast, analyse gender relations within the household within a rather different calculative frame – drawing on neoclassical approaches, exchange theory and game theory to provide an economic explanation of power relations within the conventional marriage. An important part of their argument concerns the manner in which women's investment in heterosexual partnerships that are structured around a conventional division of labour (where women provide domestic work, child rearing, emotional support and sexual commitment) is less 'liquid' or easily 'portable' than is men's investment in earning power. These inequitable investments mean that women's 'bargaining power' – to change or leave the relationship – is reduced. While men can (more or less easily) transfer their earning power to a new family, women's domestic investment in their family is more specific and less transferable. Such an account is distinctive in using rational choice analysis to develop a critical understanding of power relations. It might well be said, of course, that this account simply formalizes an argument about men's economic power over women that we don't need to be economists to be able to see. The treatment of households as proxy economic 'individuals' implies that decisions are made in this context in rational pursuit of the most efficient economic outcomes. A conventional gendered division of labour, in which men are bread-winners and women unpaid domestic workers, should in this sense represent the optimal allocation of family resources, time and skills in order to meet the needs of social reproduction. Such an approach is somewhat belied, however, by research findings that show unequal divisions of domestic labour obtain even where men are not in paid employment, or when women are. Jane Wheelock's (1990) research in the north-east of England found that in a context of economic recession and industrial restructuring, where women frequently became the chief family wage-earner, it did not simply follow that their unemployed partners would take over domestic tasks. In a significant number of Wheelock's cases, women continued to under-take the bulk of domestic labour in spite of their more limited time resources. The division of labour remained contingent on negotiation, convention and attitudes towards gender roles and relations.

Different perspectives on gender and markets point to the way that economic decisions are 'entangled' with relations of dependence, affection, duty, tradition, power and convention. These factors, it should be noted, operate on both sides of a partnership, if not always evenly: in 'gendering' accounts of economic life, feminist theorists have at times left the male partner as an unreconstructed economic cipher – while women are out making hard choices in the supermar-ket or the labour market, a behaviourist conception of economic man has been left largely undisturbed. In recent years, such factors as an ageing population, changing family and household structures, greater reproductive choice and increasing female employment have worked to frame labour, property, finance and insurance markets in radically changing ways. A labour market in which as many women as men are active, or 'markets' in marriage and children in which fewer women see the utility of marrying, and a significant minority of parents must be prevailed upon by the state to provide financially for their children, present very real challenges to the economic analysis of gender and the family. Certain elements of these changes will be consonant with an economic approach based on a model of rational calculation (see Becker 1991) – for example, professional women might be seen to trade off between market income and time (especially in terms of buying other women's domestic labour time) in balancing the demands of work and household. However, the changing relation of women in general to labour, consumer and property markets, and the diverse market locations of particular women, point to the way in which individuals' market positions and market calculations are shaped by power relations that both form outside market contexts, and in turn determine and are reproduced within market forms and processes. The attempt to bring such social factors into the market 'frame', then, is not simply a technical strategy, but marries economic arrangements with political arguments. In the framing and reframing of gender in market terms, one is continually *led out* of the market into other sites of social power, and from market calculations to alternative rationalities of social action.

Conclusion

Our starting-point for this discussion was the notion that economic processes are embedded in the social and cultural contexts in which they emerge. Taking our cue from Polanyi, this simple premise offered a corrective to the abstract market models central to formal economic theory. However, thinking about how markets are related to wider social structures necessarily goes beyond any simple or 'organic' conception of embeddedness, or a straight opposition between formal and substantive economics. In very basic terms, economic exchange is by definition a mode – however minimal at times – of social exchange. Moreover, the category of embeddedness does not serve to distinguish between modern and 'non-modern' forms of economic organization. Modern market order does not arise from the disembedding of markets from cultural practices and social norms, but indicates a series of alternative ways in which markets are *instituted* through social networks, legal and political regulations, and organizational arrangements. Market action takes place in institutional contexts that shape such behaviour in terms of rules, norms, customs, relations of power and certain expectations about the behaviour of others. If market institutions may in part be explained in relation to principles of efficiency and maximization, institutions also are shaped by legal, political and conventional constraints that are not always designed with economic outcomes in mind. As Callon's account suggests, the framing of market action and market institutions involves not only certain technologies of calculation, but struggles over meaning and power. This raises questions concerning the political constitution of markets. In the following chapter, we take up such questions in examining a powerful instance of the way that markets are instituted as modes of political order: via the actions of the state.

5

States and Markets

Introduction

One of the dominant ways in which conceptions of the market have entered social analysis is in terms of its relationship to government. A distinction between the state and the market is central both to the forms in which markets have been theorized and to ongoing debates regarding the appropriate extent of government intervention into market economies. While fairly idealized versions of 'state' and 'market' stand in opposition to each other, the ways in which markets and states are instituted help to shape each other's practical limits and formal features. Perspectives on state–market relations tend to polarize between those which hold that markets operate best when freed from wider forms of regulation (as in liberal political economy and neoliberalism) and those which hold that economic well-being depends on public measures to correct the effects of market failure and to curtail the inequalities produced by economic competition (as in welfare economics). The following discussion summarizes key approaches, both as theoretical positions and in relation to different programmes of government that have sought to limit or extend the regulatory reach of the state with regard to market processes.

In this chapter, then, we are concerned with the order of market society as a problem of *political* order. Such a problem is posed both within theoretical approaches to the market and the state, and via the practical interventions of capitalist governments. Theories of the market, in this context, shape market realities in powerful ways. The consonance between economic theory and political practice was especially evident in the links between neoliberal economics and New

Right governments during the 1980s and 1990s. However, the relationship between ways of thinking about markets and ways of acting upon them has been an enduring feature of modern market societies. We begin with a brief discussion of the classical liberal approach to states and markets. The discussion then turns to macroeconomic theory as a series of attempts to formalize the economic capacities of the state. Marxist and regulation theories of the capitalist state offer a critical alternative to the liberal view that 'state' and 'market' constitute distinct arenas, analysing the crucial role of the state within processes of capitalist reproduction. The latter part of the discussion considers specific strategies for the government of market societies, examining welfarism and corporatism as modes of 'managed capitalism', and the market reforms that characterized neoliberalism and post-communist transition. Recent theories of governance and governmentality, finally, represent theoretical approaches to social and economic regulation that go beyond any simple distinction between market and state.

Governing a market society: classical liberalism

In its pure conception, a market economy is one where all decisions regarding investment, allocation and consumption are directed by market forces. The free market, simply, is the chief instrument of economic and social organization. Economic decisions are settled in and through the market, whether these relate to large questions about what is to be produced, or small questions about what an individual is to consume. State intervention is limited to a set of minimum conditions for markets to operate effectively. These include the provision of a national system of defence, law and order, and a legal framework for the making and enforcement of contracts. The general principle, however, is that government intervention in the market is minimized. Within an ideal free market model, there should be virtually no government intervention in market processes. In effect, most existing capitalist societies evince a much higher degree of government intervention in the economy. However, the ideal is always to minimize state activity in economic life. In this context, a theory of the market as the basis of economic organization goes along with a minimal theory of the state. If this represents an idealtype of the free market economy, however, it has always been more a standard against which greater or lesser degrees of state intervention might be measured than a blueprint for any economic reality.

The emergence of modern market societies brought with it questions about the relationship of governments to the putatively 'free' operations of market exchange. Liberal social theory was premised on a separation of the political and economic spheres: in this context, the market as a private realm of accumulation was differentiated from the state as a public realm of authority. To take a key example: moving away from earlier political philosophies that were addressed to the political role of the state, Smith's political economy founded social order in relations of exchange between private individuals, rather than in a structure of vertical relations to a sovereign state. The market economy, in this way, became the organizing principle for society itself (see Meuret 1988). Smith retained a concern with the proper role of the state, but this was recast in terms of the limits of political intervention in economic life. The differentiation of economy from government, however, was taken to be problematic from the start: it is precisely because this boundary is insecure that thinkers from Smith onward must issue warnings against its trespass. Throughout the nineteenth century, politicians and political theorists were concerned to mark out the ways in which the state might intervene in the workings of the economy without impinging too far on market freedoms.

We saw in chapter 2 how Smith's account in *The Wealth of Nations* established the economy as a distinct object of inquiry. At the same time, it circumscribed the field of that knowledge to such a degree that the possibilities for government in this domain were extremely limited:

> The sovereign is completely discharged from a duty, in the attempting to perform which he must always be exposed to numerous delusions, and for the proper performance of which no human wisdom or knowledge could ever be sufficient; the duty of superintending the industry of private people, and of directing it towards the employments most suitable to the interest of society. (Smith 1991 [1776]: 180)

Private economic action, that is, cannot be governed in any wise or even properly informed way. The market economy is understood as distinct from, and ultimately impenetrable by, procedures of government. The portion that remained to government concerned the protection of the realm, the legal system of justice, the erection and maintenance of public works and, although this is less often commented upon, 'certain publick institutions'. In the absence of political controls on the operations of the market, 'the obvious and simple system of natural liberty establishes itself of its own accord' (p. 9).

Obvious and simple as the system of natural liberty might have appeared, Smith's argument for *laissez-faire* in respect to industry and commerce was complicated throughout the nineteenth century by a trio of rather intractable problems. The first of these was the need to ensure national economic stability in a context of both international trade pressures and the periodic downturns that characterize capitalist economies. Second, the development of industrial capitalism saw the organization of a mass labour movement, which rejected a pure model of individual exchange within the wage relation, and based its claims on notions of collective (class) interest and a robust critique of the exploitative nature of capital. Third, rather than securing the general good, the market economy proved unable to ensure the prosperity of a sizeable minority who continued to live in conditions of severe and even worsening poverty. From the earliest responses to Smithian political economy, a practical concern developed with respect to those members of society who were excluded or victimized by the unfettered market.

Economic science, as we saw in chapter 2, in this way became an important occasion for thinking about the nature of the 'social'. In this connection, nineteenth-century liberal thought reveals a kind of ambivalence towards the market. In one set of views (say, those of Ricardo), free and private exchange was held to result in both individual and collective well-being. In another (Mill), market relations were seen as an imperfect mechanism for ensuring welfare. It was therefore both necessary and right for governments to intervene to ensure people's well-being, given the inequitable effects of market processes. We therefore see emerging dual principles for the social management of capitalism: on one side, economic liberalism and a *laissez-faire* commitment to free trade and market self-regulation; on the other, government measures to provide social protection from the punitive effects of the market system (Polanyi 1957 [1944]: 132). There is a further argument, however, that poverty or unemployment are not simply the baleful side-effects of market processes, containable by social policy, but are technical problems that can be solved through intervention in the way that market processes *work*. It is this technical construction of economic problems that sits at the centre of modern macro-economic approaches to the market.

Governing a market system: liberal macro-economics

The analysis of large-scale social and economic co-ordination through markets has been broadly organized around two major schools of modern macro-economic thought (see Snowdon and Vane

1997). The classical approach, derived from liberal political economy, based its macro-economic analysis on assumptions regarding the optimization of private economic actors in an unfettered market system. Market processes, co-ordinated through free competition, achieve a condition of general equilibrium of supply and demand, via the mediation of relative prices. Such a perspective reveals its debt both to Smithian political economy and to Walras' notion of market clearance. Its most obvious import, even stripped to these essentials, is in seeing market processes as self-regulating. Economic order and market efficiency stem from the dynamic interplay of supply and demand. Indeed, the main threat to this virtuous market dynamic lies in obstructions – whether in the form of state interventions or of corporate monopoly – to the logic of free competitive activity. This classical approach to economic co-ordination was evident in Smith's free market views on the regulation of grain and in Ricardo's vigorous opposition to the Corn Laws. Where the natural law tradition had advocated state regulation of the grain trade in terms of the poor's natural right to sustenance, Smith argued that their interests would be served not by the benevolence of the higher orders, but via the distributive virtues of the market.

Classical and neoclassical approaches conceive the market as a bounded, self-regulating system with an inherent tendency towards equilibrium. Market fluctuations are understood as 'shocks' that are largely exogenous to the free market system itself, whether resulting from natural or human causes. While modern economics no longer evinces the political economists' interest in the fertility of different pieces of land, similar problems of harvest failure, drought or flood – from the grain shortages of pre-revolutionary France, to the effects of the Kobe earthquake on East Asian markets in the 1990s – have long been key factors in economic crisis. War represents a damaging shock to the market system, at odds with fundamental liberal principles concerning the benefits of international trade. The most obvious and systematic cause of market fluctuations, however, is ill-conceived policy interventions – government interference in the workings of the market. Clearly these different kinds of factor tend to work in tandem: for example, as government policies attempt to respond to crises of scarcity. The central point is that markets will – over the short or long run – bring themselves back into balance following these shocks, without intervention from government.

Policy activism: Keynes and after

This macro-economic orthodoxy was brought into serious question in the 1920s and 1930s. Early in this period a decline in aggregate levels of demand – particularly pronounced in the United States – coincided with a contraction in the supply of dollars. Given the operation of the Gold Standard in linking different currencies, the problems facing the dollar had severe implications for other national economies, which together were drawn into a general economic recession. The experience of the Great Depression was formative of Keynes' economic theory. In his *General Theory of Employment, Interest and Money*, Keynes contested the basic concept of market clearance, arguing that market economies are intrinsically unstable and possess the ability to maintain chronic downturn for a considerable period of time, without tending either to recovery or to complete collapse (Keynes 1936). The Walrasian notion that markets clear in the long run is fairly meaningless – given that in the long run, as Keynes famously noted, we are all dead.

Within the new orthodoxy that Keynes' macro-economics came to represent, fiscal policy (tax and public spending) and monetary policy (the supply and price of money) were necessary to maintain conditions of stability and market efficiency. Keynes developed his ideas as a set of 'improvements in the techniques of modern capitalism', central to which was an expansion of the economic functions of government. Particular emphasis fell on government measures to ensure full employment. Prolonged periods of recession and unemployment – such as during the Great Depression – were characteristic of a market economy that was 'demand constrained', where overall levels of demand were low due to low wages, unemployment or economic insecurity. The burden on government here is to promote aggregate demand by ensuring full employment through a range of strategies (employer subsidies, public employment programmes and so on). Keynesian demand management also extends to a different set of economic conditions wherein the market is 'supply constrained'. Such a situation obtains in boom periods of peak employment and inflationary growth. Under these conditions, economic policy may be used with the aim of restraining aggregate demand – through increases in income or consumption taxes, or hikes in interest rates in order to avoid inflation. Such strategies underpinned British economic policy from the late 1990s, as interest rate increases were used to stem consumer demand and stop the domestic economy from 'overheating'. While the Labour government had precluded itself from using income tax instruments to control demand, calls for the workforce to exercise wage restraint represented an appeal that people effectively 'tax' themselves.

While the Keynesian pedigree of this second set of policy strategies may be little acknowledged, by the 1950s Keynesian macro-economics had been integrated into a 'neoclassical–Keynesian consensus' in which it sat alongside marginalist approaches to the micro-economics of choice (see Snowdon and Vane 1997). This orthodox consensus was augmented in the 1950s by the work of the British economist A. W. Phillips, specifically his concept of an inverse relation, or trade-off, between wage inflation and unemployment. When unemployment fell, wages rose and vice versa (Phillips 1958). This is a simple idea; however, Phillips' innovation was to render this notion technical and predictable. A marginal trade-off between inflation and unemployment could be modelled along the 'Phillips curve', allowing policy-makers to calculate the inflation rate that would obtain at different levels of unemployment. Strategies for demand management, that is, could be informed by technical predictions about the behaviour of markets. The inverse relation held whether policy-makers were interested in promoting full employment or – as was the case under neoliberal governments in the 1980s and 1990s – saw rising unemployment as the price that had to be paid for low inflation.

Monetarism and rational expectations

Keynesian economics came under serious challenge in the 1970s from alternative approaches which held that government intervention served to damage rather than to correct market processes. A key influence here was the work of the Chicago economist Milton Friedman. Two elements of Friedman's work are especially relevant. First, he disputed the idea that levels of demand were central to market fluctuations; rather, the problem lay with changes in the money supply (Friedman 1956). Friedman's account was based on empirical research showing that market fluctuations over the long term were linked to changes in the rate of growth of money – as in the case of the Great Depression, when the US Federal Reserve had presided over a decreasing money supply. The key impact of Friedman's work was in his arguments against government intervention into markets. Given that a time lag existed between policy interventions and their economic effects, government activity served only to compound market fluctuations and instability.

Second, Friedman questioned the state's role in promoting full employment within the market economy. He rejected the idea of a trade-off between inflation and unemployment over the long term, arguing that there existed a 'natural rate of unemployment' which held irrespective of the rate of inflation. While there was, Friedman argued, evidence of a short-run trade-off between inflation and unemployment (say, two to five years), this was based not on inflation itself, but on *unexpected* inflation. Unemployment resulted, Friedman held, from sudden changes in the rate of inflation that destabilized markets. Although a sudden rise in the rate of inflation might therefore produce short-term effects on employment levels, a high but stable rate of inflation will not in itself do so. It is not the level of inflation, but the rate of change that matters – Friedman noted that people, including some economists, are given to confuse something that is 'high' with something that is 'rising' (Friedman 1968). This points to a crucial idea in Friedman's approach. Market actors, he suggested, not only respond to price signals in the market, but also adjust their market behaviour in response to signals from government. Workers, for instance, respond to government measures, such as using budget deficits to push up demand, by factoring these inflationary trends into their wage demands. Inflation would rise without there being any permanent knock-on effect on unemployment. Over the proverbial long run, expected inflation adjusts to actual rates of inflation with little impact on unemployment levels.

Friedman's monetarism gained particular credence during the period of 'stagflation' in the 1970s when market economies evinced high levels of both unemployment and inflation, helping to break up the Keynesian consensus on activist demand management. The lag between policy interventions and their real economic effects, and the fact that people rationally adjusted their behaviour in line with government signals, confounded governments' efforts to intervene effectively in market processes. The space left for policy lay in the management of supply. That is, governments could promote growth in output and higher levels of employment by fostering productivity in industry and efficiency in labour markets. Such supply-side strategies, which became increasingly popular in Anglo-Saxon economies after the 1970s, were primarily geared to making markets in labour, goods, services and capital more 'flexible' through programmes of deregulation, including the abolition of currency controls, the privatization of national industries, the curbing of trade union powers and the abolition of wages policies and forms of employment protection.

Monetarism provided the basis for a new conservative economic orthodoxy in the 1970s and 1980s. Associated with economists such as Robert Lucas and Robert Barro of the University of Chicago, this 'new classical' or 'rational expectations' approach took the expected rate of inflation hypothesis from Friedman, together with a Walrasian model of market clearance. Moreover, this perspective integrated the assumptions of marginalist theory into a macro-economic analysis. While standard neoclassical or textbook economics in the latter half of the twentieth century had been based on models of utility and maximization in the micro-economic sphere, and a broadly Keynesian approach to macro-economics, thinkers such as Lucas and Barro used micro-economic assumptions to explain macro-economic effects. This revised version of neoclassical economics assumed a strong link between the rational expectations of market actors (whether firms, workforces or individuals) and real market effects over the long term. The decisions of firms and workers are based on optimizing behaviour in light of all the information available to them, including what they know about government policy. The problem with initiatives that tried to predict the trade-off between given levels of inflation and unemployment was that they did not include the impact of such policies themselves in adjusting expectations and shaping behaviour in markets. If governments were credibly committed to low-inflationary policies, for example, market actors would adjust their expectations (downward) accordingly. The chief importance of the theorists of rational expectations was in their influence over neoliberal monetary policy. Monetary policy (including the sale of government bonds, controls over bank reserves, and changes in interest rates) could be used to bring about low inflation – as happened (pretty drastically) in the United States during the 1980s and the United Kingdom during the 1990s – independently of strategies of demand management.

Neo-Keynesians and the return to growth

Monetarist and rational expectations economics, therefore, emphasize the factors influencing aggregate supply, in contrast to Keynes' focus on aggregate demand. Furthermore, these neoclassical approaches represent a return to a fundamental notion of market clearance and equilibrium. In the 1980s, a neo-Keynesian approach to macro-economics developed (associated with theorists such as Akerlof and Stiglitz) which incorporated many of the assumptions of the new orthodoxy. Neo-Keynesians tended to accept the rational expectations hypothesis and the notion of a 'natural rate' of unemployment – a commitment to full employment, that is, had been largely abandoned by mainstream economists and their political counterparts by the beginning of the 1990s. Like Keynes himself, however, the neo-Keynesians rejected the notion of market clearing. Market instability was expressed in terms of prices and incomes 'stickiness' – that is, supply and demand were slow to adjust to changes in market conditions. What is more, prolonged periods of unemployment were not followed by a return to equilibrium. Rather, they dragged the natural rate of unemployment up – as they grow increasingly de-skilled, the jobless are unable to price themselves back into the labour market and the natural rate of unemployment within an economy tends to rise, taking into account what has become structural unemployment. Policy interventions are therefore both possible and desirable to stimulate employment growth, largely taking the form of labour market strategies to foster human capital through training and education, rather than through active job creation.

If the 1990s saw a return to a (rather heavily revised) version of Keynesian macro-economics, there has also been a revival of a classical economic interest in questions of growth. Theories of economic growth since the 1980s have been centrally concerned with comparative growth in different national contexts, as developing market economies have been drawn into an increasingly global market system. Initially, these perspectives on growth emphasized the role of technology in facilitating economic growth. In particular, technical innovation underpinned a convergence hypothesis that predicted developing economies – given access to new technical systems – should 'catch up' with their competitors (see Solow 1994). However, the evidence of continuing productive disparities suggests that such convergence is not inevitable. In the 1990s, theories of 'endogenous growth' held that growth lags between economies are due as much to differences in human capital as to physical capital, as much to 'ideas gaps' as to 'object gaps' (Romer 1993). Human capital – skills, knowledge, aptitude – is the main factor in explaining differential growth rates. In this connection, a role for government was set out in terms of promoting the development of human capital through programmes of education and training (Shaw 1997). Such programmes indicate a shift in emphasis away from state interventions into the operations of markets. Rather, they represent an approach that 'frees' markets, while steering the economic behaviour of individuals.

State and market: Marxist theories of the capitalist state

These various debates within liberal macro-economics share the basic premise that state forms are, and should be, distinct from the market economy. The nature of state intervention into economic processes, then, is understood in terms of purposive action from one autonomous sphere directed towards another, separately constituted sphere. Such a conception of the relationship between states and markets has been challenged most robustly by Marxist theories of the capitalist state. Marxist state theory aims to explain political forms in relation to the economic basis of social organization. The particular features of the capitalist state are to be analysed in terms of processes of economic accumulation and capitalist reproduction. From this starting-point, Marxist theorists have debated such questions as the precise function of the state in the reproduction of capital, its relative degree of autonomy from economic forces, the role of class struggle in determining political forms, and the potential for systemic change at the level of the state (for an overview, see Jessop 1990).

Marx himself did not develop a fully realized theory of the state. His analysis of contemporary state forms extends across different pieces of work, including his early philosophical writings and later journalism and correspondence. Marx's initial view of the state emerges in the critique of bourgeois notions of civil society in his work on Hegel's *Philosophy of Right* (Marx 1975b [1843]). For Marx at this time, as for Hegel, the proper role of the state was as the expression of a social totality – there should, in this sense, be no distinction between the political and the civil realms (see Tonkiss 1998). As it stood, the modern state embodied the hostile interests and egoistic conflicts of an atomized civil society. Rather than representing the common interest of the people, state officials constituted a powerful sectional grouping dedicated to serving their own interests. This early view of the state appears prior to Marx's analysis of capital; in this sense, it is developed as an account of the modern representative state (specifically that of nineteenth-century Prussia), rather than of a distinctly *capitalist* state form. The state is not seen to play any particular role within processes of economic reproduction, but rather has a parasitic relation to civil society.

Marx's better-known observation regarding the capitalist state is that it forms part of a legal and political superstructure which may be explained as the reflection of an economic base. Such an account appears in Marx's (1976b [1859]) 'Preface to "Contribution to the critique of political economy"', where the model of base and superstructure is briefly expounded. Another important statement appears in Engels' *Anti-Dühring*, where he argues that – while the actions of the state may impede processes of capital accumulation (for example, through redistributive tax measures or legal restraints on market activities) – the economy is always determinant, in the last instance, for broader social reproduction (see Engels 1975 [1878]). The representative functions of the democratic state are reduced to a formal expression of the struggle between economic classes. These class struggles, furthermore, are fundamentally economic rather than political in character. This notion that the form of the capitalist state can be derived from the needs of the economic base has been a primary target for critiques of the 'economic determinism' of Marxist theory, and has been a source of intense debate within Marxist and neo-Marxist circles.

The question of the capitalist state's relationship to the economy has been addressed from a number of different standpoints. A key focus has been the state's role within social reproduction (as well as economic accumulation), and the complexity of the relation between state and economy (in contrast to a reductive base–superstructure model). Structuralist approaches in the 1960s and 1970s centred on the interrelation of the political, ideological and economic features of capitalist organization. These perspectives placed new emphasis on the state as an object of analysis. Political structures could not simply be explained as expressions of an economic base. In Althusser's words, the state had a degree of 'relative autonomy' from the economy – while political structures were ultimately shaped by economic structures, they were not completely dependent on them. In particular, the state had a distinctive and crucial role to play in maintaining the stability and orderly reproduction of a class society through such institutions as the police, military, legal and education systems (Althusser 1969, 1971). While such a function served the interests of capital in providing a stable social context for economic accumulation, the ability of the state to maintain order and to secure consent represents a specific political role that cannot be assured through economic means. Poulantzas, similarly, analysed the function of the capitalist state in securing cohesion between antagonistic social classes. Class conflict was obscured by the neutral appearance of a representative state that claimed to speak for the popular interest (Poulantzas 1973). These arguments have affinities with Lenin's view that the democratic state provided the best 'political shell' for capitalism, in protecting the long-term interests of capital while securing an apparent balance of class forces at a political level (see Lenin 1970 [1917]).

Lenin's comment also echoes in Altvater's argument that the state acts as a form of ideal collective capitalist, in that it serves to maintain the general interests of capitalist reproduction in contrast to the destructive factional interests that arise from capitalist competition (Altvater 1973). Such a perspective has interesting parallels with Adam Smith's appeal to the eighteenth-century political elite to protect the workings of the market from those who would distort it in their own interest through the creation of monopolies and cartels – that is, from capitalists themselves. In a more extended sense, for Altvater, the capitalist state secured the conditions for capital accumulation that the market did or could not itself provide; in particular, the legal and monetary systems. The state as an ideal collective capitalist was also active in the social reproduction of labour, both through regulating working conditions and through the provision of education and social welfare. The functional role of these reformist social policies in ensuring stable social reproduction in a capitalist context forms the basis of Marxist critiques of the welfare state (see Altvater 1973; Block 1987; Offe 1984).

Ralph Miliband's instrumentalist theory of the capitalist state is remembered most famously in opposition to Nicos Poulantzas' functionalist analysis. However, Miliband's work was originally developed in criticism of the liberal pluralist democratic theory of the 1950s and 1960s. In *The State in Capitalist Society* (1968), Miliband contested liberal conceptions of the neutral or disinterested democratic state via a focus on the shared backgrounds, social networks and values of political and economic elites, and with an analysis of the effects of government policy on patterns of income, wealth and inequality. The actions of democratic governments in a capitalist society, then, might be analysed in terms of the relation between the political elite and the ruling economic class. While Miliband's classic work, however, was concerned with the manner in which political managers came to share and serve the interests of capital, other theorists have been concerned with analysing distinct state interests and the specific powers of state personnel (see Block 1977; cf. Evans, Rueschmeyer and Skocpol 1985). Such perspectives have been especially relevant to the analysis of developing capitalist economies, particularly in Central and South America, where the impact and interests of state elites have been particularly pronounced (see Sklair 1994).

Markets and plans

Such arguments concerning the economic role of the state appear in a different form within debates over economic planning, as these developed in a European context from the 1920s to the 1940s. Liberal accounts, originating with economists of the Austrian School such as Mises and Hayek, rejected planning – following the failure of the wartime economy, as well as the Soviet model – on grounds of both political philosophy and economic inefficiency. The arguments, then, were both moral and technical. Hayek's opposition to planning in large part arose from the priority he gave to individual freedom as a chief social good. This sat alongside his analysis of the way that prices act as information signals within markets, allowing economic actors to make free and rational choices, and co-ordinating their actions through networks of exchange. In contrast, planning bodies such as GOSPLAN in the Soviet Union set prices and wage differentials according to collective decisions. Centralized planning, Hayek held, could never produce rational, efficient economic outcomes because it could not replicate the spontaneous knowledge produced within markets in the form of price signals (see Hayek 1945, 1976 [1949]). Hayek rejected the terms of a straight opposition between markets and plans, arguing that market allocation should itself be seen as a form of economic planning: the matter then 'is not a dispute about whether planning is to be done or not. It is a dispute as to whether planning is to be done centrally, by one authority for the whole economic system, or is to be divided among many individuals. . . . Competition . . . means decentralized planning by many separate persons' (Hayek 1976 [1949]: 79).

It is interesting to note, in this context, the extent to which forms of 'bargaining' entered into the planning process in the Soviet Union, as trade-offs occurred between central planners, whose 'interest' was to set production targets at high levels, and representatives of state enterprises, whose 'interest' it was to keep targets achievably low. In this light, a straight distinction between markets and plans can be too crude a construction to account for the complicated ways in which economic decisions are negotiated and enacted. Schumpeter, who was more sympathetic to socialist systems than was Hayek, was also concerned less with questions of allocation than with issues of economic growth. In his influential view, entrepreneurship was a crucial element of dynamic market processes. Planning systems served to bureaucratize economic activity in ways that stifled the forms of 'creative destruction' through which market innovation and expansion occurred (Schumpeter 1943).

These perspectives on planning were answered by thinkers on the left who addressed the potential uses of market forms in a socialist context (see, classically, Lange 1994 [1938]; Lange and Taylor 1964; see also Lange 1970; Nove and Thatcher 1994). Such a project, which had something of a precedent in the limited markets allowed under Lenin's New Economic Policy of the 1920s, attempted to detach the market model from an extended system of capitalist ownership and exploitation. Interest in forms of market socialism revived in relation to the reform of eastern European economies – particularly Hungary, Czechoslovakia and Yugoslavia – after the 1950s (see Brus and Laski 1989; Nove 1983; Prout 1985), opening up the possibility of a 'third way' between capitalism and state socialism (see Sik 1976). Such currents can also be found in debates over the development since the late 1970s of 'socialism with Chinese characteristics', and over more recent economic reform in Cuba (for the Chinese case, see Weils 1996; Zhang 1996; for Cuba see Centeno and Font 1997). These ideas fed into a western European context within debates over Eurocommunism in the 1970s, and in attempts on the left to regroup in opposition to neoliberalism in the 1980s (see Boggs and Plotke 1980; Childs 1980; Filo della Torre, Mortimer and Story 1979; Godson and Haseler 1978; McNally 1993; Mandel 1978; Miller 1989; Nove 1983; see also Bardhan and Roemer 1993; Gould 1985; Hindess 1990; Le Grand and Estrin 1989). The Eurocommunist debate reflected the prospect of communist parties gaining significant electoral presence during the 1970s in such places as Italy, France, Spain and Portugal, raising attendant questions of how communist priorities and policies might be realized in a liberal democratic and market context, and receiving some rather worried attention in a United States on a cold war footing (see, for example, Kriegel 1978; Ranney and Sartori 1978). The collapse of Soviet communism after 1989, however, was followed by the transformation of western European parties into (very weakened) movements of a 'democratic left', whose economic policies aspired to a kind of market socialism (see Blackburn 1991b; Bull and Heywood 1994; Elson 1991).

Broader debates over market socialism, or 'socialized markets', as these developed in the 1980s in response to a dominant neoliberalism, addressed the mixed economy from a left perspective (see Hodgson 1984; Nove 1983). Rather than seeing values of social and economic justice or positive freedom as antithetical to market processes, advocates of a socialized market argued for the 'pursuit of socialist ends through market means' (Le Grand and Estrin 1989: 2). In line with Hayek's earlier arguments, markets were seen to provide distinct economic benefits in terms of information, innovation and incentive. In an extended sense, the market might positively be viewed in terms of its potential for dispersing and decentralizing economic power. If market socialism now represents something of a historical novelty, its approach to markets prefigured the remaking of the mainstream left from the 1990s, even down to providing the language of a 'third way' in government between state control and *laissez-faire*. The form of social democracy that gained ascendancy in the United Kingdom, the United States and much of continental Europe by the beginning of the twenty-first century – if it represented an accommodation to neoliberalism – was nonetheless informed by prior thinking on the socialist left. Above all, a modern politics of 'left' and 'right' could no longer be read off from any simple distinction between state and market, as the socialist left sought to adapt itself to market forms (Blair 1998; Giddens 1994, 1998).

Managed capitalism: welfare and corporatism

The 'socialized' market found its more obvious expression in the forms of managed capitalism that dominated liberal market societies in the second half of the twentieth century. Our discussion of Keynes' ideas considered welfarist measures in terms of a technical approach to macro-economic management. As markets were only imperfectly self-regulating, government intervention was not only justified but necessary when market failures produced undesirable economic effects. In an interwar context, Keynes' particular concern was with problems of falling demand and unemployment – and he considered these as specifically economic problems, amenable to technical economic fixes. However, welfarist government, as this developed in a range of capitalist democracies after 1945, was based not simply on economic considerations, but on an extended conception of the rights of citizens. The welfare consensus that prevailed in advanced capitalist democracies from the postwar period until the 1980s represents a mode of economic government that addressed people primarily as citizens, rather than merely as market actors. While a governmental interest in the welfare of citizens was not invented at this time – such an impulse drove political debates regarding poverty and pauperism in the nineteenth century, and might be linked to an earlier notion of 'police' (see Polanyi 1957 [1944]; Procacci 1991) – it assumed systematic form in the development of postwar welfare states. These systems varied in different national and regional contexts, but a generic form of the 'welfare state' might be understood to refer to governmental arrangements where the economic and social welfare of a population is secured through state intervention, and through public provision and services. As a minimum, modern welfare states provided systems of social insurance against the risks attaching to unemployment, old age, illness and disability. This basic provision was augmented to varying degrees by an extended welfare machinery that provided social goods which did not compete with commodities in the market, such as education, public housing and health care; created jobs through public works and employment schemes; or supported people's working and domestic lives through such measures as child allowances, public childcare provision and systems of parental leave.

Different forms of welfare provision reflected larger assumptions regarding the terms of liberal citizenship. If Keynes' arguments were made principally in economic terms, the politics of the welfare state carried with it a freight of values regarding questions of social justice and the nature of a good society. Principles of welfarism extend the notion of citizenship beyond civil and political rights to include 'social rights' that provide for economic security and social welfare (Commission on Social Justice 1994; Marshall 1950; Titmuss 1958). This is because the abstract equality of legal citizenship remains quite compatible with the inequalities of a market society – as, indeed, Karl Marx could have told us (see Marx 1935 [1875]; see also Engels 1975 [1878]). Within a welfarist politics, the right of citizens to meet their basic needs is seen as the substantive corollary to the formal rights of citizenship. Welfarism, then, should be understood both as a mode of economic government directed towards the market – as Keynes would have it, a set of 'improvements in the techniques of modern capitalism' – and as a mode of social government directed towards the care and improvement of the population (see Procacci 1991). This running together of the economic and social moments of modern government has provided the basis for critiques of the welfare state from the left (and, although in a different way, from the right – as we go on to discuss below). Critics of the welfare state have pointed to the manner in which these reformist measures worked to ensure long-term market stability at the same time as they secured orderly social reproduction (Gough 1979; cf. Offe 1984). Welfare provision in this light may be viewed as offering a sop to the working and non-working poor, while it increases the capacity for state surveillance and regulation of their economic and domestic arrangements (see Gordon 1990; Piven and Cloward 1972; Wilson 1977).

The development of welfare states in market societies during the postwar period formed part of a larger project of 'managed capitalism'. A welfare consensus was allied during this time with a corporatist consensus that brought national states into partnership with the peak organizations of labour and industry. Theories of corporatism – the idea, broadly speaking, that power and government should incorporate different interests in economy and society – have a long history in European social thought, and may be traced through the work of such figures as Hegel, Sismondi and Durkheim, as well as that of Keynes and Laski (see Cawson 1986; Scholten 1987). Different versions of corporatism have been associated with the political role of the Catholic Church in various national contexts, and with communist, fascist and nationalist forms of government. The specific forms of corporatism that were institutionalized in advanced capitalist governments after 1945, however, were based on agreements between the state, labour and capital to manage the market economy in the interests of social stability, national security and economic prosperity (see Berger 1981; Cox and O'Sullivan 1988; Scholten 1987; Streeck and Schmitter 1985). Welfare corporatism, if it has links with prewar communist and fascist models, represented the dominant state form of the second half of the twentieth century, both for advanced capitalist democracies and for many postcolonial states, particularly in South America.

Government had a dual role to play within corporatist structures. On one hand, it performed as a key economic actor, both providing macro-economic steering and acting as a large-scale public investor and employer. As well as centralizing planning functions, the state's role as an economic actor meant that significant sectors of the economy were taken partly or wholly out of the market – from extractive industries such as coal and steel, to telecommunications, aviation and railways. On the other hand, the state acted as mediator between different economic interests – notably between capital and labour within tripartite bargaining arrangements. Agreements on wages and price controls, for example, could be brokered outside a 'free' market context, as within the Social Contract in the United Kingdom in the 1970s, or the Accord in Australia in the 1980s. The corporatist consensus that obtained from the 1950s to the 1980s – under capitalist governments of different political stripe, what is more – represents a mode of 'managed capitalism' that went beyond conventional distinctions between state and market (see Streeck and Schmitter 1985).

Corporatism, then, marks the high point of a period of 'organized capitalism' within which labour, production and distribution to a significant degree were co-ordinated by national states and large corporate organizations (see Lash and Urry 1987). By the 1970s, however, corporatist structures were buckling under the pressure of a number of economic, social and political factors, including:

(a) the emergence of new economic players, particularly in South-East Asia, promoting new structures of international competition and trade;

(b) the rapid internationalization of finance capital, challenging the capacity of national governments and banks to control capital flows across space and to ensure economic security;

(c) new interests that did not fit with the class basis of corporatism, articulated through social movements including feminism, environmentalism, lesbian and gay movements, peace and anti-nuclear movements – neither could these groups' claims be answered through the primarily economic objectives of corporatist politics;

(d) the increasing cost of welfare bureaucracy, as unemployment re-emerged as a severe social and economic problem, accompanied by attacks on the bureaucratic welfare state from both left and right;

(e) a gathering Friedmanite orthodoxy, which held that government intervention in markets was ineffective or positively damaging – as the evidence of entrenched inflation and unemployment seemed to suggest.

An important response to these political and economic changes was provided by the work of the French regulation school (see Aglietta 1979; Boyer 1990; Boyer and Durand, 1997; Lipietz 1987). This approach was partly a response to the sway of neoclassical economics, and specifically to the notion that markets in themselves tended towards a state of general equilibrium (see Aglietta 1979: 13). In contrast, the regulation theorists were interested in the complex of factors, both economic and social, that shaped economic accumulation. In this way, regulation theory also departed from structuralist Marxist approaches that saw processes of capitalist reproduction as impersonal, objective or self-sustaining (see Jessop 1995: 309–10). Both neoclassical and structural Marxist perspectives, it was argued, were concerned with the *internal* logic of economic processes: their tendency to stability, on the one hand, and crisis, on the other. Regulation theory instead focused on the relation between economic co-ordination, political regulation and social normalization in processes of capitalist reproduction. The idea of 'regulation' refers here not simply to formal structures of government or law, or to the 'self-regulation' of capitalist markets. Rather, it is concerned with a range of regulatory mechanisms that operate at different levels and in different social and economic domains. These represent broad institutional structures that make up an overall 'mode of regulation', including the monetary system, the wage relation, forms of competition, consumption norms, international regimes and state formations (see Boyer 1990: 37–42). We might note that these involve a mix of economic, political and social factors. In Aglietta's own account, the regulation approach is interested in 'the transformation of social relations as it creates new forms that are both economic and non-economic, that are organized in structures and themselves reproduce a determinant structure, the mode of production' (1979: 16).

The origins of regulation theory lay in an attempt to explain the long-term stability of capitalism, given (from a Marxist standpoint) its structural tendencies to crisis. The immediate occasion for these concerns was the crisis of Atlantic Fordism in the early 1970s, and efforts to analyse a post-Fordist mode of economic regulation (see Aglietta 1979; Boyer and Durand 1997; Lipietz 1987; see also our discussion in chapter 7). In this case, Aglietta and others were interested in how an economic transition from Fordism to post-Fordism related to changing forms of political and economic governance. Such questions regarding the relation between economic and political change assumed particular relevance during the 1970s and 1980s, given the consonance, in this period, between broad processes of capitalist restructuring and the emergence of neoliberal governments. Within the regulationist view, the stability of national states and Fordist economies had been based on a complex set of institutional structures, including (a) corporatist agreements between government, capital and labour; (b) an Atlantic state system; (c) production for domestic markets; and (d) Keynesian structures of welfare. In contrast, the shift to a post-Fordist regime of accumulation was marked by (a) the breakdown of postwar consensus in government; (b) the hollowing-out of the nation-state; (c) internationalization of corporate ownership, production and distribution; and the (d) retrenchment of welfare provision. 'Fordism' and 'post-Fordism', then, did not simply indicate alternative systems of production, but extended regimes of economic and social regulation through which capital accumulation was secured.

In a different neo-Marxist account, Harvey (1989) views this economic and political crisis as one of over-accumulation in the Fordist system of mass production. The increasing efficiency of large-scale production systems had led, by the early 1970s, to a situation where fewer workers were needed, at the same time as output continued to expand. Growing unemployment, however, produced a fall in demand in mass consumer markets. These problems of unemployment and oversupply severely undermined the capacities of corporatist states as economic managers. As rising unemployment placed added strain on welfare budgets, governments responded to the crisis in demand and stagnation in the economy by printing more money, resulting in rapid inflation. The period of 'stagflation' that gripped capitalist economies in the 1970s – combining high unemployment and high inflation – discredited Keynesian orthodoxies and led to the eventual breakdown of the corporatist consensus. A weakening of corporatist state structures and the forms of economic management with which they were associated provided the basis for a radical revision of the relation between governments and markets. This was marked by a move away from the managed capitalism that had mediated between state and market, and a return to classical liberal precepts regarding the proper separation of economy from government.

Neoliberalism: government through the market

Over the 1970s and 1980s a number of liberal democracies witnessed an accelerated shift in their governmental arrangements away from an emphasis on state economic management and service provision, to an ethos of 'privatism' in the provisioning and regulation of social and economic life (see Barnekov, Boyle and Rich 1989). The rise of neoliberalism was closely associated with the radical agenda of Conservative governments in the United Kingdom after 1979, and Republican administrations in the United States after 1980. However, the hold that neoliberal ideas took on a range of European, North American and Australasian governments in the 1980s and 1990s (see, for example, Massey 1995; Pusey 1991) suggests that the political expression of neoliberalism is not necessarily conservative – at least in a partisan sense. Meanwhile, the emergence of neoliberal governments in Central and South America, and the post-communist transition to a crude neoliberalism in countries such as Poland and Russia, indicate that this approach to economic government is not the preserve of already liberal societies (see Martinez and Diaz 1996; Przeworski 1991; Smith and Korzeniewicz 1997; Weeks 1995). The rhetoric of a new economic liberalism – of markets, competition and deregulation – if it became a central element of New Right ideology in advanced capitalist societies after the 1970s, later came to represent an orthodox agenda for policymaking on an increasingly international scale.

Neoliberal approaches to government, which had emerged in the 1970s as a critique of welfarism, nevertheless responded to a similar problematic: how and to what extent may a market society be governed? The forms of neoliberalism developed under the Thatcher governments in the United Kingdom and Reagan administrations in the United States were heavily influenced by Friedman's monetarist theories – particularly the caution against excessive government intervention in the economy – and an antipathy towards welfare systems that were seen to create a 'culture of dependency' among their clients (see Friedman and Friedman 1980). A commitment to free markets and a minimal state was given added impetus by the conviction that increasingly global market processes escaped the regulatory reach of nation-states. This emergent political rationality subscribed to fairly orthodox neoclassical principles, based on a view of the disembedded free market as the crucible for economic success and for general social good. Neoliberal administrations in different national contexts tended to address a common set of economic conditions (the crisis of Fordism, industrial decline, globalization); developed common strategies of government (deregulation, privatization, welfare retrenchment); and understood these changes in terms of a limited number of discourses (such as enterprise, competition and flexibility).

In a general sense, the policy reforms associated with neoliberalism might be viewed as expressions of a more enduring problematic for the government of market societies. The 'reform' of the Keynesian welfare state and the onward march (more or less) of privatization can each be understood as attempts to establish a proper relationship between government and the market economy. These strategies, moreover, were based on a 'differentiation out' of the economy, which in turn placed certain limits upon government. Neoliberalism can be characterized in terms of its orientation to the market and state based on: (a) a political commitment to the free market in principle; and (b) the 'rolling back' of the state's role in economic and social life. Such an ethos found expression in a range of different policy programmes, including the sale of public assets and enterprises (nationalized utilities, industries and telecommunications); deregulation of private enterprises (broadcasting, financial services, air transport, construction and urban development); 'flexible' labour market strategies (curbs on trade union activities, relaxation of employment protection, workfare programmes); and contracting out of public functions to private providers (security and penal services, local government services). The list is extendible and – as expressions of a larger political ethos – irreducible to a finite set of policies. Specific government 'sell-offs' rather may be seen as aspects of a more general political rationality which held that the private sector was best equipped to generate the conditions for individual and collective prosperity in a social as well as an economic sense (see Barnekov, Boyle and Rich 1989). Neoliberal government, then, has both technical and ethical dimensions; it refers not only to the transfer or elimination of public functions, but also to the creation of a policy environment that is conducive to private sector growth and encourages individual, familial and community forms of private activity (see Heelas and Morris 1992). Market efficiency and individual prosperity emerge as the principal criteria for assessing policy outcomes.

This produces a mode of government that both gives priority to economic processes and seeks to govern social life in a frugal or economic way. A particular version of the market economy, that is, comes to be seen 'as the obligatory framework for *all* policy' (Pusey 1991: 18), whether of an explicitly economic character or not. Market rationalities, imperatives and instruments made up a neoliberal policy approach that was not confined to more obviously 'economic' problems, such as inflation or unemployment, but also was applied to conventionally 'social' domains, such as health or education. In this latter respect, neoliberal programmes involved a particular approach to welfare policy. One of the keynotes of neoliberal programmes of government, particularly in Anglo-democracies, was the 'rolling-back' of the welfare state. These programmes were prompted not simply by a practical desire to reduce levels of public spending, but by certain convictions about the proper tasks of government and the duties of individuals. Specifically, welfare structures were seen to encourage a culture of 'dependency', within which individuals came to rely on the state for a range of social and economic provisions, stifling individual initiative, independence and choice (see Mead 1986). It is interesting to note the contrast, here, with earlier arguments that welfare provision was *necessary* to allow individuals to realize their capacities as independent citizens (see Marshall 1950). The response of neoliberal governments was both to reduce the size of welfare states through cuts, privatization and contracting out; and to redefine the relation between state and citizen in market terms. Within a bastardized language of the market, the users of public services were repositioned as customers, such that one might 'consume' health or higher education much as you would holidays or hi-fis.

It is not clear, in this context, how far neoliberalism represented a 'rolling-back' of the state, if by this one understands something like the relaxation of the dead hand of government upon the market. While an opposition to 'big government' was a crucial element of neoliberal rhetoric, this ignores two important points about the regulation of economic life. First, the market is itself a regulatory form – as most liberal economists would aver (see Hayek 1976 [1949]: 79). What is more, competitive market forms are secured in significant part through the actions of the state. Polanyi (1957 [1944]: 147–52) shows how free market liberalism as a matter of economic policy prosecuted by the state has a long, if discontinuous, history. Rather than representing a realm of 'freedom' from government (much less a system of 'natural liberty'), the market is instituted through specific forms of regulation. Privatization and deregulation under neoliberal governments in this sense worked not simply to 'free' incipient markets, but positively to create them in spheres such as energy, public transport or health. Where markets did not previously exist, that is, it was necessary to invent them. The market forms that resulted were distorted, managed and limited in a number of ways – from the role of majority public shareholders to controls on consumer charges and the use of statutory regulators. Viewed in this context, neoliberalism represented an approach to economic government that is necessarily statist in disposition, using policy instruments to create, secure and control market structures, rather than simply 'freeing' them.

Second, neoliberal deregulation tended to result in a dense thicket of 're-regulation'; in a proliferation of quangos, industry regulators, public contracts, consumer charters, ombudsmen, 'watchdog' bodies and audit processes. Neoliberal programmes involved not only the privatization of public enterprises and the deregulation of many market activities, but the 'marketization' of various public services – that is, the introduction of market models into the organization and conduct of government. Marketization assumed different forms in different contexts, but notably included the use of competition and contract between public agencies, a corporate-style model of 'new public management', the development of public–private partnerships and the use of value-for-money and performance measurements (see Hood 1991; Osborne and Gaebler 1992). The list might be extended, but the general point to be taken from this one is that such elements are only loosely related to any clear model of a market. Perhaps the most salient market feature at work here is the requirement that different agencies should (be seen to) compete for public funding – the market in this way provides a model for the allocation of public, as well as private, resources. However, it is a peculiarly portable and ill-defined market model that comes to be applied to the domain of policy. Precisely because the conception of the market that underlies public sector reforms is always highly variable and often very weak – sometimes involving little more than a rhetoric of efficiency or added value – it translates into a number of different policy contexts, from transport to urban development and unemployment. Moreover, the notion that market measures are *by definition* deregulatory obscures the tight forms of economic and political regulation that have attended neoliberal reforms. While owing much of their impetus to the 'big government' critiques of neoclassical thought, market reforms provide new ways of managing government agencies, as well as producing a 'second-order market of governmental goods and services' – whether in health, education or prison services – that mediates between the public and private spheres (Gordon 1991: 36).

New market economies: problems of post-communist transition

The doctrinaire approach to free markets typical of neoliberalism seemed to be borne out by the collapse of communist economic planning in central and eastern Europe in the late 1980s and early 1990s. Soviet-style communism had rested on the idea that an economy could be rationally organized through the application of human reason, technological progress, control over nature and the elimination of scarcity. Within this model, co-ordinated decisions over economic planning were intended to replace what Engels called the 'anarchy' of the market, while social incentives for economic activity displaced the profit motive. Centralized planning, however, proved insufficient to the complex, unpredictable and changing nature of economic life – particularly the challenges of 'post-indus-trial' economic organization after the 1970s (see Bauman 1992; Habermas 1990). Meanwhile Soviet communism proved incompat-ible with principles of democracy and freedom – as evidenced by the brutal suppression of movements that sought to realize a form of 'socialism with a human face', most notably in Czechoslovakia in 1968. The eventual failure of the Soviet project at great human and economic cost appeared to some eyes to represent the exhaustion of planning as a viable alternative to free markets, and more generally to indicate the 'triumph' of liberal capitalism as a mode of economic and political organization (see Fukuyama 1992). In a more qualified way, its critics on the left acknowledged the unparalleled if imperfect ability of liberal capitalism to provide democratic freedoms together with relative material well-being (see Blackburn 1991a and especially Enzensberger 1991).

The experiences of post-communist transition, however, put into question any easy linkage between liberal democracy and free markets (see Blackburn 1991a; Crawford 1995; Holmes 1997; Lavigne 1995). In broad terms, the shift to a market economy involved the removal of political controls over economic activities, without any corresponding process of effective industrial restructuring (see Crawford 1995). Privatization programmes, as exemplified by the Russian or Polish cases, functioned as a massive seizure of public assets that produced only notional 'shares' for ordinary people, with no real shareholder control and little prospect of actual dividends. The economics of transition in many of the former Soviet states was marked by a mixture of fierce speculation and powerful capitalist ideology, such that the challenges facing these transitional economies could be reduced to a crude choice between free markets and a reversion to communism. However, deregulation and privatization could not in themselves ensure economic efficiency, let alone political stability or social and economic welfare (for an alternative view of the Polish case, see Johnson and Loveman 1995). The 'shock therapy' introduction of economic liberalism in national contexts, such as Russia or Poland, that had no existing traditions of political or civic liberalism (see Sidorenko 1999) proved an insufficient condition for the development of a market culture. It was not clear, for example, how individuals might understand their market 'interests', or how these might best be represented. While the informal economy had provided a type of market incentive under communism, it was vulnerable to forms of bribery, exploitation and menace that became a model for conduct in the new market economy more generally. Such relations within the informal economy are often as hostile to free market exchange as they are to legal regulation, and can undermine the effects of liberalization as mistrust and cronyism reduce the efficiency of market processes. In-group networks, patronage and racketeering have been used to explain the problems of transition in a Russian economy within which corruption had by the end of the 1990s become so prevalent as to render honest economic behaviour *irrational* (see Woolcock 1998). Russia's problems, in particular, would seem to bear out an argument that forms of public legitimacy and norms of market conduct are crucial to economic efficiency. The notion of a free market was defined in the Russian context largely in opposition to centralized state control – that is, without positive characteristics in itself – and in practice indicated markets controlled by politicians and their business cronies (see Crawford 1995). Economic liberalization in this sense is quite distinct from the creation of a liberal state whose role, as Adam Smith would have it, is to defend market principles against those who wish to distort markets for their own gain. This represents a *positive* theory of the state that, if it should act as no more than a nightwatchman, should also act as no less.

Beyond states and markets

Governance . . .

The forms of liberalization that shaped advanced capitalist governments over the 1980s and 1990s, and dominated the economics of transition, have been reflected in a growing analytic interest in questions of 'governance'. This term designates rather loosely a field that takes in debates over private interest government, neocorporatism, mesocorporatism, corporative democracy, private interest government, socio-economics and associative governance (see Amin and Thrift 1995; Berger 1981; Cawson 1985; Cohen and Rogers 1995; Etzioni 1988; Etzioni and Lawrence 1991; Hirst 1994; Matzner and Streeck 1991; Scholten 1987; Streeck 1988; Streeck and Schmitter 1985; see also Jessop 1995). What these different perspectives share is an interest in new patterns of association between political, economic and civil institutions in regulating social and economic life. A common concern is with how relations between these sectors are restructured, or their respective tasks redivided, in order to create new governance institutions and networks that go beyond conventional distinctions between state and market.

'Governance' in this context may be distinguished from 'government' in that the former is not restricted to the practices of a formal public authority, but emphasizes 'private' modes of regulating social and economic life. In this sense, 'government' represents the formal or official moment in more general processes of 'governance'. On one level, then, approaches to governance involve a critique of conventional ways of analysing modern social structures – disturbing the classical separation between state, market and society (see, for example, Streeck and Schmitter 1985). On a different level, one finds a historical argument about changing state capacities (see, for example, Streeck 1995). Perspectives on governance in this second sense share in a more general anxiety about problems of political and economic regulation in a global context, or a perceived 'crisis' of the nation-state in respect of the latter's command and control functions. Approaches to neocorporatism, in particular, have been concerned with how governments might steer economic processes in a situation where footloose capital has been freed from the tripartite planning arrangements that typified the high moment of corporatist capitalism (see Streeck 1995; cf. Hirst and Thompson 1996; Matzner and Streeck 1991). At another scale, notions of governance have been useful for analysing the proliferation of semi-public agencies, private development corporations and quasi-market bodies that have cluttered the regulatory field in the wake of neoliberal efforts to privatize and disaggregate the central and local state.

This diverse field of work is especially interesting in bringing together currents from political theory and from economic analysis. An important impetus for the development of governance theory came from institutional economics, and specifically from transaction cost economics (see Coase 1937, 1960, 1984; Williamson 1975, 1985). These perspectives centre on forms of corporate regulation and interaction within markets that involve a variable 'governance mix' of market exchanges, relational contracting and internal hierarchies (see Williamson 1985). An economic language of 'governance' in turn has been taken up to describe modes of democratic organization and representation that go beyond the official politics of the state (see, for example, Cohen and Rogers 1995; Hirst 1994). While these represent very different strands of governance theory with quite distinct concerns, their commonality lies in displacing what conventionally have been seen as the tasks of *government* – economic management, the representation of interests, mediation between the economic and civil spheres – across an extended sphere of social and economic *governance*. In so doing, they put into question not only the formal coherence of the state, but the separation of a market sphere seen as the site of free association and private economic interest.

. . . and governmentality

Rather different work on issues of governance has developed in response to Michel Foucault's work on government rationalities or 'governmentality' (Barry, Osborne and Rose 1996; Burchell, Gordon and Miller 1991; Foucault 1991; Gane and Johnson 1994; Rose 1999). Such accounts are distinctive in focusing on local practices of regulation in diverse social domains, which may have only loose or incidental links with more formal government processes. Broadly speaking, studies of *governance* derive from work in institutional economics and state theory, and are concerned with issues of policy problem solving, questions of institutional design and mechanisms of representation. Perspectives on *governmentality* have different origins in Foucault's study of modern systems of rule, addressing the manner in which particular objects of regulation – such as the market – are constituted through the very discourses and practices that seek to govern them. These arguments range across a number of sites, but share a critical attitude towards such normative categories as civil society (Burchell 1991), welfare (Donzelot 1979, 1991), the economy (Meuret 1988; Miller and Rose 1990; Procacci 1991), the state (Rose and Miller 1992) or culture (Hunter 1988).

Governmentality, in Foucault's account, refers to a particular form of reflection upon the practices of government, a way of conceiving the ends and techniques of governing oneself and others. Foucault's analysis of government does not reduce to the formal realm of the state, but refers in an extended way to the range of practices that seek to regulate individual and collective conduct through various institutions, discourses, rules, norms and practices. Furthermore, 'government' is not confined to its technical elements – edicts, actors, organizations, buildings. Rather, it includes the values and knowledge that shape technical practices of governing. Foucault was particularly interested in forms of liberal governmentality, and specifically what he calls – following the French physiocratic thinker Quesnay – 'economic government' (Foucault 1991: 92). Quesnay was concerned with the place of the economy within matters of state; primarily in the form of an injunction to governors not to interfere with the free conduct of trade – 'to govern,' he advised, 'one should do nothing' (Procacci 1991: 243). At the same time, he was interested in how a new statistical science of economics might inform policy (see Polanyi 1957 [1944]: 135). In this respect, Quesnay was occupied with similar questions about the limits of government intervention into an emergent market society as exercised Adam Smith. Quesnay's approach hinged upon a dual understanding of 'economy', as referring both to a substantive domain and to a formal model of conduct. In the latter sense, 'economic government' required that governors economize on their own activities – as Polanyi (1957 [1944]: 117) writes, 'laissez-faire was simply a principle of the ensurance of law and order, with the minimum cost and effort.' Such a frugal mode of government is one where minimal inputs in terms of official or coercive activity produce maximum outputs in terms of orderly social reproduction. Foucault (1991: 92) puts it another way: 'the art of government', he writes, 'is just the art of exercising power in the form and according to the model of the economy.'

Classical liberal theory viewed the market as a system that operates subject to an intrinsic logic and provides an independent field of activity. The separation of the economic from other spheres of social life introduces a new problem of government: how to understand and regulate the relationship between these different domains of economy and society. The emergence of such questions by the end of the eighteenth century turned upon a particular view of the object and functions of government. Foucault argues that a concept of 'population' is constituted during this period, through a developing statistical science, as a datum – an entity that might be recorded, monitored and adjusted in respect of its size, distribution, growth and a plethora of local rates of health, marriage, age, work, wealth, birth, death and so on (Foucault 1991: 99–100; see Hacking 1990). It is this premise that provides the basis for Foucault's treatment of 'bio-politics' as the government of populations, and for much of the work that has taken up a governmentality perspective on the contemporary regulation of social life. A less noted aspect of Foucault's work concerns the way that the government of the population was linked to the emergence of a market economy (for later work that develops the economic dimensions of Foucault's ideas, see Burchell 1991; Defert 1991; Donzelot 1991; Ewald 1991; Miller and Rose 1990; Procacci 1991). Foucault's own account links emerging programmes of social administration with discourses of economy. The population that became the key site for government in the modern period is understood in *economic* terms as a social matrix of exchange relations in the market. It is this relationship between population and economy – and the contradiction posed by the fact that the population is construed as a site of intervention and the market as a site of non-intervention – that produces the new problematic of government: how to, and how far to, regulate the market for the benefit and improvement of the population.

Foucault's reflections on liberal governmentality – and specifically his notion of economic government – are firmly based on this earlier modern period. However, the notion that a liberal art of government is both directed towards the economy and adopts economic models for its own activities has proved well suited to the study of neoliberalism (Barry, Osborne and Rose 1996; Rose 1992, 1993, 1999). Neoliberal 'economic government' understands both the ends and means of government as primarily economic in character. Market prosperity is seen as the surest basis for social good, while economic principles ensure that government agencies pursue market-based standards of efficiency, value for money and frugality. Market imperatives, that is, constitute both the ends (deregulation, privatization) and the means (internal markets, the contract culture) of government. A neoliberal art of government, then, can be seen as 'the art of exercising power in the form and according to the model of the economy'. Perspectives on governmentality require one to think about government in an extended way, as programmes of calculation and regulation directed toward the conduct of social and economic life that do not necessarily sit within an established architecture of the state. The forms of authority that operate in notionally 'non-state' institutions have often been obscured by a public–private fix in political and economic discourse. The planning, steering and control of social and economic life, however, are purposive practices of governing, whether these originate within a state apparatus, a private firm or a public–private 'partnership'.

Conclusion

This chapter has considered a number of ways of thinking about the relationship between states and markets. Our aim has been to provide an overview of how different theorists have sought to delimit the proper role of the state in respect of market processes, and how these theories link to specific political and economic arrangements. How have the limits of political authority over market structures, relations and activities been understood and marked out? The discussion involved a further aim, however, which is more critical in orientation. That is, the contested nature of state–market relations suggests that the boundary between them is highly permeable. This is not simply to suggest that, in a market society, the state is only 'relatively autonomous' from the economy (or vice versa), but that the margin between them is a site of interaction, regulation and mediation. The interface between the state and the market is relative to specific forms of economic government at different political moments. At one such moment, for example, economic government is organized around corporatist relations between the state, industry and labour unions which serve to curtail 'free' market processes in the setting of prices and incomes. At another, labour or financial markets are in turn 'freed' from the dead hand of government. In each case, state strategy is accompanied by an argument that it will promote greater market efficiency ('efficiency', in this context, being something of a movable feast). However, these strategies do less to reveal the proper functioning of markets (or of states for that matter) than the variable ways in which markets are shaped by different tactics of regulation. In this context, the order of a market society can be understood as a problem of political order; one constituted both at the level of social theory and via techniques of government.

6

Commerce and Culture

Introduction

We have noted throughout our discussions that the study of the market has been structured by a division of intellectual labour. It is perhaps still best characterized in Weber's terms of formal and substantive rationality: formally rational market behaviour and mechanisms constituted the separate object of economic analysis; the substantive values, social relationships and forms of social order that could not be understood in this way formed the external context of markets, or the basis of a critique of markets, or the essential conditions for market order, economic order and indeed social order in general. The term 'culture' has played a strategic role in defining this 'other' of rational economic action in a market society. It has been used as a label for the context of markets in the sense of labelling the wider world of meaning and sociality in which such things as tastes and desires, expectations and economic motives are formed. It has also grounded critiques of market society by repre-senting all those values, identities and spheres of life (for example, the 'ideal' as opposed to the 'material') that seemed to be excluded from action dominated by utilitarian self-interest, and therefore provided a basis for defending all that is deemed to possess true worth as opposed to merely economic value. Finally, culture has done service as a label for the 'social glue', the traditions and habits, allegiances and ethical obligations that might constitute social life in solidarity rather than anomie.

This chapter is particularly concerned with the notion of culture as a critique of and defence against market society. More specifically, this critique and defence has been closely bound up with a definition of culture as 'expressive forms': that is to say, aesthetic objects such as art and literature, expressive domains such as philosophy, religion and indeed social theory, everyday forms such as dress, the media and lifestyles as they are reflected in one's housing or leisure or even work. The term 'culture' registers the fact that these forms are both the expression of and vehicle for constructing meaningful social life. Indeed, at its widest definition, sometimes dubbed an 'anthropological' view, culture is the meaningfully patterned character of social life and action as glimpsed through the material and objective forms ('material culture') that a society produces. Hence, culture as a critique of market society might take the form of defending art against the incursions of commercialization or arguments to the effect that the meaningful constitution of the everyday has become increasingly dominated by commodification in the form of a consumer culture.

We will frame this discussion in terms of a tension within modern thinking over the relationship between market forces and culture. On the one hand, market forces appear as manipulating or corroding culture, making it a functional element of economic domination, whereas the 'truth' of culture seems to lie in its autonomy from material interests. On the other hand, market mechanisms have also appeared as liberating in two senses: they seem to provide a basis for a populist culture by undermining cultural elites and authorities and bringing culture closer to everyday life; and they seem to provide a vastly expanded material culture that provides symbolic resources for meaningful social life. From the critical side of these divides, the incursion of market rationality into the domain of culture has been theorized as producing quite a variety of social pathologies. We will look particularly at mass culture theories, at the fate of the artist and other cultural practitioners, and at the Marxist concept of reification. At the same time, diverse new intellectual streams – postmodernism, cultural studies, theories of consumer culture – have fed into newer conceptualizations of the relationship of markets to culture, many of which have emphasized the capacity of individuals, even as consumers, to translate the products of market society into their own individual or even oppositional terms. Many of these themes will be developed in the concluding chapter of this book: recent re-evaluations of culture under market conditions are part of an even broader re-evaluation of the relation between economics and its (cultural) others, forming part of what has been labelled a general 'cultural turn' in social theory.

Markets and mass society

The relation between 'commerce' and 'culture' has been profoundly uncomfortable from the beginnings of market society, as is perhaps most starkly summed up in Leavis' (1930: 26) pronouncement that ' "Civilization" and "culture" are coming to be antithetical terms.' The materialistic, self-serving, standardized individual of the industrial and market society ('civilization') battles with the idealist, organic, authentic individual of romantic and artistic mythology. These feelings have been mutual. From the viewpoint of culture, capitalist civilization is a debasing force to be kept at bay; while from the standpoint of (liberal and neoclassical) economics, formally rational market behaviour must be insulated from the cultural forces that constitute its always external backdrop. We need now to look more closely at what has been meant by 'culture' within alternative, more critical traditions, both radical and conservative. These have been less concerned with keeping markets safe from culture and more concerned with keeping culture 'safe' from markets. In particular, over the modern period much critical thought has come to constitute the concept of culture as the barometer of society's ethical status as it becomes increasingly typified by market relations: it has regularly been argued that market society 'debases' culture or subordinates it to commercial ends. Conversely, it is in the supposed 'decline' of culture that one can read the true evils of marketization.

Indeed, the very idea of 'culture', and the word itself, came into existence in response to the emergence of market society and consumer culture, specifically as a way of differentiating special and privileged forms of value, experience and meaning from economic value, market behaviour and utilitarian calculation (see summary in Slater 1997a). In brief, the idea of 'culture' arose largely to deal with the fear that the development of market society would debase or erode 'true' or 'authentic' values, 'traditional' or 'organic' forms of expression, 'high' or 'universal' and 'autonomous' forms of art and thought. At the same time, 'culture' is not only a response to market relations; or rather, commercialization is only one of a series of modern assaults on traditional social order and status hierarchies of value and distinction. Raymond Williams (1985), who set off this line of analysis, regards the 'culture and society' tradition as reacting against a wide range of new entrants to the modern stage – above all, the rise of those 'masses' and 'mobs' who were congregated via urbanization and the industrial concentration of labour; who take an increasingly political form through the gains or claims of democracy and public voice; and who are increasingly addressed by new communications channels and media.

In Williams' (1985) classic account of the 'culture and society' tradition from the late eighteenth century onwards, the term 'culture' registers a wide range of fears (as well as appreciation of some new modern opportunities) that marketization and democratic demands are destroying a traditional order in which people knew their place, in which values were inscribed in tradition and organic relations that evolved over time and experience, in which work and reproduction were in close touch with the natural order. Leavis is generally identified as the author who most clearly captured and celebrated the romantic longing for a world we have lost, one somehow more authentic than that manufactured by industrial modernity and which now confronts modern subjects in the form of alienable commodities. It is lost through such forces as individualism, utilitarian and self-interested calculation; through mechanization and mass production; through the recontextualizing of expressive forms in industrial, profit-oriented production rather than folk ways of life, individual vision or religious devotion; and in the predominance of acts of individual purchase and consumption over collective traditions, rituals and ways of life.

Culture is defined as that sphere in which the values that are lost from market society are either preserved from the past or prefigured for a non-alienated, post-capitalist future (much as the family – women and children – are constituted as compensations for the emotional deficits of the public world). In the case of Leavis, whereas a certain authenticity and quality of language and response once inhered in everyday life, it is now only to be found in a more rarefied sphere of great art and literature which – in a commercial society – is entered not through socialization into practical life but rather through an education in English literature. Culture now exists in the form of great literary works that preserve values and transmit 'all that is best in what has been thought and felt', and not in an everyday life dominated by the false culture of advertising and cheap media thrills (see also Hoggart 1977 [1957]) that pander to the lowest common denominator. Whereas the truth of culture, and the authentic values in the name of which people might properly act, formerly emerged organically from their practical life, the truth of culture now depends upon its autonomy from a practical life increasingly dominated by instrumental calculation, individual self-interest and manufacturing. Autonomy of culture here means at least two things: first, autonomy from economic values, the creation of art in relation to its own inner gods rather than the idols of the marketplace; and second, autonomy from the false and inauthentic 'culture' that arises in and through this marketplace, the seedy demon born when the ignorant tastes of the people mate with the fiscal lust of the capitalist. One can contrast this with the romantic figure of the artist, freed from aristocratic and commercial patronage and pandering by listening to his or her inner voice, or – in the case of high modernism – by following the autonomous logic and nature of the artistic medium.

The market mediation of culture was only part of a picture of moral decline through the intrusion of economic forces where they did not belong. The problem of the commodification of culture was also linked to its mass production. Whereas culture was once seen as produced through craft-like relations between people and materials, the need to produce for a market and at a profit necessarily required cultural producers to employ the same technical advances as any other commodity production: a technical division of labour, stand-ardization and bureaucratic rationalization of processes that were seen as properly intuitive, non-rational, personal and organic (that is, 'creative'). This shift was thematized by both conservatives such as Leavis and neo-Marxists such as Adorno in the notion of 'the culture industry', to which we will return below.

Significantly, Williams talks of a 'culture *and society*' tradition because, although these critical discourses sought a solution to the problems of commercial and industrial society in the autonomy of art from society, their underlying concern was nonetheless urgently social and indeed political in character. We might take as examples Edmund Burke's argument that economic and cultural rationalism leads directly to the destruction of social order (and soon after that to the guillotine), or Matthew Arnold's choice between 'culture and anarchy', which posed starkly the worry that the powers unleashed by market liberalism not only brought down artistic standards but precluded social order as such. The *ancien régime* anchored social status in a cosmic order that also laid out bonds of mutual obligation and loyalty; marketization implicitly carried an assumption of formal equality between freely contracting individuals and brought with it the practical force of monetarization through which anyone could buy anything – status, culture, land, rank and office – purely by virtue of having money (rather than customary entitlement) and anything could be put up for sale. Hence, both the movement of the arts from their courtly context of patronage to the marketplace of bourgeois and then popular taste, as well as the rise of *nouveau riche* lifestyles and consumer culture, sounded the death knell of traditional status hierarchies as guarantors of both quality and order. If anyone with the wherewithal could buy an estate, an education, a place at the fashionable resort, a ticket to the opera, then it was market power rather than inherited status or aesthetic nobility (whether born or bred) that now governed both social and cultural order.

The artist in the marketplace

Various modern figures have had vested interests both in decrying the 'debased' culture of everyday modern life and in mapping out an opposing field of autonomous culture: artists thrown into dependency on the marketplace, aristocrats looking down on the moneyed *nouveaux riches*, and comfortable bourgeois worried about the urban mobs, democratic publics and vulgar new mass audiences unleashed by market capitalism. However, if we look more closely at the social position of these various social actors, we find an ambivalence in that both artists and audiences may be condemning the market while at the same time depending on it for their very ability to engage with culture at all.

For example, John Brewer's (1997) study of emerging definitions of culture and taste in eighteenth-century Britain argues that, over the course of the century, the arts moved, though never entirely, from the court to the city, from patronage to market. Through this process, the arts became 'the property of a larger public' in the form of a 'more commercial and less courtly culture' (p. xvii). This process included a wide range of cultural entrepreneurs who expanded the public's encounter with the arts: commercial enterprises such as networks of publishers, printers and booksellers, theatre and opera by ticket or subscription, assembly halls, pleasure gardens and public art exhibitions. On the one hand, this was welcomed, as ' "The fine arts" were viewed as one of the defining features of modern commercial society' (p. xix), rather than as threatened by commercialization. Indeed, commerce and culture were eminently compatible in the eyes of optimistic Enlightenment thinkers such as Hume and Smith, for whom markets formed part of a civilizing process that brought real progress in the domain of taste, civility, refinement and the arts.

On the other hand, as Brewer argues, even those who enthused about these developments were nonetheless at pains to distinguish the artistic from the commercial, the 'pleasures of the imagination' from 'the gratification of appetite' (p. 87): they sought to define 'a field of human endeavour which was neither utilitarian nor rational but pleasing because it affected people's feelings'. Such distinctions were crucial for the newly professionalized and market-dependent artists who 'were at once dependent on paying audiences and resentful of their power' (p. 96) and their money-empowered vulgarity. These distinctions were if anything more important for the new paying publics themselves, who sought to distinguish their refined aesthetic experience from the more vulgar popular entertainment being opened up by the same cultural and urban marketplace. In the end, however, in a line of thought that persists to this day, the (fine) arts were redefined as the best cure for (rather than cause of) the vices of luxury and materialism arising from a successful market society – so long as they are distanced from 'lust and mammon', from 'gratification of appetite' and 'pursuit of gain' (p. 89). This idea was most powerfully formulated in terms of proper culture as an autonomous and other-worldly aesthetic experience, including the contemplation of the artwork from a 'disinterested' point of view. Cue both the romantic artist and the bourgeois opera-going audience capable by the mid-nineteenth century of sitting through seven hours of Wagner without squirming.

In these accounts, marketization involves a cultural dialectic: at once the autonomization of culture and its commercialization. The idea that special artefacts be called 'art', special people and practices deemed 'artists' or 'artistic', has a contradictory relation to commerce. On one level, such specialization is partly legitimated as a way of safeguarding 'genuine' values from commercial ones (or from the popular, debased tastes empowered by cultural spending power in the marketplace). Simply, artists and their work should be *different* from everyday life and labour. In its avant-gardist forms, the artist's role is to *épater la bourgeoisie*, insulting the world of both commercial public values and respectable domestic ones, while at the same time exuding contempt for, and independence from, the bourgeois audience who generally formed the market and material basis for their art. On another level, so-called autonomized culture was nevertheless made possible partly by the new cultural marketplaces of early modernity which released so many art forms from traditional contexts of religious and aristocratic patronage by allowing them to engage with the new commodity-buying audiences. In recent theory, this dialectic has been developed in relation to the work of Bourdieu: for example, by Mike Featherstone (1991, 1995). This work focuses on the specific interests and strategies of emergent cultural specialists, and how they use particular institutional and market opportunities to secure social power and position. Modern cultural producers move between the twin poles of protecting their privileged cultural enclaves and embracing markets as means of disseminating and supporting their work, even though this threatens to de-monopolize and de-differentiate the autonomous aesthetic sphere they are also trying to carve out. Contemporary cultural analysts (such as Habermas 1985 and Huyssen 1986) have located this dialectic in the fault-line between modernism and postmodernism. High modernism in particular sought to make an absolute distinction between art and everyday life by locating artistic integrity in dedication to the internal logic and properties of the specific aesthetic medium (for example, 'being painterly'); a move which rejected all external pressures on artistic practice, and especially the financial pressures of selling to audiences. Postmodernism acknowledged that closing the gap between art and everyday life necessarily entailed settling accounts with the commercial culture and market processes that made up modern lived experience. In short, it meant 'learning from Las Vegas', as Robert Venturi put it, and even embracing and savouring popular and commercial culture, whether by making it into the subject matter of art (as in the case of Dada or Pop Art), or more radically moving out of the artistic academy altogether and into the marketplace.

As theorized by Bourdieu or Featherstone, what is at stake in this dialectic is the struggle of cultural practitioners and audiences to legitimate their own social, cultural and economic capital in the social marketplace:

> Conditions that favour the autonomization of the cultural sphere will better allow cultural specialists to monopolize, regulate and control cultural production, to seek to place cultural production above economic production. . . . Alternatively, conditions that threaten the autonomy of the cultural sphere . . . will tend to allow outsider groups of cultural specialists, or encourage new alliances of particular groups of cultural specialists with other powerful groups of economic specialists. . . . (Featherstone 1995: 16)

In line with Bourdieu's overall framework, the culture sphere is depicted as structured by competitive strategies in which terms like 'markets', 'capital' and 'competition' are used in both literal and metaphoric senses. Cultural competition to legitimate one's own aesthetic capital (whether through autonomization from, or embrace of, market society) is conducted 'just like' economic competition, with rational and strategic use of resources, with processes of valuation and devaluation, with attempts to convert different forms of capital into one another. At the same time, new cultural tastes, expertise and legitimations can be quite literally means by which to advance one's market position and social status. Cultural specialists are in competition both with other social groups and capitals (including the industrial bourgeoisie, who nonetheless frequently form their audience and market) and with other *cultural* specialists. Hence postmodernism is partly interpreted as a series of strategies for legitimating the consumption tastes and productive output of new cultural intermediaries, largely drawn from an aspiring lower middle class and positioned in opposition to the high modernist culture that excluded them. New tastes and taste structures – for example, an ironic taste for kitsch – are legitimated through a combination of market populism and anti-elitism, a merger of culture with everyday life, new academic and intellectual discourses such as postmodernism and cultural studies, and new forms of work such as advertising, design or multi-media.

Finally, and as Featherstone notes, Bourdieu (1983) usefully distinguishes a range of culture–market relations in terms that bring out clearly the connections between social, cultural and economic competition. He distinguishes broadly between a 'field of restricted cultural production' (enclaved, sacral, high art) and a 'field of large-scale cultural production' (culture that is opened out through the market); a distinction based on whether symbolic or economic considerations come first for the producers involved. At the same time, we can place aesthetic practices along a continuum between these two points (Bourdieu 1983: 329; Featherstone 1995: 30). We can distinguish, first, avant-gardists and bohemians whose identity depends on declaring great autonomy from the market; second, cultural institutions such as academies and museums that are relatively autonomous from the market and establish their own symbolic hierarchies and canons; third, cultural producers who are endorsed by 'high society' and upper class patrons and whose cultural success is therefore 'closely tied to economic profit and market success'; fourth, cultural producers who achieve mass audience or popular success and whose production is closely tied to dictates of the market (Featherstone 1995: 30).

We should, however, add to this picture the role of the state in maintaining the cultural autonomy of the artist (and indeed in maintaining 'quality' culture against market forces, as in the idea of public service in broadcasting or 'intellectual freedom' in academia). At least within the European social democratic and British welfarist tradition, it was recognized from fairly early on that market forces did not do a great job of materially supporting the artist or of sustaining the kinds of culture that were increasingly seen as necessary for national identity and national prestige. State subsidies for the arts – whether in the European form of funding bodies or the American form of tax breaks on donations – insulate the artist from the market (they also create jobs, as in the New Deal in America) and sustain 'heritage'. During the cold war they also came to propagandize for a 'pure' freedom that only the affluent and liberal market society of the West seemed able to offer (Fuller 1980).

To summarize: The presence of the market in modern social thought and experience has produced a very powerful cultural dialectic. On the one hand, the desire to constitute culture as an autonomous and pure sphere, as a utopian prefiguration or nostalgic archaism, as an ideal defined *against* market society, has fed the western cultural and political imaginary throughout modernity and produced many romantically starving artists. On the other hand, the market emerges – not just in the minds of doctrinaire liberals – as a site of populist pleasures, cultural and political renewal and excitement, and democratic egalitarianism and anti-elitism. It is a source of liberation as much for postmodernists who desire to 'learn from Las Vegas' – so much more playful and profitable than the autonomous artistic citadels of modernist architecture – as for the entrepreneurial publishers and painters of the eighteenth century, for whom the market empowered a release from artistic patronage.

Markets and reification

An alternative intellectual trajectory concerned with the autonomy of culture from market society is represented by the Marxist tradition, particularly in the form of critical theory. In this account, the tension between market autonomy and dependence determines the very form or internal structure of culture, and in particular its critical distance from capitalist social structures. It determines, indeed, the ability of culture (in the broadest sense of consciousness and ideas as well as aesthetic practices) to carry out the function of critique. The crude formulation of this structuration process runs along the lines of 'the ideas of the ruling class are in every epoch the ruling ideas' (Marx 1974 [1845–6]: 64), a notion whose enduring force is too often sidestepped: market power translates into cultural power through ownership of the means of cultural production and distribution (as evidenced in figures such as Murdoch, Turner and Gates). Moreover, the commercial power of dominant classes – allied with and transmitted through state power – can secure the co-operation of ostensibly autonomous intellectuals: for example, in education, the Church, the 'objective' laboratory of the scientist and so on, as Gramsci argued.

Nonetheless, the coincidence of ownership of the means of cultural production and the cultural hegemony of economically powerful classes does not answer all the questions: *what* are their ideas and where do they come from? and why should the mere power to transmit these ideas secure the consent of the less culturally empowered classes? In later Marxism – largely starting from Lukács – the concepts of fetishism and reification look at the effects of marketization on culture not so much in terms of a political economy of ownership, or (as in the previous section) in terms of class structures of cultural value and taste. Rather, the concern is to trace the effects of the very structure of market exchange on the kinds of culture that can be produced and experienced – indeed, on what can be thought and said in a market society.

Objectification, fetishism and reification

In the Hegelian tradition that forms the backdrop to Marx, Lukács, Benjamin and Adorno, cultural crisis and distortion are to be understood primarily in relation to alienation. As discussed in chapter 3, this tradition identifies authentic culture and human identity with praxis: through their labour, social actors shape the world in relation to their needs, desires, ideas and imagination, and therefore the products of their labour – their material culture and transformed environment – can be treated as the objectification of their subjectivity (see also Berger and Luckman 1966). Culture is best understood as material culture: the transformation of things, through praxis, in relation to social values. At the same time, people are also determined or mediated through this material culture, their subjectivities are structured by the objective world they have themselves historically constructed. Authentic culture is then identified with the ability of social agents consciously to enter into this dialectic of making and self-making, knowing that the world they inhabit is one that they have produced and can alter, and thereby becoming able both to command and to know themselves.

In this tradition, the problem of capitalist and rational modernity is that the objective world becomes split off from any sense of agency: people are unable to connect their own labour to the ever greater world of objects surrounding them. The objective world that they have made comes to appear as if it were a natural order rather than a social or historical one. This alienation and consequent fetishization (treating objects as if they were subjects endowed with will and agency) is theorized in various ways. Marx (1976a [1867]) understood it specifically in relation to the way in which the mediation of markets creates a split between production and consumption such that objects appear to come out of nowhere, endowed with intrinsic values that are not connected to human labour. Indeed, human labour itself becomes alienated from its human subject in the form of a commodity that can be traded. Hence, the market appears as a central structural principle of mystification: it generates a view of the social order – a culture – which is false and which impedes the modern subject's self-understanding and empowerment.

The traditional point of departure for this kind of analysis is Marx's chapter on 'the fetishism of the commodity and its secret' in the first volume of *Capital*; an account of why political economists – who attend only to markets and therefore to these false appearances – are wrong. The chapter aims – as do later accounts of reification and capitalist culture – to provide simultaneously an economic sociology and a sociology of knowledge. Marx's central distinction (as we discussed in chapter 3) is the split between use value and exchange value in the commodity form. Whereas Marx (dubiously) treats use value as physical, sensuous, concrete, 'nothing mysterious' (1976a [1867]: 163), exchange value has 'absolutely no connection with the physical nature of the commodity and the material [*dinglich*] relations arising out of this' (p. 165). Rather, it is a social relation between men – the social relations of production by which the products of labour are alienated from their producers and are exchanged in terms of quantities of abstract labour (as opposed to qualitative relations of concrete labour) expended in them. Exchange value arises from these social relations and stands for those social acts of production but appears independently of them, as simple numeric ratios of exchange between things. The social relations between men 'assumes here, for them, the fantastic form of a relation between things' (p. 165). Marx immediately likens this effect to religion, echoing the already well-developed Feuerbachian critique, but now following a parallel anthropological trail through the term 'fetishism', in which gods and supernatural forces – the products of men's minds – are misconstrued as real entities with their own proper qualities and powers. They – and, like them, commodities – are 'fetishes' in the literal sense of totemic objects that are endowed with powers of agency and subjectivity: 'The mysterious character of the commodity-form consists therefore simply in the fact that the commodity reflects the social characteristics of men's own labour as objective characteristics of the products of labour themselves, as the socio-natural properties of these things' (Marx 1976a [1867]: 164–5).

It is important to emphasize how, for Marx, it is the market and its strategic position that is decisive for contemporary consciousness, culture and knowledge. It is the market – above all, the market in labour power – that splits off the making of things from the purchase and consumption of ready-made objects, such that they happen at different times and in different places and cannot be placed within the same conceptual framework, either by social actors within everyday life or by intellectuals (economists, pundits, moralists) within the elite cultural sphere. What we all actually perceive and experience in a market society is the relation of exchange value between object and object: the value of the objects we desire appears in the form of relative quantities of money, rather than the quantities of labour that went into their production. Under capitalist property relations, production is carried out privately and in isolation; producers come into social contact only through exchanging their wares in the market. Hence it is only in the market that 'the specific social characteristics of their private labours appear. . . . In other words, the labour of the private individual manifests itself as an element of the total labour of society only through the relations which the act of exchange establishes between the products, and, through their mediation, between the producers' (p. 165). Labour is conducted privately and in isolation and only gains a social form through the act of exchange. However, because it is only exchange that brings labour into a social relationship, it does so in a very abstract form, equating labour through the abstract common denominator of exchange value:

> It is only by being exchanged that products of labour acquire a socially uniform objectivity as values, which is distinct from their sensuously varied objectivity as articles of utility. This division of the product of labour into a useful thing and a thing possessing value appears in practice only when exchange has already acquired a sufficient extension and importance to allow useful things to be produced for the purpose of being exchanged, so that their character as values has already to be taken into consideration during production. (p. 166)

Market exchange, then, brings objectified human labour together socially, but at the cost of abstracting and emptying it of all substantive content. There is nothing left but quantitative equivalences (prices) and a competitive drive to accumulate value that turns around to dominate use value (the substantive needs and material culture of a society). This is what is meant by the domination of exchange value over use value: the generalization of markets means the rationalization of all production in relation to the accumulation of abstract value rather than specific use values. Moreover, this infiltration of exchange value into the very substance of all our useful things also means the obliteration of their substance and specificity, their uniqueness as things. Everything is rendered equivalent as a commodity, in the sense that everything is viewed as a commodity in its production as well as exchange. And everything is viewed in terms of quantities; everything is simply a sum of value realized or hoped for.

Although, as we saw in chapter 3, Marx treats the market as economically epiphenomenal, he accords it the leading role both in the mystification of human subjectivity and in the emptying out of our objective or material culture. One point should be very clear, however: Marx is aiming at a theory of *socially necessary* illusion. The false understandings and warped object relations of market society are to be explained neither as individual error and mistake nor as self-interested conspiracy. They are structurally produced as a normal and inevitable aspect of market relations. Hence, Adorno's criticism of the way Benjamin sought to account for capitalist culture in terms of myths and 'dialectical images' – that he reduced fetishism to an issue of consciousness (the 'dream world') rather than one of structure (Bloch et al. 1980: 110–33). For Marx, we are dealing here with the way things look and the way people behave when their lives depend on meeting their needs through markets. Value is opaque; it 'does not have its description branded on its forehead; it rather transforms every product of labour into a social hieroglyphic' (Marx 1976a [1867]: 167). Under these conditions people, including intellectuals, *cannot* see the real forces determining their existence (relations of production rather than exchange) and therefore cannot act effectively to pursue their interests politically or economically.

Adorno: the culture industry

This line of structural analysis is developed into a general theory of culture and consciousness largely through the notion of 'reification', the term through which later Marxists – starting with Lukács and in dialogue with Weber and Simmel – move from commodity fetishism to a theory of capitalist culture (see, for example, Frisby 1988; Rose 1978). In many respects, the most developed and most influential attempt to use the concept of reification to extrapolate from a theory of market relations to a characterization of modern consciousness and culture is to be found in the work of Theodor Adorno. For Adorno, the cultural iniquities of the market are one instance of the broader domination of instrumental rationality (thus extending the work of Weber and Simmel, discussed in chapter 3), which Max Horkheimer and he (1979) delineated through the slogan the 'dialectic of enlightenment'. At a philosophical and cultural level, Adorno characterizes instrumental rationality through the concept of 'identity thinking'. Identity thinking represents the complete subsumption of the particular under the universal. It is exemplified in positivism, that scientistic modern belief that the vast diversity of the natural and social object world in all its particularity of sensuous properties, historical circumstances and social relations can be captured without loss by scientific principles, neutral observation languages, quantification or abstract exchange value. In the abstract language of the German philosophical tradition, all of these diverse manifestations of modern *ratio* represent the assumption that objects may be treated as identical with their 'concepts'. For Adorno, truth and critique arise in the realization of the gap between object and concept, in the contradiction between that which is and that which could be. Market institutions (as we explored in chapter 3) rest on the formal assumption that economic actors are free and equal. Non-identity thinking, or 'negative dialectics', confronts the real object with its concept; in this case it is to confront – as Marx did – the formal freedoms of the capitalist market with the concepts or promises of freedom implicit within it, to confront what the object is with what it 'would itself like to be'. For example, the figure of the sovereign consumer ideologically embodies a notion of freedom and supports the (false) claim that this freedom has already been achieved in the marketplace. The critical theorist's task is to elaborate the utopian moment embodied in market relations ('freedom') and confront it with 'what is': the obscene gap between the formal equality of freely contracting market actors and the compulsions of exploitation, non-ownership of the means of production and income inequality. Indeed, the fiction of consumer sovereignty is perversely one means by which real unfreedom is sustained and by which the social conditions of that unfreedom (the relations of production) are obscured from view.

Non-identity thinking crucially concerns the split between formal and substantive rationality: the problem with the dominance of identity thinking is precisely the way in which the subsumption of the particular under the general empties the former of its specific value and properties. All particulars become means to ends rather than ends in themselves. All are rendered equivalent from the point of view of a god-like scientific or philosophical *cogito*, or from the point of view of utilitarian market actors who empty out all (substantive, particular) use values in the manic drive to accumulate (general, abstract) exchange values. Non-identity thinking, by returning to 'the concept', is seeking to return meaning as well as truth to the object, to return to questions of values, goals and desires rather than simply to issues of mastery and efficiency. The tragedy of the dialectics of

enlightenment is that the same process of subsumption that demythi-
fied nature through rationality and empirical observation also
reduced it to a meaningless object of domination, replacing all
questions of substantive value with pure manipulation.

The market is recognized by Adorno as a particular instance of
this process of domination, but also as a privileged mechanism for
accomplishing it. Adorno employs a fairly literal version of Marx
here: market mediation means the domination of exchange value
over use value, which means the domination of the universal (quantities of money as the 'abstract form of wealth') over the particular
(use values as the unique sensuous properties of specific *things*).
Indeed, in the process made so clear by utilitarianism, with its
reduction of the diversity of human drives and their objects to
quantities of a single substance, utility, the market reduces the
heterogeneous object world to complete equivalence, differing only
as to quantity. Capitalist production is necessarily market-oriented
and hence is characterized by production for profit not use. It is
unconcerned (or concerned only in a highly mediated way) with
particular human needs and desires, with the intrinsic properties of
objects and with the sensuous relation between humans and things.
It treats all these things purely from the point of view of maximizing
a quantum of abstract value (accumulation). The abstract logic of
exchange value rules over the elaboration of substantive culture and
value (use value). Capitalism's subsumption of use value under
exchange value, then, is just one instance of Enlightenment rationality's subsumption of the sensuous particularity of things under
universals.

What really exercises Adorno, however, is the way in which this
subsumption permeates all aspects of the circulation of all objects; a
formulation that Adorno and Horkheimer theorized as the 'culture
industry'. As often reiterated (for example, in Adorno 1991: 87), this
phrase is not meant to suggest that culture is now literally produced
through manufacturing processes. Rather, the argument is that all
aspects of the production, distribution and consumption of culture
are increasingly rationalized in relation to exchange value. While
commodification and market exchange are far from new, nonetheless
the appearance of the culture industry represents a fundamental
qualitative shift from liberal bourgeois society into the era of monopoly capitalism. In the earlier period,

> Culture, in the true sense, did not simply accommodate itself to human
> beings; but it always simultaneously raised a protest against the petri-
> fied relations under which they lived, thereby honouring them. In so

far as culture becomes wholly assimilated to and integrated in those petrified relations, human beings are once more debased. Cultural entities typical of the culture industry are no longer *also* commodities, they are commodities through and through. (p. 87)

Whereas, for example, artistic technique once referred to the 'internal organization' or 'inner logic' of the art work (as in high modernism), technique in the context of the culture industry refers to market distribution and industrial-mechanical reproduction, hence to something that 'always remains external to its object'. In this manner, culture and society become one with each other, rather than autonomous and intrinsically opposed. In practical and sociological terms, culture is no longer 'external to its object' in the sense that it now plays an integrative and functional – rather than critical and distanced – role within social order: culture is assimilated to advertising, sales, leisure and recreation. It is a means at once to increase sales and profits and at the same time to integrate modern citizens as consumers into the capitalist order through forms of escapism and amusement that both keep them content and allow them to recuperate their mental and physical energies for more labour.

Contemporary culture is thereby characterized by both false universality and false particularity. Despite the appearance of pluralism and diversity, the culture industries subsume cultural products under various kinds of generality. First, they produce all culture as commodities and through rationalized processes. Second, in functional terms the apparent diversity of cultural goods reduces to the same experiences of entertainment, recuperation and escapism – all integrative functions. Third, this is accomplished through the formal qualities of the cultural object itself, which again presents a real equivalence in the guise of a merely apparent diversity. Adorno and Horkheimer stress the ways in which 'pseudo-individualism' obscures the lack of any real individuality in the products of the culture industry: they are in fact standardized goods, but are given little twists and quirks to give them the appearance of difference. The Spice Girls carry meaningless icons of 'girl power', while All Saints pitch their femininity in terms of street cred. Culture industry products are in fact dominated by the 'formula', in which all particulars have their functional place in fulfilling generic expectations – the jazz riff, the sitcom structure and plot, the iconic form of movie stars, all make for ease of consumption and therefore maximization of sales. However, it is essential to the cultural industry – to legitimate their claim to supply cultural pleasures – that the illusion of use value and particularity is preserved in all these cases.

The difference between culture industry products and their opposite, autonomous art, is not to be mistaken for the difference between commodities and non-commodities or between market production and autonomous creative genius. Quite the contrary, Adorno argues that a great period of autonomous and critical art was possible during the bourgeois era precisely because the artist's ability to support him- or herself through sales allowed a mediated relationship to audiences that contrasted with direct dependence on Church, state or patrons. This is precisely the cultural dialectic we examined in Brewer's and Featherstone's accounts. Adorno argues that high art gained a paying audience among the bourgeoisie precisely because it claimed (hypocritically) to be pure, above the game of use and exchange, need and profit. Moreover, it is also important for Adorno that high art and autonomous art are not the same thing: high art – exemplified in the despised figure of the conductor Toscanini, a most marketable signifier of high cultural legitimacy – is eminently susceptible to commodification in depth, to the subsumption of all particulars under the rationality of industrial production, to functional integration, formulaic standardization and pseudo-individualization. Autonomous art, in contrast to marketable high art, is represented by a very few works that manage to maintain a critical distance from commodification. In this sense, Adorno is definitely not an elitist in the Leavisite mould, but rather a thoroughgoing – indeed obsessive – dialectician. Above all, it would be a crass betrayal of first principles for him to take one side or the other of the great divide between autonomous and consumerist culture (represented by both high and popular arts), for 'The division itself is the truth' of market capitalism (Horkheimer and Adorno 1979: 6). Neither autonomous nor high art is inherently either good or true, but at best they represent a schism which manifests the social contradictions of the market society that produced it. Even where autonomous art maintains its critical distance from the laws of equivalence and identity in a market society, it does so precisely on the basis of – or at cost of – restrictive, unequal, limited 'social premises', the system of class and exploitation. Neither high nor autonomous art is simply to be appreciated, in an elitist manner, as the last refuge of truth; they are rather one vantage from which to perceive that – in the moving formulation Adorno offered to Benjamin – both high art and industrially produced consumer art 'bear the stigmata of capitalism, both contain elements of change. Both are torn halves of an integral freedom, to which, however, they do not add up' (Bloch et al. 1980: 123).

This is also Adorno's reply to the conservative cultural critics who disdain the impurity of culture when it is sullied by commerce and materialism: 'all culture shares the guilt of society' (Adorno 1967: 19), is complicit with and structured by the capitalist modernity which constitutes it. In the simplest terms, however critical culture may be, it is always a privileged domain. Indeed, the more critical it is, the more remote it is from those who are oppressed because its critical edge is achieved only at the cost of being technically 'difficult', resisting easy consumption (and hence its integrative function) and distancing itself from everyday life. The real aims of culture can be achieved only when culture is itself abolished within a free society that allows it to rejoin the actual life-processes of the social order, a society beyond the division between mental and manual labour and beyond the principle of domination by false universals such as money.

Markets, culture and agency

Adorno's work explains the domination of the system over human agency and critical consciousness in terms of the domination of exchange value over use value. It can be taken as one of the most sophisticated expressions of mass society and manipulationist views of the relation between markets and cultures. It is also now considerably at odds with contemporary positions, both right and left, all of which stress the active and even subversive agency of the consumer of market goods and experiences. Moreover, the contemporary focus is on discontinuities between production and consumption, which give the latter social moment some real autonomy and unpredictability. Indeed, there are uncanny convergences between neoliberals and postmodernists, both of whom regard people's engagement with commercially produced culture not as a sell-out or impurity, but rather as a basis for real pleasures, real autonomy and real assaults on cultural and social elites (a theme they share with the very earliest proponents of marketization as an assault on the traditional order of the *ancien régime*).

However, this concern with the complexity and agency involved in people's engagement with market culture pre-dates 1980s cultural movements; indeed, it hails from the earlier revolutions of the 1960s, and most notably from the rise of youth culture and disciplines like cultural studies which emerged out of that experience. The emergence of the teenager in the 1950s and of a range of spectacular style subcultures over the following decades all involved a central focus on the cultural consumption of commercially produced goods, whether music, new leisure spaces, dress, motorcycles, film or marketed visual styles. While this could be viewed by some critics merely as more manipulation by businesses that saw new markets in these consumer groups and then manufactured styles for them, it was clear that even such power as producers had was caught up in a more complex dynamic. Above all, most subcultures involved the reinterpretation of mass manufactured goods. The literature is replete with recodings: for example, mods (in Hebdige's landmark studies of 1979 and 1988) used Italian styling to translate suits from an office uniform into the basis of a new dandyism that helped them negotiate shifting class cultures and social mobility; they appropriated for their own purposes a vehicle (the moped) which was designed for Italian ladies' shopping trips around Rome; punks transformed bin-liners and safety pins into clothing and fashion.

In each case of youth culture, the very products of commercial capitalism were turned into an embodied commentary on, and generally a critique of, contemporary society. At the same time, each rebellious reappropriation of commercial products did indeed take a material and stylized form that could also be reappropriated by capitalism. Street subcultures were tremendous sources of new ideas and products for the many culture industries, while also helping to create new markets to whom these products could be sold. This produced a quite different view of the market and its relationship to culture. On the one hand, manipulationist models of the unidirectional determination of consumption by production were modified into a more complex image of cycling and recycling of culture through the market, from the street to the capitalist and back again (see, for example, Frith 1983). To use the imagery of the 1960s, the market is a different place if it is Carnaby Street, the King's Road or Portobello market, as opposed to your local supermarket. On the other hand, the same model of recycling and cultural diversity could also be seen as simply a more subtle and insidious manipulation. In the imagery of Marcuse's (1964) 'one-dimensional man', the Situationist's 'society of the spectacle' or – later – Baudrillard's 'code' and 'black hole' of the masses, the complicit relationship between youth culture and capitalism testified to the latter's power to assimilate all consciousness and critique. Even revolution could be translated into marketable style, as in the ubiquitous posters of Che Guevara that went up in every trendy bar.

These doubts aside, a view of modern consumer capitalism was possible in which marketed goods were at the centre of a new cultural populism (see McGuigan 1992), and markets appeared as places of diversity, play and anti-elitism. Paul Willis' (1990) *Common Culture*, for example, a piece of research originally commissioned as an inquiry into young people's relationship to art, argues that it is wrong to assess people's culture in terms of their (minimal) engagement with official art and its legitimated objects. A broader notion of 'symbolic creativity' is required that identifies culture in terms of 'grounded aesthetics', the constant effort of meaning making and interpretation that is constitutive of everyday life. This aspect of life centrally includes the 'necessary symbolic work' that is involved in all acts of consumption, from the most mundane to the most 'cultural': 'interpretation, symbolic action and creativity' are necessary in order for people to assimilate any objects into their everyday lives, and these interpretive acts of assimilation are the basis for the construction of new meanings that might never have been anticipated or desired by the manufacturers or marketers: 'Why shouldn't bedroom decoration and personal styles, combinations of others' "productions", be viewed along with creative writing or song and music compositions as fields of aesthetic realization?' (p. 20). To the extent that 'common culture', as opposed to official and elite culture, is grounded in mundane symbolic work, then it is naturally to the modern marketplace, as opposed to the museum or academy, that people will turn for their symbolic resources, and Willis propounds a modified and qualified market populism on this basis:

> If it ever existed at all, the old 'mass' has been culturally emancipated into popularly differentiated cultural citizens through exposure to a widened circle of commodity relations. These things have supplied a much widened range of usable symbolic resources for the development and emancipation of everyday culture. Certainly this emancipation has been partial and contradictory because the consumer industries have sought to provide some of the contents and certainly the forms as well as the possibilities for cultural activity. But, in this, commerce discovered, *by exploiting*, the realm of necessary symbolic production within the undiscovered continent of the informal. No other agency has recognized this realm or supplied it with usable symbolic materials. (p. 18)

Willis himself identifies the term 'postmodernism' with its nihilistic, Baudrillardian variety, in which the explosion of cultural resources – aestheticization, as discussed in the next chapter – promotes an implosion of meaning and the death of the social. However, his own account is quite consonant both with more optimistic renderings of postmodernism and with many themes within liberalism and neo-liberalism. As we saw earlier, the relationship between market and culture has been understood since the eighteenth century as a positively – not just negatively – levelling force, which is anti-elitist and which closes the distance between aesthetic practices and the ordinary life of ordinary people. Despite the profound reservations that authors like Willis might have about the power relations between producer and consumer, the marketplace nonetheless offers not only a wealth and diversity of usable culture, but also a breathing space in which this can be reinterpreted around new and even oppositional uses. The same themes have been a focal point within media studies and research into explicitly cultural consumption (see, for example, Ang 1985, 1991; Morley 1980, 1986; Radway 1987; Storey 1999).

In this context, the market no longer appears as the thin end of the capitalist wedge, or as an economic taint on true culture. Indeed, it tends to be divorced from economic analysis entirely. The trajectory of 'culturalism' within culture studies has followed a path that began with a focus on popular culture as ideology, to be investigated through close textual analysis. An example might be the study of advertising: although emblematic of advanced capitalism, studies of advertising (Brown 1977; Cook 1992; Dyer 1982; Goffman 1976; Goldman 1992; Leiss, Kline and Jhally 1986; Messaris 1997; Packard 1977; Schudson 1984; Vestergaard and Schroder 1985; Williams 1980; Williamson 1978; Winship 1980) were in fact almost entirely textual studies of advertisements, with little reference to the commercial practices in which they were produced or the competitive market contexts in which they operated. In fact, studies of advertising still routinely start by arguing that, while the commercial effects of advertising may be unknown or unimportant, the primary concern should be with the 'broader' cultural or ideological impact of advertising (for example, Myers 1999: 3–5). Where the literature has shifted away from this focus, it has tended to be in the direction of a re-evaluation of advertising and consumption in a more positive and subversive light rather than in a more economically informed one. On the one hand, work by Fiske (1989) examines the way in which ordinary consumers use market-produced culture as means of empowerment; on the other, figures like Nava (1987, 1992) explicitly link consumption and the market to political activism and resistance, to the extent that even the US black civil rights movement of the 1960s can be interpreted as a consumer rights movement (it involved equal rights to goods such as buses).

By contrast, more recent work indicates a re-engagement with the economic and indeed a need to look at the complexity of cultural-economic phenomena. For example, McRobbie (1998, 1999; see also Ross 1997, 1998) focuses on the structure of work and employment in culture industries. This is particularly important for cultural workers such as young musicians and fashion designers, for whom production and consumption are closely intertwined within club cultures, street styles and small economic sectors in which they are likely to be both producers and consumers, having to interpret the conditions of their existence both economically and culturally. Moreover, it is clear from these sectors that cultural promises (as a self-employed designer, you can do creatively rewarding work, with real autonomy and the possibility of cultural influence and glamour) can act to establish economic exploitation and self-exploitation. Similarly, du Gay (1996, 1997) and Nixon (1997) have tried to show how culture enters the economic sphere itself through the dual role of the worker as both consumer and producer.

However, perhaps the most revealing focus for all of these debates has been shopping – the modern marketplace, as discussed in chapter 1. Once regarded as intellectually trivial or as the preserve of applied researchers, the institutions, locations and activities of shopping and retailing have generated a huge volume of literature since the late 1980s (for a comprehensive survey, see Falk and Campbell 1997), precisely because they were newly perceived as a major site of cultural experience, rather than as a narrowly economic moment that fulfils utilitarian functions (distribution, provisioning). The spirits presiding over this re-evaluation were undoubtedly Walter Benjamin and Georg Simmel, both of whom emphasized the phenomenology of modern life depicted as a consumable spectacle or sensorium of objects and sociality, which they identified with both the city and shopping. The encounter between consumer and commodity is a densely cultural one; indeed (as discussed in chapter 1), the congregation of people through and around commodities produces specific, but highly diverse, forms of sociality, civic identity, regulation and so on (Slater 1993). Above all, shopping itself emerges as a site of diverse pleasures and freedoms that are connected to but independent of the act of buying or consuming: pleasures of fantasy, desire, looking and feeling, longing and so on. These are promoted and, one could say, exploited by increasingly sophisticated retailers, yet at the same time they provide a space in which experiences are released that may not be so easily controlled. Moreover, the very validation of public hedonism that shopping presumes can itself be construed as legitimating a kind of utopian moment within capitalist market culture. Finally, given the close relation between gender and shopping, this has particular consequences for women. Hence, the emergence of new shopping spaces such as department stores in the nineteenth century can be interpreted as a significant gain for (bourgeois) women, who were empowered to traverse public spaces (the city, the shopping street, the shop) on the basis of their desires and pleasures. Similarly, Fiske (1989) analyses contemporary shopping as women's use of the opportunities at hand to empower themselves.

In this view of shopping, the marketplace is not a site of fetishization, but rather an empowering cultural resource. Oddly, the image of cultural empowerment offered in these largely postmodernist accounts is very consumerist in a conventional liberal sense: the focus is on the individual as a desiring subject (though obviously not a utilitarian subject). We might usefully contrast this image with an alternative formulation of the culture of the marketplace that can be found in Daniel Miller's (1998b) *A Theory of Shopping*, which is equally concerned with market actors as active and socially embedded, but contextualizes them within mundane rather than spectacular cultural activity. In Miller's ethnography of everyday supermarket shopping in north London, people certainly articulate views of shopping as utopian, hedonistic, imaginative and liberating, and indeed can construe it as a largely cultural activity. However, this seems to be belied by their actions and by the ways in which they articulate the market experience at more practical levels. In this context, the culture of shopping is not postmodern but intimate and familial – people are concerned with thrift, care, the needs of loved others. Indeed, shopping, in Miller's account, is an act of love and (literally) sacrifice, in which the other (child, partner, parent) is constructed as an object of need in order that one can offer up purchased provisions as a kind of devotion. From this perspective, market culture has to be seen within the context of gendered power and the meanings of domestic relations.

Conclusion

Over the course of this chapter we have traced a set of relations drawn between markets and culture within modern social thought: market forces can be seen as a threat to culture or as a mechanism for releasing it from elites and domination (including the domination of capitalist firms themselves). Indeed, they can be both at once. The nature of culture under these conditions is equally ambivalent. One use of the term 'culture' invokes a defensive retreat of aesthetic production ever further from both material interests and everyday life in order to preserve critical consciousness or non-utilitarian values within the modern order. Alternatively, both early modern and postmodern cultural strategies have involved a settling of accounts with the market and everyday material life, focusing on the potentials of culture in its commodity forms. This particular point in the dialectic of autonomy and dependence between markets and culture also directs us towards an even broader development in thinking about the market, the so-called 'cultural turn', which will be the subject of the final chapter of this book. Whereas the positions we have just outlined continue to assume a separation and external relationship between economy and culture, and are largely concerned to register the impact of market forces on culture, the 'cultural turn' indicates a different kind of relationship in which the market economy itself is understood as increasingly cultural in its nature and operation.

7

The Cultural Turn

Whereas the central preoccupation of critical social analysis has traditionally been the way in which economic rationality dominates culture, contemporary social theory has been increasingly concerned with the central role of cultural processes and institutions in organizing and controlling the economic. This has been labelled by some the 'cultural turn' in social thought (for example, Ray and Sayer 1999). In some respects, these developments echo the embeddedness perspectives outlined in chapter 4, but the claims made here are rather stronger, arguing not simply that we have to recognize the cultural and social embeddedness of economic process, but that the economy itself, and the 'things' that flow through it, are now largely constituted through informational and symbolic processes.

For example, Philip Crang (1997: 4), considering the 'cultural turn' in the context of economic geography, delineates five options for thinking about the relation between economics and culture. First, one can continue to oppose the economic to the cultural as distinctive entities, considering the impact of one on the other. Ray and Sayer (1999; see also Sayer 1997) argue that one can distinguish an economic moment that involves means–ends relations from a cultural one concerned with ends in themselves, a rerun of the formal/ substantive split we have already dealt with in several guises. Second, one can 'export the economic into the cultural' in various ways: for example, by arguing for the determination of new cultural formations by the economic (as in Harvey 1989, or Jameson 1984) or for the operation of culture along economic lines (in the case of Bourdieu). However, at this point it becomes clear that 'there is no one-way economization of cultural practice; economic practice and product is also reworked as it gets entangled in cultural life' (Crang 1997: 10), an issue which is placed centre stage in the third option. Here we view the economic as embedded or contextualized in the cultural. Embeddedness approaches, as we have already seen in chapter 4, place the economic in a broader cultural order; yet such approaches raise questions about the nature of the economic that they cannot themselves answer: as Crang puts it, we need to do more than merely locate economic activity within the cultural order; we need to 'shift our focus away from concerns of contextualization and embedding and towards the representational and discursive constitution of economic life':

> To speak of embedding is to speak of situating the economy in a cultural context, in a placed culture, whether its cultural place be the individual . . . , the firm, the region or the nation-state. To speak of representing the economic in the cultural is to highlight how all these 'places' are themselves cultural constructions, and how as constructions they sit alongside and help to constitute a host of other constructed economic entities that make up what an economy is (labour, work, home, the harvest, profit, and so on). (p. 12)

Below we will look at some of these representations and constructions of the market, particularly the role of economics itself as a cultural constitution of the economy. However, Crang also delineates a fifth step. It is not just that economic entities are represented and that this is important to their constitution; more than this, economies are seen increasingly to be comprised of 'the production, circulation and consumption of "materials" that are cultural' (p. 4). In many respects, this theme represents the bulk of the literature generated by the cultural turn, for it is linked to a wide range of claims concerning what are often formulated as epochal changes in the nature of market society: a shift from Fordism to post-Fordism; the aestheticization of everyday life through advertising, marketing, design and lifestyle imagery; the increasing centrality of marketing and information in the management of economic institutions and processes; and the increasing 'dematerialization' of commodities. For some writers, these themes map out a revolution in socio-economic thought; for others, they mark a revolution in the economy itself and its relation to the rest of social life.

In this chapter we will be mainly concerned with the last two options discussed by Crang. We will first look at arguments to the effect that market economies increasingly comprise cultural goods and cultural logics. This discussion particularly focuses on the notions of post-Fordism, postmodernism, consumer culture and globalization. Finally, we will take up the increasing concern with the way in which economics itself constitutes a cultural force that plays a decisive role in producing economies and economic entities.

Cultural economies

Much current writing within the cultural turn, particularly under the impact of post-Fordist and postmodern arguments, envisages something akin to an 'implosion' of the economic and the cultural (Ray and Sayer 1999: 5–9) to the extent that the distinction between the two is no longer meaningful. This claim is partly based on arguing that the economy seems increasingly made up of informational and symbolic work on goods that are themselves increasingly 'non-material' (whether because they are conceived as services or as predominately cultural commodities such as media and entertainment goods). This gives, it is argued, a new character to the economy: the logic of economic flows and processes is better understood in terms of the nature of signs, information and cultural dynamics. Moreover, such developments place cultural experts in the driving seat of economic institutions, in particular those who specialize in knowledge, design, conceptualization and marketing. Despite the apparent deconstruction of the economic moment, however, the cultural turn has yet again placed the market at the very centre of social life, if anything more extremely than ever before. On the one hand, from the firm's point of view, the cultural turn is associated with the predominance of marketing – the cultural specification and signification of goods, an intensive knowledge of and orientation to the consumer, the potential commodification of ever more aspects of social experience and meaning, and the increasing importance of cultural, informational and interpersonal expertise in the labour market. On the other hand, as intimated in the previous chapter, in relation to the consumer the market is increasingly seen as the locus of identity formation and the construction of meaningful social life through its provision of symbolic resources and the cultural elaboration of social difference and distinction.

The centrality of culture within modern economy is actually a long-term theme. Above all, there has been a consistent (and problematic) association between enculturation and affluence (see, for example, Berry 1994; Scitovsky 1976, 1986; Sekora 1977; Slater 1997a, 1997b). This is an argument, taking many forms, that with increasing material welfare, western societies move from a preoccupation with the production and consumption of material necessities to a concern with cultural goods. A greater distance from the urgency of physical reproduction places goods increasingly in a context of social reproduction, where their importance is not so much in keeping bodies alive and healthy, but rather in marking social distinction, relative status and cultural sophistication. In this context, small differences of meaning between goods are more important than differences in function or price. Indeed, function and price themselves come to signify identity and status, as when people will aspire to buy an expensive fur coat from a prestige department store rather than a cheaper overcoat from a high street retailer on the basis of what it might signify. In arguments from as far afield as Veblen (1953 [1899]) and Bataille (1991), market behaviour is theorized in terms of conspicuous waste rather than economizing rationality on the grounds of a cultural distancing from 'natural' and functional necessity. The capacity of the market to act as the cultural locus of identity and distinction is therefore often treated as a natural outcome of the general affluence and economic success of modern economies (for example, Galbraith 1969).

This overarching theme has been replayed in more specific analyses of transitions within contemporary capitalism. First, a range of theorists from the 1960s onwards (Bell 1976; Block 1990; Galbraith 1972; Lyotard 1986; Piore and Sabel 1984; Poster 1990; Touraine 1971) have given central significance to the shift of the economic centre of gravity from manufacturing to service and informational industries. Economic activity seems to be involved less in the transformation of material things and more in producing or commodifying activities, interpersonal relations and knowledge. This is evidenced both in the kinds of commodity that increasingly dominate the consumer marketplace and in the kinds of 'raw material' that go into production, in particular information and socioculturally skilled labour. Moreover, this involves a new kind of labour market, with consequences for cultural and economic life: as originally argued by Riesman (1961), more recently by Bell (1976, 1979), Bourdieu (1984), Featherstone (1987, 1991, 1995), Hochschild (1983), du Gay (1996) and Sennett (1998), the skills and capital required of the ever-growing ranks of knowledge workers and cultural intermediaries are quite different from those required of manual or agricultural workers in terms of things like interpersonal skills, taste and style, cognitive, affective and social flexibility, and so on. Many of these skills are very close to the self: to succeed in these fields requires presenting *oneself*, not merely one's material labour power, as a commodity in the labour market, a development exacerbated by the increasing prevalence of short-term contracts, subcontracting, self-employment and consultancy arrangements in so many of these economic sectors (for an example that deals with this in specifically gendered contexts, see Entwistle 1997a, 1997b, 2000a, 2000b). Being a knowledge worker or cultural intermediary requires aestheticized work on the self and its presentation; being either kind of worker also implicates one in taste structures and relations to culture as a worker which spill over into one's relationship to culture as a consumer (see especially Featherstone 1991). Hence if postmodernization has become a recognizable feature of modern marketing and consumption, this is at least partly attributable to the way in which knowledge workers and cultural intermediaries market goods to themselves as consumers, or to 'virtual consumers' constructed in their own image. The relations between cultural production and consumption are nicely explored for advertising in Nixon (1996, 1997), for retail in du Gay (1996) and more generally in du Gay (1997).

In recent years, this kind of argument has been subsumed within broader theses about transformations from Fordism to post-Fordism, or from organized to disorganized capitalism or to new regimes of 'flexible accumulation' (Aglietta 1979; Amin 1994; Harvey 1989; Lash and Urry 1987, 1994). 'Fordism' is used to characterize capitalist economies from the turn of the twentieth century to the 1970s (see the related discussion in chapter 5), in which mass production based on increasingly rationalized manufacturing processes was linked to a culture of mass consumption involving the construction of national and international markets around rationalized distribution of standardized goods. Consumers were understood in terms of masses, in the sense that marketing aimed at the largest possible aggregates of homogeneous consumers, at most differentiated through blunt demographics such as class, gender or age. Cultural differentiation of either goods or consumers is argued to be minimal under this system because of the dictates of production: as in Henry Ford's statement that the consumer could have any colour of car they wanted so long as it was black, the economics of scale, high output and decreasing unit cost governed the logic of market sales. Fordism is therefore associated in this type of analysis with a separation between production and marketing, in which the production of goods was governed by the engineers and designers rather than by cultural intermediaries, who – in the form of advertising agencies – had an entirely separate and subordinate role, instructed to give a cultural coating to objects whose shape was already determined by the producers. Finally, Fordism is associated with a broader sense of the division of production and consumption: rationalization of mass production processes required the complete subordination of labour to cybernetic systems of manufacture (exemplified in the flow-past assembly line). The worker was to give up all control over the labour process in exchange for steadily increasing wages and ever-cheaper mass-produced goods; that is to say, to locate their identity and empowerment in the realm of consumption rather than production.

According to theorists of post-Fordism, this system reached its limits in the 1960s and 1970s. Mass production was facing decreasing economies of scale and increasing risk associated with large investment in dedicated plant. It was facing increasing labour militancy in the form of a rejection of both alienation at work and compensation in the form of mass consumption at home. It was also facing increasing saturation of core consumer markets. At the same time, it is argued, new technological, organizational and social opportunities were emerging that have refocused the logic of production away from mass manufacture and mass consumption to flexible, responsive production of more differentiated ranges of goods to ever more culturally differentiated consumers. For example, in the world of Benetton capitalism (Murray 1989a, 1989b) (or indeed Nike capitalism), the firm may no longer directly own any means of production or even retail outlets. Instead, the firm comprises a continuous flow of up-to-the second information about sources of supply and levels of demand for highly specific versions of its products. The aim is flexible response to culturally differentiated, rather than massed, consumers. The corresponding idea of 'niche marketing' indicates that sales and profits are to be sought in identifying consumer needs in terms of lifestyles, tastes and other cultural dimensions which not only cut across more 'objective' demographics such as class or gender, but are obviously more fluid and can be operated on through cultural expertise in design and interpretation of consumer trends. Finally, the disaggregation of both production and consumption that is associated with post-Fordism is echoed in the disaggregation of the mass media, advertising and retailing, which increasingly target culturally defined consumer segments and experiences.

All of these developments would lead both theorists and practitioners to understand markets more in terms of the production and flow of signs than simply the selling of goods, and would place cultural knowledges and skills at the centre of both production and consumption. In fact, the extent of this sense of increasing enculturation of markets can be summarized through the term 'dematerialization', a word that covers at least four developments: a shift from the production of material to non-material goods, evidenced in the move from manufacturing to service as core industries; the greater non-material composition of even material goods, in the form of 'commodity aesthetics' and 'sign values' constructed through design and promotion; the increasing symbolic mediation of goods through objectified cultural forms (advertising, media, retail spectacles); the increasing centrality of non-material raw materials – information, planning, managerial expertise and corporate culture – in economic processes (Slater 1997a: 193–5). Lash and Urry (1994) group these various processes under two headings:

> What is increasingly produced are not material objects, but *signs*. These signs are of two types. Either they have a primarily cognitive content and are post-industrial or informational goods. Or they have primarily an aesthetic content and are what can be termed postmodern goods. The development of the latter can be seen not only in the proliferation of objects which possess a substantial aesthetic component (such as pop music, cinema, leisure, magazines, video and so on), but also in the increasing component of sign-value or image embodied *in* material objects. The aestheticization of material objects takes place in the production, the circulation or the consumption of such goods. (p. 4)

The last point is worth emphasizing: aestheticization features in all stages of a commodity's life cycle and indeed draws together processual moments – production, circulation and consumption – which have been regarded as separate by earlier economic and social thought. The necessary integration of these moments in relation to the circulation of signs can be thought about in terms of marketing. As we have seen, it is argued that both producers and consumers have moved away from the idea that firms are engaged in the technical production and distribution of things with self-evident uses to consumers with self-evident needs. Through the discourses and institutions of marketing, corporate culture – like social science – acknowledges that consumers assimilate goods into their lives in meaningful forms, and that these meanings are produced through multiple and overlapping processes: by the consumers themselves as an integral aspect of their consumption, through processes of circulation such as the spectacles of retail display and advertising, and in the very heart of production through R & D and design. Meaning as an integral aspect of economic flows is *not* something new to modernity or postmodernity: we cannot conceptualize any production, consumption or exchange as a brute materialism (Douglas and Isherwood 1979; Sahlins 1976). However, the argument here is that this aspect of commodity circulation is both increasingly central to economic action and intensified through the reflexivity of economic actors and institutions. Consumers in a post- or late-modern world, it is argued, are bound up with the meanings of things – and relate them to core issues of identity and social place – to a degree and with a reflexive understanding hitherto inconceivable. Moreover, firms have increasingly come to understand and strategize their activities in terms of the production of meaning – the term 'marketing' again encapsulates this, denominating an approach to market competition that integrates production and distribution of goods in terms of orientation to the self-understandings of consumers.

What Lash and Urry refer to as post-industrial or informational goods – signs with a predominantly cognitive content – feature first as forms of data or information within the traditional 'economic moment'. This includes forms of expertise; cybernetic and planning functions; financial, organizational and technical statistics that increase the rational accounting and control of the enterprise; the increasingly sign-like or 'tokenized' (Waters 1995) form taken by money, which now flows electronically through networks in the form of digital representations. Informational goods constitute not only major aspects of production and co-ordination within firms, but also huge commodity markets comprising information and databases, news, expertise, consultancies, provision and maintenance of information systems (for example, electronic trading systems). Moreover, techno-panics – for example, about the role of automatic trading systems in triggering the 1987 stock market crash, or doomsday scenarios in which the global economic system is brought to its knees by the millennium bug – are indications that the high ground of economic activity is no longer monopolized by steel mills and car assembly plants.

Sign value and social order

The progressive enculturation of the market can be seen as part of a process of increasing abstraction that arises out of the market, yet turns around to engulf and transform the landscape of market capitalism. Baudrillard's (1975, 1981, 1998 [1970]) radical semiotic rewriting of economic history is doubtless the clearest example of this approach, albeit one of the most extreme. Market exchange has long been understood, particularly within Marxism, as a triumph of abstraction through the dominance of abstract exchange value over use value. In Baudrillard's argument, this process of abstraction is overtaken by yet another: the commodity, freed from its use value and hence from the concrete particularity of needs, labour and real material properties, is able to take on a different kind of value, a 'sign value'. Sign value derives neither from the object's place in the real order of needs and objects, nor from its value in exchange relations, but rather from its position within codes of meaning and semiotic processes. Moreover, the production and manipulation of such codes and sign values can become a matter of functional specialization (or 'commodity aesthetics' (Haug 1986)): institutions and processes arise that specialize in semiotic expertise. These include not only advertising, but also the entire 'dream world' (Williams 1982) of consumer capitalism comprising shop display, malls, exhibitions and other images through which modernity made a spectacle of itself (Slater 1993, 1995).

Signs and the logic of their production take on a high degree of autonomy both from their objects and from the material production of those objects. Indeed, the order of things is reversed. This train of thought, developing partly out of Marx's analysis of fetishism, argues that such intensive mediation of both world and desire through commercially generated images ultimately 'de-realize[s] reality' (Featherstone 1991: 68). Postmodernism, in one of its many definitions, is the culture of a market society that has become completely abstract through aestheticization, in which 'it is the build-up, density and seamless, all-encompassing extent of the production of images in contemporary society which has pushed us towards a qualitatively new society in which the distinction between reality and image becomes effaced and everyday life becomes aestheticized' (p. 68). Rather, capitalist postmodernity generates a hyperreality, an aesthetic coating of the world with images that replace, displace and themselves generate what used to be called 'society'. We can no longer conceive of the social order as arising from the interactions of autonomous subjects; it is rather bound together through relations of meaning: the sign itself is what effects the social bonds between people (Kellner 1989). Even labour has become a 'sign among signs': not a material force of production and commodification, but a sign that marks one's social position within 'the system'. 'Labour power is no longer violently bought and sold; it is designed, it is marketed, it is merchandised. Production thus joins the consumerist system of signs' (p. 61). Objective structures that were previously deemed to generate social reality (for example, the social relations of production that determined class and therefore market position) or frame it (for example, time and history) are now reduced to mere signs within overarching codes that organize reality through the meaningful interrelation of terms within semiotic structures.

Indeed, although this situation arises out of market capitalism, ultimately the very notion of a market within postmodernity would seem inconceivable to Baudrillard (1981, 1983): the demise of the market, competition, exchange and use value are part of the generic death of the social. For markets to work, the value contained in them would have to continue to represent certain realities beyond representation (such as labour and utility), around which real social contests could persist; in fact these realities are subsumed within representation and persist only as simulacra or artefacts of the code. There are no longer markets, but rather shopping malls that simulate the old marketplace, making us imagine – culturally – that we live in a market society when in fact we live in a society of signs, a space of flows (Ritzer 1999; Slater 1993). In the form of the marketplace and shopping, the market is no longer properly to be understood in terms of technical relations between quantities of value, but rather as a fluid magma of signified difference that becomes the raw material of equally fluid identities, pleasures and desires.

Both the cultural critics and critics of reification whom we discussed in chapter 6 raised huge doubts about the very possibility of 'culture' existing in any meaningful sense within a market society: they strove to differentiate the signs and appearances thrown up by marketization from alternative and oppositional notions of culture. Particularly in Baudrillard's formulation, the idea of aestheticization – of a world awash with signs and of the functional centrality of sign production to contemporary production and consumption – can be seen as adding urgency to these themes. And yet they also mark a potentially radical break. In the case of postmodernism, as we have just seen, the triumph of the sign threatens the very notion of social reality as a basis for either social analysis or critique, let alone as a source of alternative cultural values. The notion of consumer society or consumer culture has registered these worries very clearly. As with the term 'culture' itself, 'consumer culture' may be identified with the achievement through marketization of self-determined choice; or it may represent a bitter irony – consumer culture is a contradiction in terms, since no real culture is possible on the basis of individual choice mediated through commodities (Slater 1997a: 63–83). Moreover, consumer culture comes to represent the cultural manipulation of the consumer through the market and non-market powers (for example, advertising) of firms, as well as indirectly through the commodification and monetarization of everyday life.

The term 'consumer culture' first tends to argue that core values and identities are now bound up with or negotiated through consumption and commodities. Hence, we constantly talk about values such as choice, desire and pleasure, privacy and freedom, appearance, fashion and style, materialism and rising material standards, comforts and conveniences, and so on. All of these are seriously important to modern citizens as ideals (whether or not they can afford them), are understood in relation to the market, and tend to be experienced in terms more of the role of 'consumer' than of alternative prestigious social roles (citizen, family member, worker, religious adherent), which themselves tend to be recast in terms of being a consumer (a vote is like a purchase decision, religions are matters of personal choice, marriages can legitimately be dissolved if they do not give personal satisfaction, and so on). Similarly, market society is corrosive of stable social hierarchies that ascribe identities to individuals; instead consumer culture both embodies market society's promises of egalitarian and socially mobile identity while at the same time destabilizing status systems. We are incited to construct our identities through the assemblage of commodities into personal lifestyles or shared subcultures or communities of taste. For many commentators (for example, Marcuse 1964) this means that it is through consumer culture that we are integrated within market society, locked into commodity exchange through a desperate and insatiable need for identities and pleasures that can be secured only through the marketed goods that inflame these needs in the first place; and that we are led – in a classic manifestation of market-derived false consciousness – to identify our personal and political interests not with power over the relations of production that really rule our lives, but rather with the mystifying games of consumption (Williamson 1978). Both individual and more collective identities then seem to be 'made up' out of market choices, producing a condition of instability and anxiety that may be met by yet more market-oriented aesthetic products: advertising, magazines and films offer not only images of specific desirable commodities, but also endless images of how to assemble these commodities into meaningful identities and lifestyles, expert advice, self-help suggestions for dealing with the anxieties of choice (Bauman 1990; Beck 1992; Giddens 1991; Warde 1994a, 1994b).

   Second, the possibility of consumption playing this role in personal and social identity rests on its cultural character and the kinds of aestheticizing process it can participate in and sustain. That is to say, although consumption goods and processes always have cultural meaning, under consumer culture those meanings become essential raw material both for producers to use for increased sales and for consumers to use to negotiate their identities, aspirations and choices. The 'meanings of things', as we have seen, become the site of enormous specialist labour by designers, advertisers, sales forces, the media and leisure industries, labour which is directed towards moulding these meanings in the direction of increasing sales, engaging wider or larger consumer constituencies, and building synergies between products (such as through lifestyle concepts spread across different markets and media). The ability to deal with marketable things through their capacity as signs seems to free them or destabilize them: this gives us the characteristic modern cultural landscape in which we are all awash with a dazzling and constantly changing flow of images, fashions, styles, ways of relating things to our everyday lives, identities and relationships. Because it is a flow of signs, it allows objects, identities and markets to be constantly redefined, recontextualized and renewed, hence producing a dynamic of both insatiable need (because new needs and new things can always be dreamed up) and unstoppable economic and cultural growth.

Third, both the values inscribed in consumer culture and the instability of meaning that it exploits and intensifies raise a range of issues concerning the reproduction of everyday life under market capitalism and the rule of the commodity. This is often construed as a largely postmodern matter: part of the seeming autonomy of commercial culture, as we have seen, is a sense that it is no longer anchored in external social realities, and can no longer be questioned or challenged by realities such as class, gender or race, or by history or a philosophically realist understanding of economic and political forces as objective and external – all of these can be and have been absorbed within autonomous, and generally market-driven, sign systems. As in Baudrillard, the triumph of market forces is reflected in the capacity of a consumer culture to dematerialize social structure and process by absorbing them within the ambit of infinitely malleable commercial signs.

These developments continue to raise questions about the freedom or manipulation of social actors. On the one hand, Baudrillard's (1983) characterization of modern populations as a 'black hole' or silent majority whose only possible strategy of resistance is to passively absorb the aesthetic outpouring of consumer capitalism fits unproblematically into older mass culture and manipulationist views of consumption. Consumers and their innermost desires march in step with the beat of advertising: we have passive commercial psyches structured by instrumentally rational sign systems. On the other hand, as we have seen in the previous chapter, we can argue that commercialization has produced – for whatever nefarious reasons of its own – an unprecedented range of symbolic resources for common (everyday) culture (Willis 1990), through which people necessarily construct their own symbolic universes. This does not mean (as authors like de Certeau 1984 and Fiske 1989 would have it) that people's use of goods is necessarily rebellious, oppositional or significantly autonomous; simply that announcements as to the death of the social might be somewhat premature.

Enculturation as flow, mobility and velocity

Crang (1997: 13) argues that 'the materialization of economic activities matters for the character of these activities themselves. . . . So, whether one is producing/circulating/consuming crude oil, or a piece of music, or a car, or some polite conversation, matters to those moments of production, circulation and consumption, and, indeed, to the character of the cultural circuits through which those moments are interconnected.' On this basis it would be no surprise that the dematerialization of the economy and its objects would have dramatic consequences. A central one is the claim that dematerialization intensifies the mobility and velocity of the flow of 'things' through space and across time. Dematerialization is associated with 'deterritorialization' and the disembedding of things and people from their localities: things increasingly flow around the world without regard for territorial boundaries or for places. Indeed, it is argued that an older twentieth-century sense of the world as a 'space of places' is being replaced by a postmodern experience of the world as a 'space of flows' (Castells 1996). Waters (1995: 9) states the case most baldly: 'material exchanges localize; political exchanges internationalize; and symbolic exchanges globalize'. This is because 'symbolic exchanges liberate relationships from spatial referents. Symbols can be produced anywhere and any time and there are relatively few resource constraints on their production and reproduction. Moreover they are easily transportable. Importantly, because they frequently seek to appeal to human fundamentals they can often claim universal significance' (p. 9). Waters sees two economic processes, already discussed, which have promoted the dematerialization of commodity production and therefore the predominance of symbolic exchange: post-industrialization (the shift from manufacturing to services) and 'hypercommodification and the industrialization of culture' (p. 75). Both imply 'the production of more mobile and easily tradeable products', hence 'generally speaking, globalization will increase to the extent that world production is devoted to these non-material commodities precisely because they are so mobile' (p. 75).

The notion of 'flows' becomes a central analytic, one which – much like 'networks' – subsumes hitherto more segregated social processes. The notion of a market could once crudely denote the circulation of commodities at the spatio-temporal meeting point of buyers and sellers, as in the marketplace we discussed in chapter 1. In the new 'economies of signs and space' (Lash and Urry 1994), however, it is difficult to separate the circulation of commodities from the circulation of, say, media messages or data flows. This is not simply because media messages and databases can be sold as commodities, but also because commodities circulate in represented form within media representations of lifestyles or in data representations of, for example, design specifications or production statistics. Rather than thinking of the market as one separate process or institution, this line of thinking would present it as one flow of things with its own characteristics, but nonetheless intertwined with other flows of political, cultural and social representations. This is captured in Appadurai's (1990) seminal article, in which he thinks through the 'imagined worlds' (p. 296) that people inhabit in terms of five 'global cultural flows' – ethnoscapes, mediascapes, technoscapes, finanscapes and ideoscapes – in which the flows of (respectively) people, representations, technologies, capital and ideas constitute different social landscapes that are at once internally driven and mutually disjunctive, yet always interconnected and rubbing shoulders, often tensely, in the same social spaces. For example, the notion of a market as a separate institution does scant justice to the kind of situation he describes, in which transnational flows of money and people may lead residents of both Bombay and London to worry about affluent Arabs altering their local leisure amenities – hotels, restaurants and other services:

> Yet, most residents of Bombay are ambivalent about the Arab presence there, for the flip side of their presence is the absence of friends and kinsmen earning big money in the Middle East and bringing back both money and luxury commodities to Bombay and other cities in India. Such commodities transform consumer taste in these cities, and also often end up smuggled through air and sea ports and peddled in the gray markets of Bombay's streets. In these gray markets, some members of Bombay's middle-classes and of its lumpenproletariat can buy some of these goods, ranging from cartons of Marlboro cigarettes, to Old Spice shaving cream and tapes of Madonna. Similarly gray routes, often subsidized by the moonlighting activities of sailors, diplomats and airline stewardesses who get to move in and out of the country regularly, keep gray markets of Bombay, Madras and Calcutta filled with goods not only from the West, but also from the Middle East, Hong Kong and Singapore. (p. 302)

What Appadurai is pointing to goes beyond the simple idea of a marketplace to the description of spaces defined by various flows:

the flows of people (through international labour markets and tourist markets, and through ethnic drifts that might be political, economic, cultural or even religious in nature); the flows of goods (not only as exchanged commodities, but also as personal consumption goods, souvenirs and cultural icons); the flows of cultural/media experiences (images of self and other, and the different and changing meanings of things as they are recontextualized in different times and spaces).

The metaphor that hovers over all these developments is that of 'globalization'. Although there is sometimes an assumption that globalization is a recent concept, the idea that markets have inherent tendencies to ignore national boundaries, to expand beyond localities and to dominate local ethnicities stretches back to early modernity. For example, the interlinked extension of markets and the social division of labour, as we discussed in chapter 1, could be related to the pacification of international relations and to awareness of inter-dependencies as a new basis for solidarities. Marx had a rather more pessimistic view in which the structural necessity for capitalism to expand leads it to seek markets throughout the globe, hence bringing all human and natural resources within the ambit of exploitation, competition and monetarization. Even Marx sees a positive side to this, in that the technical forces of capitalist production drive society into a world of expanded needs and goods, greater technical know-ledge and wealth. In this sense, globalization is part of the progressive mission of capitalism, in which it develops society's productive power in advance of the more egalitarian society beyond the 'realm of necessity' that will emerge after its own demise. More immediately, however, globalization is associated with an imperialism that requires markets to be secured whether through political domination, military adventure or economic and technical advantages, through which market society displays no more respect for the traditional cultures it encounters abroad than for those at home: 'all that is solid melts into air' as lifeworlds are transformed by the systematization of world market relations. The idea of marketization as a basis for the global power of capitalism and capitalist culture was made very clear in arguments about media and cultural imperialism (as in the notion of Americanization): American economic, military and ideological power secured it overwhelming advantages in the marketplace for cultural goods such as film and television; while its role in marketiz-ing foreign cultures in turn secured economic, military and ideolo-gical hegemony. Above all, it spread marketization through the powerful seduction exercised by images of consumer culture.

Given such enduring arguments that markets transform cultures at the global or transnational scale, the cultural turn approaches to globalization represent a reversal: rather than markets being the driving force behind capitalist domination at a global scale, they are merely one aspect of a more complex and multidirectional dynamic, one among a range of flows and drives. First, as we have seen in Appadurai's work, globalization is generally grasped through a range of flows rather than through marketization (or rationalization or division of labour) as a monocausal explanation. Second, in the current debates, 'globalization' does not refer to analysis of an already assumed domination, or to a one-way process of convergence or homogenization of culture at a global level. Rather, it commonly refers to a dialectic in which forces that operate transnationally nonetheless have to be domesticated or assimilated in particular locales. As Robins (1997: 14) puts it, 'globalization is about growing mobility across frontiers – mobility of goods and commodities, mobility of information and communications, products and services, and mobility of people', and 'with mobility, comes encounter' (p. 18). The upshot of the cultural encounters effected by globalization is not in principle uniform, predictable or unambiguous: all that can be said in general is that a range of globalizing developments – including marketization – increasingly place people, goods and events in common spaces, bring them into contact, where previously they would have been kept separate through constraints of space (distance, borders, costs of movement) and time. Moreover, as Giddens notes through the concept of time-space distanciation, people increasingly inhabit common abstractions or representations of time and space, such as a single map and single clock-time. These common spaces and the encounters that occur within them are not dominated by a single global player, nor do they result in cultural homogeneity. Indeed, the major focus has been on hybridization: older local or regionally dominant cultural forms are challenged and transformed out of all recognition by new encounters, often with the cultures they previously dominated.

Hence – in contrast to earlier perspectives – it is as important to consider globalization as a context for the transformation of market behaviours and institutions as to think of marketization as a force for globalization. How does the flow of commodities fit within deterritorialized flows of people, information, money and so on (the 'scapes' that Appadurai defined)? For example, Theodor Levitt's (1983) classic and much cited article on 'The globalization of markets' argued that firms must think through their brands at the international level, seeking to produce global brands for global consumers. This formulation, while acknowledging a common consumerist marketplace, characterized it under the older notion of homogenization, as if firms could create international markets on the same model as the national markets of the Fordist heyday. As Kline (1995: 108) notes, 'global marketing was destined to lead to "cultural convergence" as corporations re-positioned themselves to take advantage of global reach, larger markets and advanced production technologies', along the old lines of economies of scale. The classic example is Coca-Cola's 1960s attempt to 'teach the world to sing in perfect harmony', which, as Kline notes, addressed an 'international youth consumer' through optimistic global village imagery of a universal consumer 'who was really American at heart' (p. 109). This approach has been widely overtaken by ' "glo-local", or "glocal", marketing strategies, by which merchants customize products, brand names, packages, distribution channels and even advertising appeals to the particularities of the domestic social milieu in which they are sought and used' (p. 122), and which Kline investigates through the example of the international marketing of children's games.

Such marketing approaches seem to recognize both that consumer goods are consumed not by global consumers but by particular people assimilating things within local everyday cultures, and that at the same time these goods and consumers inhabit a cultural space vastly expanded and complexified by globalizing forces of which markets and marketers are merely one element. There is no global market as a homogeneous cultural space: the more global the market becomes, the more localities a marketer must contend with; and yet also the more hybrid and complex those localities become as their range of encounters, and responses to encounters, expands. New media technologies such as the Internet, which are also seen as new transnational marketplaces, intensify such dialectics. For example, Miller and Slater (2000), in an ethnographic study of the Internet in relation to Trinidad, found that while Internet media broadened the range and immediacy of Trinidadians' encounters with other parts of the world, it simultaneously heightened their sense of national identity and locality. The dominant metaphor for contemporary engagements with markets and commodities is not homogenization but rather 'creolization' (see Howes 1996), in which the focus is on the shifting means of goods when they flow across borders and are recontextualized in new contexts, when market behaviours have to contend with the disjunctures between the cultures in which things might be produced, exchanged and consumed. Hence, Classen (1996), writing about the place of remote north-west Argentina in world consumer markets, focuses on the surreal quality of the seemingly random juxtaposition of goods that result from global flows such as 'Japanese recordings of Argentine tangos and American television shows dubbed in Mexican Spanish' (p. 39). The specific local conditions were partly structured by the introduction of neo-liberal free market policies in Argentina, which opened up the north-west to new goods after a long period of protectionism:

> As I travel between my homes in Canada and Argentina, I hardly know what to take or bring as presents any more, for the same goods are for sale in both places. To comparison-shop for goods between cities in the northern and southern hemispheres seems absurd, yet in the late twentieth-century global village it is entirely possible. My mother takes chocolate replicas of Canadian dollar coins for her great-nieces and nephews in Argentina only to find them for sale there – and at a lower price than in Canada. (p. 45)

In fact, in Classen's account the surrealism of global consumer culture is not all that far from Marxist accounts of fetishization: the products that enter Argentianian life not only enter a new world of meaning, discontinuous from the (metropolitan) culture in which they were produced, they also 'enter Northwest Argentina *without* a history. . . . Notions such as laptop computers, breakfast cereal, or shopping centres have no indigenous roots in the region, they simply appear on the scene as if materialized from a Hollywood movie. . . . As a result, there appears to be little continuity between the tra-ditional way of life in the Northwest and the new – just a surreal juxtaposition' (p. 52). As Classen points out, this surrealism is actu-ally not new but central to the marketing of goods in consumer culture: all goods are advertised as 'an eruption of the extraordinary into the everyday' (p. 52).

Economics *as* culture

The very fact that markets are not natural events but social ones implies that they are the results of meaningful human action and deploy cultural beliefs about human nature, social action and rela-tions. More specifically, markets are, as Polanyi argued, 'instituted' by social agencies and therefore involve programmes based on rep-resentations of the social and theories of social cause and effect. Markets arise where particular social actors, operating through institutions such as governments, states, legal systems and businesses, produce and reproduce market institutions. In this sense, we especially need to think about economics and economic theory *as culture*, whether formulated in academic discourses, policy statements or common sense and lay knowledge. Hence, economic theory is not simply a commentary upon 'real' economic processes that are external to it; it is part of the constitution and operation of markets. Indeed, economics as culture is a powerful element within modern social life and governance precisely by virtue of the way it provides actionable and convincing representations of social actions, flows and networks. This is reflected in the forms of rhetoric and linguistic construction it employs and helps to maintain its prestige (Klamer, McCloskey and Solow 1988; Lavoie 1990; McCloskey 1986, 1994). Economics as culture includes not only ideologies such as neo-Keynesianism and neoliberalism, which can act as universalizing cosmologies and belief systems in the same sense as, say, the cultural framework of *kula* circuits (Carrier 1997). It also involves powerful technologies of representation that produce highly specific perceptual schemas for seeing society: above all, economics involves a culture of quantification, of modelling and of abstraction from particular cases.

For example, Dodd (1995) examines the reaction of financial markets to the publication of treasury figures or announcements of interest rate changes by national banks. As information, these announcements do not provoke either automatic or predictable responses; instead market actors process market information not only through their own theories of economic cause and effect ('what impact should a fractional rise in rates have on medium-term expectations of economic growth?'), but even more complexly and confusingly through their assumptions about *other actors'* economic theorizations ('how do I calculate a situation in which predicting the impact of an interest rate rise depends in large measure on how other people with market power answer the question, "what impact will a fractional rise in rates have . . . ?", an answer which depends on their theoretical framework – thus requiring that my theoretical framework include theirs as datum?'). Rational expectations must include, within their 'horizon' of available knowledge, information concerning other people's rational expectations, which in turn depend on *their* social beliefs, theories and values.

From this point of view, we are considering economic theory – whether formal, practical, commonsensical or tacit – as part of the culture of the market, beliefs that enter into the 'real' market. In Dodd's argument, a direct line is drawn between this sense of economics as culture and the 'postmodern' idea – discussed in the last section – that economies are increasingly cultural. However, Dodd's direct line is possibly not the usual one. Whereas many postmodern theorists (Dodd cites Lash and Urry 1994) see the economy as increasingly cultural because of the new pre-eminence of sign value, Dodd argues that this has always been the case: taking the specific issue of money, he demonstrates that the symbolic properties of money – including beliefs about the nature of money – have always been inherent in the operation of money. What is new today is the extraordinary 'media-driven *acceleration* in the constitutive role of theories, perceptions and ideas about money in the operation of money itself' (Dodd 1995: 3). One element of this acceleration is the actual speed-up of information flows. But a crucial element is the enhanced role of the media: Dodd explores this in relation to 1980s consumerism, which he defines in terms of an orgy of spending fuelled by massive increases in personal indebtedness. The transformed relation of consumers to money and to markets which underlay the decade's frenzy needs to be understood in terms of how the very idea of markets was sold to western publics through the media-transmitted ideal of 'passive enrichment', the idea that money begets more money without any connection to a productive economy. On the basis of these media-transmitted versions of neo-liberal culture, it could be deemed rational for ordinary citizens to borrow money in order to buy shares in privatized public utilities such as British Telecom, in the expectation of automatic rises in share value on the very day of issue, hence making a huge market in privatized public companies.

As Callon (1998a: 2) puts it, 'economics, in the broad sense of the term, shapes and formats the economy, rather than observing how it functions.' It is a point within economic process, an economic actor as it were, rather than an external vantage point. Moreover, Callon does not define economics in terms of the higher-level academic discipline, the dismal science, but additionally in terms of marketing, accountancy, management studies and other forms of knowledge that both formalize the knowledges and practices already to be found within market institutions and at the same time feed them back into market behaviour through professional training and education. As discussed in chapter 4, Callon is concerned with this economic knowledge not simply as a 'cultural influence' in the conventional sense of an external framework of meanings that leads economic actors to inflect their behaviour in particular directions. Rather, economics as culture operates as a structure that constitutes the spaces in which market actors are produced and framed. In the earlier discussion, we noted Callon's example of the production of a strawberry market through the conscious application of neoclassical theory by a local bureaucrat. Callon's argument indicates that culture and social technology are inseparable in the generation of markets, reflecting a generally Foucauldian argument that we should not be considering liberal and neoliberal versions of the market as either ideologies or truth claims; rather, we should think of them as discourses that construct things like markets, economizing individuals and competitive relations as objects of governmental practices, and largely do so *through* governmental practices. Similarly, Bourdieu (1998) labels neoliberalism as a 'strong discourse', one which has 'the means of *making itself true* and empirically viable' because it orients 'the economic choices of those who dominate economic relationships' and hence constitutes a 'scientific programme, converted into a plan of political action'.

In these formulations, then, the very ideas of 'an economy' or 'the market' are part of a language through which the social world is represented and acted upon and need to be historically tracked through genealogical analysis: for example, at what point and through what movements of thought is something called 'the economy' as an independent social moment discursively identified and made into an object of 'government intervention', 'regulation' or 'statistical knowledge'? (There is also the intriguing idea that there can be a history of the market for economics, as described by Kadish and Tribe (1993), who consider the rise of economics as a taught discipline within British universities.) Articles in Burchell, Gordon and Miller (1991) are concerned with exploring Foucault's account of the transitions to liberalism as a form of governmentality from earlier notions of 'police'. These transitions involved reconfiguring a view of society as resources to be known and intensively exploited directly by state agencies into a view of society as a self-regulating entity, too complex to be known or directly managed by political agents. The Smithian view of the market emerges as the image that sums up this representation of the social. The kind of representation it typifies is neither simply 'culture' in the sense of elite intellectual thought nor 'culture' in the sense of an external framework of values or beliefs in which economic activity is embedded, by which externally existing actions are ruled. Rather, culture appears as representations that constitute the market and economy as objects of knowledge which are simultaneously objects of action.

Finally, we might compare this argument with that of contributors to Carrier and Miller (1998): commercial capitalism as the process of extreme abstraction theorized by Marx was by various means integrated or tamed over the twentieth century. Miller, over various publications, cites sociopolitical domestication through Scandinavian-style social democracy; what he terms the 'organic capitalism' of Trinidad; consumption as grounded practices through which people use commodified goods themselves to combat the alienation of market institutions and processes (see, for example, Miller 1987, 1994, 1995, 1998a, 1998b). However, Miller argues, the past twenty or so years have witnessed a major swing back to processes of abstraction that reintroduce a great distance between economic institutions and local contexts. Miller describes these institutions as 'virtualist' rather than 'capitalist'; populated by such institutional actors as economists, auditors and management consultants. Such institutions construct abstract representations of the world as objects of practice, representations that both arise within and at the same time form the objects of regulatory practices. These institutions are said to be virtual in the sense that they speak in the name of 'realities' that are entirely constituted within representation: the virtual consumer who is produced as a point within market research statistics and neoliberal constructs; the virtual economy that is represented by IMF models of normative government debt structures, and so on. What distinguishes Carrier and Miller from related arguments such as Callon's is their epistemological realism: this allows for a social dialectic in which virtual consumers and 'real consumers', virtual markets and real ones, cannot be legitimately conflated, in which the social is very far from dead and buried by the virtual. To the contrary, just as economists cannot be left outside the frame of economy because they are instrumental in constituting it, neither can we leave out of view the efforts of governments, consumers and intellectuals to concretize commodity capitalism within their own life-worlds.

Conclusion

The cultural turn in contemporary analysis of the market reformulates issues of both individual identity and social order in profoundly new ways. Above all, it would seem to render meaningless the intellectual division of labour between markets as the object of technical economic analysis and markets as the focus of cultural critique. In a sense, market practice and analysis now involves issues of meaning and order simultaneously and inseparably. At the same time, as Ray and Sayer (1999) note, it is significant that – despite their insistence on the implosion of economy and culture, the domination of culture over economy or the merging of market circulation of goods with broader flows, 'scapes' or networks – all of the various literatures discussed in this chapter continue to draw upon 'culture' and 'economy' as if they were distinct and meaningful terms. Indeed, all must pay at least some attention to the institutionalization of

particular market mechanisms and practices, whether they are concerned with flexible production, new retail organizations or the
market conditions of consumer identity formation. Even the most
apparently dematerialized market institution of all – electronic commerce over the Internet – has involved corporate reorganization,
international agreements on systems of financial settlement, and legal
and legislative deliberations on the part of national governments in
order to establish frameworks for specifically economic forms of
exchange, however closely these may be integrated with other flows
of information, communication and sociality (Miller and Slater
2000). Indeed, precisely on the basis of the developments discussed
in this chapter, we might well conclude that the market, however
transformed, persists into the twenty-first century as an institution
that urgently raises, for analysts and citizens alike, the central issues
of modern social order.

Conclusion: Markets versus Market Society

It should be clear from our discussion not only that modern social thought has been centrally preoccupied with markets, but that key conceptual building blocks of the modern social science disciplines, such as the individual, society and rationality, cannot be understood independently of the modern encounter with markets. At the same time, even within apparently technical economic thought, theorizations of the market have also been social theories in the broadest sense: they are ways of conceptualizing social action, social integration and social value. At a profound level, and whatever the ostensible division of intellectual labour between economics and its others, concepts of the market and questions of modern social order exist within the same field of inquiry.

The category that has framed our entire discussion – 'market society' – indicates just how decisive has been the role of the market in modern social thought. The term suggests that modern society can be characterized, and even explained, by the domination of market exchange from the eighteenth century onwards; and that the crucial images of social order that preoccupied modern social thought emerged from the market experience or in opposition to it. On the one hand, 'market society' was a way of imagining a modernity liberated from tradition and collective bonds, in which a rational social order could emerge spontaneously from the market-coordinated actions of free and rational individuals. On the other hand, 'market society' represented the domination of an implacable logic of quantification and formal rationality over social life, producing inequality, social disorder, loss of substantive values and a destruction of both the individual and social relations.

From a contemporary standpoint, the most striking aspect of both these uses of 'market society' as an image of modernity is their monolithic, all or nothing character: the image either proposes or criticizes a social order that is entirely dominated by one mode of exchange. The 'all or nothing' perspective that is associated with images of 'market society' is evident on both sides of the critical divide. Marx, for example, correctly castigated market proponents for the way they universalized the market as the natural foundation of social order, and grounded individual action in a 'general disposition to truck, barter and exchange' (Smith 1991 [1776]: 21), or in a reductive psychology of the rational pursuit of self-interest. It is this universalization of the market order that has allowed the 'free West' to consider all alternative social arrangements – whether in societies outside itself, or surviving or emerging within itself – as unworkable and undesirable deviations from the norms of social order and human nature, and as incompatible with constructions of freedom, reason and progress. Hence, neoliberals like Margaret Thatcher could put forward a particular model of market behaviour as the natural basis for all social life. Any hint of collectivism could only end in disaster; a cultural and political revolution was required to remove from social life anything that might reduce the centrality of market models as the basis of social order.

And yet opponents of market society – most notably followers of Marx himself – promoted a similarly absolute model of market society. When Lenin commented that the emergence of a single market stall in Soviet Russia would herald the reappearance of full-blown market capitalism (and must be stamped out), he was deploying a concept of the market that was in its own way as absolute as the normative models of the economic liberals. Markets in this context represent not a particular form of exchange that can subsist alongside others, but rather an ineluctable principle of social order that subordinates all others. Hence, there can be no complicity or compromise with markets, whether one is a socialist or an artist or a cultural critic. Moreover, this perspective assumes a radical opposition between market and non-market societies, either romanticizing premodern social order for its apparently transparent, non-mediated relationship between production and consumption or presaging a utopian post-capitalist social order in which production is governed directly by the politically articulated desires of a people.

The idea of market society, then, has been decisive in thinking about and intervening in modern social order. It has certainly proved useful in this book as a way of ordering and presenting key themes in modern social theory. And yet we want to conclude the book by casting considerable doubt on the very idea of market society and whether it maps out a fruitful intellectual strategy at all. These doubts arise from tensions in writing the book and can be clearly seen in the text itself: in the all or nothing perspective of market society, there are either markets or no markets, and there are societies that either are or are not largely organized through singular market principles. And yet this is precisely the way of thinking about markets that makes the least historical, social or even economic sense. As should be clear from our discussions of, for example, the historical emergence of modern markets, of embeddedness and of the cultural turn, no society is entirely ordered by a single mode of exchange. Moreover, even if markets in some sense dominate, they do not themselves represent a single and homogeneous principle. We have been concerned throughout to emphasize that markets actually represent a broad range of behaviours, mechanisms and institutions, which can be found embedded in an even broader range of social and historical contexts. Moreover, in presenting modern social thought in relation to the market, it has been clear that the way forward has always been pointed out not by the Titans of liberal-utilitarianism or its opponents, but rather by the messier, less totalizing, disaggregating perspectives of historical studies, economic anthropology, sociology and 'the cultural turn'.

The most convincing accounts of the market in relation to social order involve more nuanced analyses of the structuring of exchange within complex social systems. In this sense, we need to make a sharp distinction between totalizing accounts of market society, on the one hand, and analyses of markets, on the other. The former explicates modern social order on the basis of a tendency towards a single principle; the latter disaggregates an apparently singular principle into a fine-grained analysis – even into specific ethnographies – of how particular forms of exchange and social order are accomplished and institutionalized. Broad-brush accounts of market society take a world-historical perspective in which the entire social order seems to be at stake; analyses of the market take a far more pragmatic point of view, in which every instance of 'market making' involves a specific line-up of social actors, strategies, institutions and interests. Looked at this way, it might make some sense to be 'for' or 'against' market society, insofar as this concept represents attempts to project ideal (or dystopic) images of social order on the basis of a thought experiment about the dominance of one form of exchange. For example, it makes perfect sense either to oppose a neoliberal agenda that seeks to use the full power of government to reduce all social values to prices, all choices to individual consumer decisions, and all social co-ordination to a particular model of market transaction; or to oppose a state socialism that uses an equally powerful governmental apparatus (unsuccessfully) to eradicate all autonomous economic exchange. The problem would be to recognize that this dominance is never really complete.

On the other hand, it makes much less sense – either analytically or politically – to take a stance 'for' or 'against' markets as such, because that would be to assume that markets are a single and definite thing, consistent in their form and function across time and space. To the contrary, to analyse and take a stand on markets (socially, politically and economically) – *if* one wants to ground one's case in the best of economic anthropology and sociology – would necessarily involve understanding particular programmes and concepts of marketization, particular institutionalizations of exchange, particular framings of exchange (Callon) that internalize or externalize pertinent social consequences, particular technical problems of allocation, particular value conflicts and so on.

The tension between theories of market society and analyses of markets can be seen throughout most of the book. It was certainly evident in the writing of it: we found the trope of 'market society' useful in understanding much about how modern social thought has been structured; however, in trying to understand and evaluate markets in modern social life, this term ultimately proves insufficient. Indeed, the forms of social thought that were structured by it appeared more as parties to the battle than as ways of understanding it. In chapter 1, we dealt with the historical context of modernity, which observers widely explained as a rise to dominance of markets and market exchange. And yet even in order to set this context we had to indicate the diversity of market experiences and structures that might co-exist or overlap. The clash between liberal-utilitarian and economic thought, on the one hand, and the classical sociological tradition, on the other hand, conventionally appears as a conflict between a technical account of exchange and a properly social one, as well as a conflict between defenders and critics of capitalism and market society. We have indicated that this opposition is wrong – economic theory is also social theory in the broadest sense – but we can go further and say that the real opposition is between the world-historical accounts we dealt with up to chapter 3 and the theories of embeddedness that appear in chapter 4. Both economics and critical social theory accept an account of modern market society as increasingly based on abstract and formal exchange, differing only as to whether this promotes or undermines ethical individualism and rational social order. And yet it is only when we get to theories of embeddedness, of the market economy as an instituted process and beyond, that we encounter a deconstruction of the very idea of abstraction. And, as presented in terms of both Polanyi's and Callon's work, this abstraction is best approached through the concrete, specific and various means by which markets are established rather than in terms of the spread of a general principle throughout the social order. Markets are best imagined not as a viral epidemic or an organic growth, but rather as the outcome of a range of political, cultural, social and economic strategies.

In chapter 5, the opposition between markets and states is the clearest example of totalized and doctrinaire concepts of 'market society': the last century and more has been dominated by an apparently political choice between a market society and a planned one. Economic outcomes such as efficiency and political outcomes such as democracy have seemed to ride entirely on purifying whole social systems entirely of either markets or plans. In this area of debate, it could be argued that the notion of market society drops any pretence to ground coherent analysis and takes on its proper function of political programme: it is not a cogent characterization of any social order but the Jerusalem to be constructed by neoliberal revolutionaries. It is interesting, however, that whereas until the 1980s the political left's opposition to markets tended to be absolute (market solutions *must* imply a settling of accounts with capitalism) and the political mainstream was pragmatic (markets had a defined place within managerialist mixed economies), the picture has reversed since then: we have only recently emerged from the most sustained and effective attempt, since the nineteenth century, to create a pure market society, and the left-of-centre response has been to drop the kind of doctrinaire approach to markets that goes with theories of market society. Indeed, current intellectual *and* political standpoints have significantly departed from all-or-nothing versions of market society. It is notable that the fall of actually existing socialism in 1989 coincided not so much with the expected triumph of neoliberalism (which was also reaching its sell-by date) as with a range of perspectives that have increasingly understood modern social order not in terms of first principles, but rather as a mix of social mechanisms that might include markets and market behaviours without assuming that these will automatically dominate (see Thompson et al. 1991). These approaches include new models of mixed yet progressive economy (Hodgson 1984; Nove 1983; Nove and Thatcher 1994), new cultural models of order such as postmodernism (Gibson-Graham 1996), and new conceptualizations of society (particularly information society) as embracing diverse networks that might even subsume markets (Castells 1996).

Finally, it is in the realm of culture that opposition to modernity as market society has been most absolute, to the extent of framing it as an opposition between the ideal and the material, between authenticity and alienation, true selves and false consciousness. Ironically, this is also now the sphere in which the very opposition between economy and its others is being most thoroughly dismantled in the 'implosion' marked by 'the cultural turn'. There is certainly a danger that culturalist accounts of the economy as a sign system might become as total as the theories of market society that preceded them (Baudrillard looks to be simply the negative image of Marcuse). Nonetheless, the cultural turn on the whole pushes us into disaggregating markets. If economics and economic institutions partly come into being through the ways in which they are represented, and if both the means of production and their outputs have an irreducible and increasingly cultural character, then both the structure and the content of economic exchange are likely to be fluid, particular, variable. This is underlined by notions such as 'flows' and 'networks', which indicate that market exchange cannot legitimately be separated out as a pure 'type' from the myriad and shifting exchanges in which it is contingently entangled.

The focus on diverse markets as opposed to market society does not entail embracing markets, let alone giving capitalism an unqualified green light to drive down a 'third way'. Nor does it mean denying the massive power that can be exercised through marketization. To the contrary, the powers and problems involved in markets can best be understood and opposed by understanding them as diverse and localized phenomena, constructed through complex social processes, rather than by treating them as generic technical solutions or as the thin end of inevitable oppression. A prime example would be the intensity of contemporary globalization. Some of the most powerful forces operating to create the global 'free markets' that massively advantage multinational capital are ideological: arguments that the only possible model of international exchange is the *laissez-faire* version promoted by the World Trade Organization and other international bodies. If the best that opponents can muster is an equally totalizing anti-market rhetoric of self-sufficiency and local autarky, they will not get far in the contemporary context of global interdependence and division of labour. On the other hand, movements to cancel Third World debt – which bring within the market frame considerations of social stability, equity and long-term relationships as opposed to single trading transactions – point to far more complex models of how to understand exchange at an international level.

To be sure, a variety of market forms have spread ever more widely in recent years. The expanding reach of market structures and values makes them an urgent site of contest, not only as economic solutions to be embraced or rejected, but as social and political forms whose effects and purposes are open to question and susceptible to regulation. If their outcomes cannot always easily be altered, predicted or prevented (and sometimes they cannot), this does not of itself mean that markets processes are either natural or ungovernable. As powerful products of social action and interaction – and as the horizon within which more and more people live ever-larger parts of their lives – market processes represent important objects of social critique and viable domains of intervention.

Bibliography

Abercrombie, N., Hill, S. and Turner, B. (1986) *Sovereign Individuals of Capitalism*. London: Allen and Unwin.

Adburgham, A. (1979) *Shopping in Style: London from the Restoration to Edwardian Elegance*. London: Thames and Hudson.

Adorno, T. (1967) *Prisms*. London: Neville Spearman.

Adorno, T. (1991) 'Culture industry reconsidered', in T. Adorno (ed.), *The Culture Industry: Selected Essays on Mass Culture*. London: Routledge.

Aglietta, M. (1979) *A Theory of Capitalist Regulation: The US Experience*. London: Verso.

Agnew, J. (1986) *Worlds Apart: The Market and the Theater in Anglo-American Thought, 1550–1750*. New York: Cambridge University Press.

Althusser, L. (1969) *For Marx*. London: Allen Lane.

Althusser, L. (1971) *Lenin and Philosophy and Other Essays*. London: New Left Books.

Altvater, E. (1973) 'Some problems of state interventionism'. *Kapitalistate* 1–2: 96–108; 76–83.

Amin, A. (ed.) (1994) *Post-Fordism*. Oxford: Blackwell.

Amin, A. and Thrift, N. (1995) 'Institutional issues for the European regions: from markets and plans to socioeconomics and powers of association', *Economy and Society*, 24(1): 41–66.

Ang, I. (1985) *Watching 'Dallas': Soap Opera and the Melodramatic Imagination*. London: Methuen.

Ang, I. (1991) *Desperately Seeking the Audience*. London: Routledge.

Appadurai, A. (1986) *The Social Life of Things: Commodities in Cultural Perspective*. Cambridge: Cambridge University Press.

Appadurai, A. (1990) 'Disjuncture and difference in the global cultural economy', *Theory, Culture and Society*, 7: 295–310.

Arendt, H. (1958) *The Human Condition*. Chicago, IL: University of Chicago Press.

Bakhtin, M. (1984) *Rabelais and his World*. Bloomington, IN: Indiana University Press.

Banfield, E. (1958) *The Moral Basis of a Backward Society*. New York: Free Press.

Baran, P. A. and Sweezy, P. M. (1977) [1966] *Monopoly Capital: An Essay on the American Economic and Social Order*. Harmondsworth: Penguin.

Bardhan, P. K. and Roemer, J. E. (eds) (1993) *Market Socialism: The Current Debate*. Oxford: Oxford University Press.

Barnekov, T. K., Boyle, R. and Rich, D. (1989) *Privatism and Urban Policy in Britain and the United States*. Oxford: Oxford University Press.

Barry, A., Osborne, T. and Rose, N. (eds) (1996) *Foucault and Political Reason*. London: UCL Press.

Bataille, G. (1991) *The Accursed Share: An Essay on General Economy*. New York: Zone Books.

Baudrillard, J. (1975) *The Mirror of Production*. St Louis, MO: Telos.

Baudrillard, J. (1981) *For a Critique of the Political Economy of the Sign*. St Louis, MO: Telos.

Baudrillard, J. (1983) *In the Shadow of the Silent Majorities*. New York: Semiotext(e).

Baudrillard, J. (1998) [1970] *The Consumer Society: Myths and Structures*. London: Sage.

Bauman, Z. (1990) *Thinking Sociologically*. Oxford: Blackwell.

Bauman, Z. (1992) 'Communism: a post-mortem', in Z. Bauman (ed.), *Intimations of Postmodernity*. London: Routledge.

Beck, U. (1992) *Risk Society: Towards a New Modernity*. London: Sage.

Becker, G. (1976) *The Economic Approach to Human Behavior*. Chicago, IL: University of Chicago Press.

Becker, G. (1991) *A Treatise on the Family*. Cambridge, MA: Harvard University Press.

Bell, D. (1976) *The Coming of Post-Industrial Society: A Venture in Social Forecasting*. New York: Basic Books.

Bell, D. (1979) *The Cultural Contradictions of Capitalism*. London: Heinemann.

Benjamin, W. (1989) *Charles Baudelaire: A Lyric Poet in the Era of High Capitalism*. London: Verso.

Berger, P. L. (1986) *The Capitalist Revolution: Fifty Propositions about Prosperity, Equality and Liberty*. New York: Basic Books.

Berger, P. L. and Luckman, T. (1966) *The Social Construction of Reality: A Treatise in the Sociology of Knowledge*. New York: Doubleday.

Berger, S. D. (ed.) (1981) *Organizing Interests in Western Europe: Pluralism, Corporatism and the Transformation of Politics*. London: Sage.

Berry, C. J. (1994) *The Idea of Luxury: A Conceptual and Historical Investigation*. Cambridge: Cambridge University Press.

Bethell, T. (1998) *The Noblest Triumph: Property and Prosperity Through the Ages*. New York: St Martin's Press.

206   Bibliography

Bielby, D. and Bielby, W. (1988) 'She works hard for the money: household responsibilities and the allocation of work effort', *American Journal of Sociology*, 93: 1031–59.

Blackburn, R. (ed.) (1991a) *After the Fall: The Failure of Communism and the Future of Europe*. London: Verso.

Blackburn, R. (1991b) 'Fin de siècle: socialism after the crash', in R. Blackburn (ed.), *After the Fall: The Failure of Communism and the Future of Europe*. London: Verso.

Blair, T. (1998) *The Third Way: New Politics for the New Century*. London: Fabian Society.

Blaug, M. (1985) *Economic Theory in Retrospect*. Cambridge: Cambridge University Press.

Bloch, E., Lukács, G., Brecht, B., Benjamin, W. and Adorno, T. (1980) *Aesthetics and Politics*. London: Verso.

Block, F. (1977) 'The ruling class does not rule', *Socialist Revolution*, 7: 6–28.

Block, F. (1987) *Revisiting State Theory*. Philadelphia, PA: Temple University Press.

Block, F. (1990) *Postindustrial Possibilities*. Berkeley, CA: University of California Press.

Boas, F. (1974) *The Shaping of American Anthropology, 1883–1911: A Franz Boas Reader*. New York: Basic Books.

Boggs, C. and Plotke, D. (1980) *The Politics of Eurocommunism: Socialism in Transition*. Boston, MA: South End Press.

Boland, L. A. (1996) *Critical Economic Methodology: A Personal Odyssey*. London: Routledge.

Bourdieu, P. (1983) 'The field of cultural production', *Poetics*, 12: 311–56.

Bourdieu, P. (1984) *Distinction: A Social Critique of the Judgement of Taste*. Cambridge, MA: Harvard University Press.

Bourdieu, P. (1989) *Outline of a Theory of Practice*. Cambridge: Cambridge University Press.

Bourdieu, P. (1998) 'The essence of neoliberalism: What is neoliberalism? A programme for destroying collective structures which may impede the pure market logic', *Le Monde Diplomatique*, December.

Boyer, R. (1990) *The Regulation School: A Critical Approach*. New York: Columbia University Press.

Boyer, R. and Durand, J.-P. (1997) *After Fordism*. Basingstoke: Macmillan.

Braudel, F. (1977) *Afterthoughts on Material Civilization and Capitalism*. Baltimore, MD: Johns Hopkins University Press.

Braudel, F. (1981) *The Structures of Everyday Life: The Limits of the Possible*. London: Fontana.

Braudel, F. (1982) *The Wheels of Commerce*. New York: Harper and Row.

Brewer, J. (1997) *The Pleasures of the Imagination: English Culture in the Eighteenth Century*. London: HarperCollins.

Britnell, R. H. (1978) 'English markets and royal administration before 1200', *Economic History Review*, 31: 183–96

Britnell, R. H. (1993) *The Commercialisation of English Society, 1000–1500.* Cambridge: Cambridge University Press.

Brittan, S. (1988) *A Restatement of Economic Liberalism.* London: Macmillan.

Brown, J. A. C. (1977) *Techniques of Persuasion: From Propaganda to Brainwashing.* Harmondsworth: Penguin.

Brubaker, R. (1984) *The Limits of Rationality: An Essay on the Social and Moral Thought of Max Weber.* London: George Allen and Unwin.

Brus, W. O. and Laski, K. (1989) *From Marx to the Market: Socialism in Search of an Economic System.* Oxford: Clarendon Press.

Buck-Morss, S. (1981) 'Walter Benjamin – revolutionary writer', *New Left Review*, 128: 50–75.

Bull, M. J. and Heywood, P. (eds) (1994) *West European Communist Parties After the Revolutions of 1989.* New York: St Martin's Press.

Bunzel, R. (1938) 'The economic life of primitive peoples', in F. Boas (ed.), *General Anthropology.* Boston, MA: D. C. Heath.

Burchell, G. (1991) 'Peculiar interests: civil society and governing the system of natural liberty', in G. Burchell, C. Gordon and P. Miller (eds), *The Foucault Effect: Studies in Governmentality.* London: Harvester Wheatsheaf.

Burchell, G., Gordon, C. and Miller, P. (eds) (1991) *The Foucault Effect: Studies in Governmentality.* London: Harvester Wheatsheaf.

Callon, M. (1998a) 'Introduction: the embeddedness of economic markets in economics', in M. Callon (ed.), *The Laws of the Market.* Oxford: Blackwell/The Sociological Review.

Callon, M. (ed.) (1998b) *The Laws of the Market.* Oxford: Blackwell/The Sociological Review.

Campbell, C. (1989) *The Romantic Ethic and the Spirit of Modern Consumerism.* Oxford: Blackwell.

Carrier, J. G. (1994) *Gifts and Commodities: Exchange and Western Capitalism since 1700.* London: Routledge.

Carrier, J. G. (ed.) (1997) *Meanings of the Market: The Free Market in Western Culture.* Oxford: Berg.

Carrier, J. G. and Miller, D. (eds) (1998) *Virtualism: A New Political Economy.* Oxford: Berg.

Castells, M. (1996) *The Rise of Network Society.* Oxford: Blackwell.

Cawson, A. (ed.) (1985) *Organized Interests and the State: Studies in Meso-corporatism.* London: Sage.

Cawson, A. (1986) *Corporatism and Political Theory.* Oxford: Blackwell.

Centeno, M. A. and Font, M. (eds) (1997) *Towards a New Cuba? Legacies of a Revolution.* Boulder, CO: Lynne Rienner.

Chaney, D. (1991) 'Subtopia in Gateshead: the MetroCentre as a cultural form', *Theory, Culture and Society*, 7: 449–69.

Childs, D. (1980) *The Changing Face of Western Communism.* London: Croom Helm.

Clarke, S. (1982) *Marx, Marginalism and Modern Sociology: From Adam Smith to Max Weber.* London: Macmillan.

Classen, C. (1996) 'Sugar cane, Coca-Cola and hypermarkets: consumption and surrealism in the Argentine northwest', in D. Howes (ed.), *Cross-Cultural Consumption: Global Markets, Local Realities*. London: Routledge.

Coase, R. (1937) 'The nature of the firm', *Economica*, 4: 386–405.

Coase, R. (1960) 'The problem of social cost', *Journal of Law and Economics*, 3(1): 1–44.

Coase, R. (1984) 'The New Institutional Economics', *Journal of Law and Economics*, 27: 229–31.

Cohen, J. and Rogers, J. (eds) (1995) *Associations and Democracy*. London: Verso.

Coleman, J. (1988) 'Social capital in the creation of human capital', *American Journal of Sociology*, 94: S95–S120.

Commission on Social Justice (1994) *Social Justice: Strategies for National Renewal*. London: Vintage.

Cook, G. (1992) *The Discourse of Advertising*. London: Routledge.

Cox, A. and O'Sullivan, N. (eds) (1988) *The Corporate State: Corporatism and the State Tradition in Western Europe*. Aldershot: Edward Elgar.

Crang, P. (1997) 'Introduction: cultural turns and the (re)constitution of economic geography', in R. Lee and J. Wills (eds), *Geographies of Economies*. London: Arnold.

Crawford, B. (ed.) (1995) *Markets, States and Democracy: The Political Economy of Post-Communist Transition*. Boulder, CO: Westview Press.

Dalton, G. (1961) 'Economic theory and primitive society', *American Anthropologist*, 63(1/2): 1–25.

Davis, J. (1992) *Exchange*. Buckingham: Open University Press.

de Certeau, M. (1984) *The Practice of Everyday Life*. Berkeley, CA: University of California Press.

Defert, D. (1991) ' "Popular Life" and insurance technology', in G. Burchell, C. Gordon and P. Miller (eds), *The Foucault Effect: Studies in Governmentality*. London: Harvester Wheatsheaf.

Dobbin, F. (1994) *Forging Industrial Policy: The United States, Britain and France in the Railway Age*. Cambridge: Cambridge University Press.

Dodd, N. (1994) *The Sociology of Money: Economics, Reason and Contemporary Society*. Cambridge: Polity.

Dodd, N. (1995) 'Whither Mammon? Postmodern economics and passive enrichment', *Theory, Culture and Society*, 12(2): 1–24.

Donzelot, J. (1979) *The Policing of Families*. New York: Pantheon.

Donzelot, J. (1991) 'The mobilization of society', in G. Burchell, C. Gordon and P. Miller (eds), *The Foucault Effect: Studies in Governmentality*. London: Harvester Wheatsheaf.

Douglas, M. and Isherwood, B. (1979) *The World of Goods: Towards an Anthropology of Consumption*. Harmondsworth: Penguin.

du Gay, P. (1996) *Consumption and Identity at Work*. London: Sage.

du Gay, P. (ed.) (1997) *Production of Culture, Cultures of Production*. London: Sage.

Duncan, S. and Edwards, R. (1997) *Single Mothers in an International Context: Mothers or Workers?* London: UCL Press.

Durkheim, É. (1984) [1933] *The Division of Labour in Society.* London: Macmillan.

Durkheim, É. (1987) [1897] *Suicide: A Study in Sociology.* London: Routledge and Kegan Paul.

Dyer, G. (1982) *Advertising as Communication.* London: Methuen.

Eggertsson, T. (1990) *Economic Behaviour and Institutions.* Cambridge: Cambridge University Press.

Ekins, P. and Max-Neef, M. (eds) (1992) *Real-Life Economics: Understanding Wealth Creation.* London: Routledge.

Elson, D. (1991) 'The economics of a socialized market', in R. Blackburn (ed.), *After the Fall: The Failure of Communism and the Future of Europe.* London: Verso.

Engels, F. (1975) [1878] *Anti-Dühring.* Moscow: Progress Publishers.

England, P. (1993) 'The separative self: androcentric bias in neoclassical assumptions', in M. A. Ferber and J. A. Nelson (eds), *Beyond Economic Man: Feminist Theory and Economics.* Cambridge, MA: Harvard University Press.

England, P. and Kilbourne, B. S. (1990) 'Markets, marriages and other mates: the problem of power', in R. Friedland and A. F. Robertson (eds), *Beyond the Marketplace: Rethinking Economy and Society.* New York: Aldine de Gruyter.

Entwistle, J. (1997a) 'Fashioning the self: women, dress, power and situated bodily practice in the workplace', Ph.D. thesis, Goldsmiths College, University of London.

Entwistle, J. (1997b) 'Power dressing and the fashioning of the career woman', in M. Nava, I. MacRury, A. Blake and B. Richards (eds), *Buy this Book: Studies in Advertising and Consumption.* London: Routledge.

Entwistle, J. (2000a) 'Power dressing: gender, power and the "management" of the female body at work', in M. Talbot and M. Andrews (eds), *All the World and Her Husband: Women and Consumption in the Twentieth Century.* London: Cassell.

Entwistle, J. (2000b) *The Fashioned Body: Theorizing Fashion and Dress in Modern Society.* Cambridge: Polity.

Enzensberger, H. M. (1991) 'Ways of walking: a postscript to utopia', in R. Blackburn (ed.), *After the Fall: The Failure of Communism and the Future of Europe.* London: Verso.

Etzioni, A. (1988) *The Moral Dimension: Toward a New Economics.* New York: Free Press.

Etzioni, A. and Lawrence, P. R. (eds) (1991) *Socio-economics: Towards a New Synthesis.* Armonk, NY: M. E. Sharpe.

Evans, P. B., Rueschmeyer, D. and Skocpol, T. (eds) (1985) *Bringing the State Back In.* Cambridge: Cambridge University Press.

Ewald, F. (1991) 'Insurance and risk', in G. Burchell, C. Gordon and P.

Miller (eds), *The Foucault Effect: Studies in Governmentality*. London: Harvester Wheatsheaf.

Falk, P. and Campbell, C. (eds) (1997) *The Shopping Experience*. London: Sage.

Featherstone, M. (1987) 'Lifestyle and consumer culture', *Theory, Culture and Society*, 4(1): 55–70.

Featherstone, M. (1991) *Consumer Culture and Postmodernism*. London: Sage.

Featherstone, M. (1995) *Undoing Culture: Postmodernism, Globalization and Identity*. London: Sage.

Ferber, M. A. and Nelson, J. A. (eds) (1993) *Beyond Economic Man: Feminist Theory and Economics*. Cambridge, MA: Harvard University Press.

Filo della Torre, P., Mortimer, E. and Story, J. (eds) (1979) *Eurocommunism: Myth or Reality?* Harmondsworth: Penguin.

Firth, R. (1965) [1939] *Primitive Polynesian Economy*. London: Routledge and Kegan Paul.

Fiske, J. (1989) *Reading the Popular*. Boston, MA: Unwin Hyman.

Folbre, N. and Hartmann, H. (1988) 'The rhetoric of self-interest: ideology and gender in economic theory', in A. Klamer, D. N. McCloskey and R. M. Solow (eds), *The Consequences of Economic Rhetoric*. Cambridge: Cambridge University Press.

Foucault, M. (1991) 'Governmentality', in G. Burchell, C. Gordon and P. Miller (eds), *The Foucault Effect: Studies in Governmentality*. London: Harvester Wheatsheaf.

Frances, J., Levăcić, R., Mitchell, J. and Thompson, G. (1991) 'Introduction', in G. Thompson, J. Frances, R. Levačić and J. Mitchell (eds), *Markets, Hierarchies and Networks: The Coordination of Social Life*. London: Sage.

Friedland, R. and Robertson, A. F. (1990) 'Beyond the marketplace', in R. Friedland and A. F. Robertson (eds), *Beyond the Marketplace: Rethinking Economy and Society*. New York: Aldine de Gruyter.

Friedman, M. (1953) *Essays in Positive Economics*. Chicago, IL: University of Chicago Press.

Friedman, M. (1956) *Studies in the Quantity Theory of Money*. Chicago, IL: University of Chicago Press.

Friedman, M. (1968) 'The role of monetary policy', *American Economic Review*, 58: 1–17.

Friedman, M. and Friedman, R. (1980) *Free to Choose*. London: Penguin.

Frisby, D. (1988) *Fragments of Modernity*. Cambridge: Polity.

Frith, S. (1983) *Sound Effects: Youth, Leisure and the Politics of Rock'n'Roll*. London: Constable.

Fukuyama, F. (1992) *The End of History and the Last Man*. London: Penguin.

Fukuyama, F. (1995) *Trust: The Social Virtues and the Creation of Prosperity*. London: Penguin.

Fuller, P. (1980) 'The fine arts after modernism', *New Left Review*, 119: 42–59.

Galbraith, J. K. (1969) *The Affluent Society*. London: Hamish Hamilton.

Galbraith, J. K. (1972) *The New Industrial State*. Harmondsworth: Penguin.

Galbraith, J. K. (1992) *The Culture of Contentment*. London: Penguin.

Gane, M. and Johnson, T. (eds) (1994) *Foucault's New Domains*. London: Routledge.

Garcia, M.-F. (1986) 'La construction sociale d'un marché parfait: Le marché au cadran de Fontaines-en-Sologne', *Actes de la Recherche en Science Sociales*, 65: 2–13.

Geist, J. F. (1983) *Arcades: History of a Building Type*. Cambridge, MA: MIT Press.

Gellner, E. (1988) *Plough, Sword and Book: The Structure of Human History*. Chicago, IL: University of Chicago Press.

Gibson-Graham, J. (1996) *The End of Capitalism (As We Knew It?): A Feminist Critique of Political Economy*. Oxford: Blackwell.

Giddens, A. (1991) *Modernity and Self-Identity: Self and Society in the Late Modern Age*. Cambridge: Polity.

Giddens, A. (1994) *Beyond Left and Right: The Future of Radical Politics*. Cambridge: Polity.

Giddens, A. (1998) *The Third Way: The Renewal of Social Democracy*. Cambridge: Polity.

Godelier, M. (1986) *The Mental and the Material: Thought, Economy and Society*. London: Verso.

Godson, R. and Haseler, S. (1978) *Eurocommunism: Implications for East and West*. London: Macmillan.

Goffman, E. (1976) *Gender Advertisements*. London: Macmillan.

Goldman, R. (1992) *Reading Ads Socially*. London: Routledge.

Gordon, C. (1991) 'Governmental rationality: an introduction', in G. Burchell, C. Gordon and P. Miller (eds), *The Foucault Effect: Studies in Governmentality*. London: Harvester Wheatsheaf.

Gordon, L. (ed.) (1990) *Women and the Welfare State*. Madison, WI: University of Wisconsin Press.

Gough, I. (1979) *The Political Economy of the Welfare State*. London: Macmillan.

Gould, B. (1985) *Socialism and Freedom*. London: Macmillan.

Granovetter, M. (1973) 'The strength of weak ties', *American Journal of Sociology*, 78: 1360–80.

Granovetter, M. (1985) 'Economic action and social structure: the problem of embeddedness', *American Journal of Sociology*, 91: 481–510.

Granovetter, M. and Swedberg, R. (eds) (1992) *The Sociology of Economic Life*. Boulder, CO: Westview Press.

Gudeman, S. (1986) *Economics as Culture: Models and Metaphors of Livelihood*. Boston, MA: Routledge and Kegan Paul.

Habermas, J. (1970) *Toward a Rational Society: Student Protest, Science and Politics*. Boston, MA: Beacon Press.

Habermas, J. (1976) *Legitimation Crisis*. Boston, MA: Beacon Press.

Habermas, J. (1985) 'Modernity – an incomplete project', in H. Foster (ed.), *Postmodern Culture*. London: Pluto.

Habermas, J. (1987) *The Theory of Communicative Action: The Critique of Functionalist Reason*. Cambridge: Polity.

Habermas, J. (1990) 'What does socialism mean today? The rectifying revolution and the need for new thinking on the left', *New Left Review*, 183: 3–21.

Hacking, I. (1990) *The Taming of Chance*. Cambridge: Cambridge University Press.

Halévy, E. (1972) [1928] *The Growth of Philosophical Radicalism*. London: Faber and Faber.

Hall, J. (1995) 'After the vacuum: post-communism in the light of Tocqueville', in B. Crawford (ed.), *Markets, States and Democracy: The Political Economy of Post-Communist Transition*. Boulder, CO: Westview Press.

Hart, K. (1988) 'Kinship, contract and trust: the economic organization of migrants in an African city slum', in D. Gambetta (ed.), *Trust: Making and Breaking Cooperative Relations*. Oxford: Blackwell.

Harvey, D. (1989) *The Condition of Postmodernity: An Enquiry into the Origins of Culture*. Oxford: Blackwell.

Haskell, T. L. and Teichgraeber, R. F. (eds) (1996) *The Culture of the Market: Historical Essays*. Cambridge: Cambridge University Press.

Haug, W. F. (1986) *Critique of Commodity Aesthetics: Appearance, Sexuality and Advertising*. Cambridge: Polity.

Hayek, F. von (1941) *A Pure Theory of Capital*. London: Routledge and Kegan Paul.

Hayek, F. von (1945) 'The use of knowledge in society', *American Economic Review*, 35: 519–30.

Hayek, F. von (1976) [1949] *Individualism and Economic Order*. London: Routledge and Kegan Paul.

Hayek, F. von (1991) 'Spontaneous ("grown") order and organized ("made") order', in G. Thompson, J. Frances, R. Levačić and J. Mitchell (eds), *Markets, Hierarchies and Networks: The Coordination of Social Life*. London: Sage.

Hebdige, D. (1979) *Subculture: The Meaning of Style*. London: Methuen.

Hebdige, D. (1988) *Hiding in the Light: On Images and Things*. London: Routledge.

Heelas, P. and Morris, P. (eds) (1992) *The Values of the Enterprise Culture: The Moral Debate*. London: Routledge.

Heilbroner, R. L. (1953) *The Wordly Philosophers*. New York: Touchstone.

Heilbroner, R. L. (1972) *The Economic Problem*. Englewood Cliffs, NJ: Prentice Hall.

Hennis, W. (1987) 'Personality and life orders: Max Weber's theme', in S. Whimster and S. Lash (eds), *Max Weber, Rationality and Modernity*. London: Allen and Unwin.

Herskovits, M. J. (1940) *The Economic Life of Primitive Peoples*. London: A. A. Knopf.

Hindess, B. (ed.) (1990) *Reactions to the Right*. London: Routledge.

Hirschman, A. (1977) *The Passions and the Interests*. Princeton, NJ: Princeton University Press.

Hirst, P. (1994) *Associative Democracy: New Forms of Social and Economic Governance*. Cambridge: Polity.

Hirst, P. and Thompson, G. (1996) *Globalization in Question: The International Economy and the Possibilities of Governance*. Cambridge: Polity.

Hirst, P. and Zeitlin, J. (eds) (1989) *Reversing Industrial Decline?* Oxford: Berg.

Hobbes, T. (1968) [1651] *Leviathan*. Harmondsworth: Penguin.

Hochschild, A. (1983) *The Managed Heart: Commercialization of Human Feeling*. Berkeley, CA: University of California Press.

Hodgson, G. (1984) *The Democratic Economy: A New Look at Planning, Markets and Power*. Harmondsworth: Penguin.

Hodgson, G. (1988) *Economics and Institutions: A Manifesto for a Modern Institutional Economics*. Cambridge: Polity.

Hodgson, G. (1993) 'Evolution and institutional change: on the nature of selection in biology and economics', in U. Mäki, B. Gustafsson and C. Knudsen (eds), *Rationality, Institutions and Economic Methodology*. London: Routledge.

Hodgson, G. (1994) *Economics and Evolution*. Cambridge: Polity.

Hoggart, R. (1977) [1957] *The Uses of Literacy*. Harmondsworth: Penguin.

Holmes, L. (1997) *Post-Communism: An Introduction*. Cambridge: Polity.

Holton, R. J. (1992) *Economy and Society*. London: Routledge.

Holton, R. J. and Turner, B. (1986) *Talcott Parsons on Economy and Society*. London: Routledge and Kegan Paul.

Holton, R. J. and Turner, B. S. (1989) *Max Weber on Economy and Society*. London: Routledge.

Hood, C. (1991) 'A public management for all seasons?', *Public Administration*, 69: 3–19.

Horkheimer, M. and Adorno, T. (1979) *Dialectic of Enlightenment*. London: Verso.

Howes, D. (ed.) (1996) *Cross-Cultural Consumption: Global Markets, Local Realities*. London: Routledge.

Hunter, I. (1988) *Culture and Government: The Emergence of Literary Education*. Basingstoke: Macmillan.

Huyssen, A. (1986) *After the Great Divide: Modernism, Mass Culture and Postmodernism*. London: Macmillan.

Jameson, F. (1984) 'Postmodernism, or the cultural logic of late capitalism', *New Left Review*, 146: 53–92.

Jennings, A. L. (1993) 'Public or private? Institutional economics and feminism', in M. A. Ferber and J. A. Nelson (eds), *Beyond Economic Man: Feminist Theory and Economics*. Chicago, IL: University of Chicago Press.

Jessop, B. (1990) 'Recent theories of the capitalist state', in B. Jessop (ed.),
    State Theory: Putting the Capitalist State in its Place. Cambridge: Polity.
Jessop, B. (1995) 'The regulation approach, governance and post-Fordism:
    alternative perspectives on economic and political change', *Economy and
    Society*, 24(3): 307–33.
Johnson, S. and Loveman, G. (1995) *Starting Over in Eastern Europe:
    Entrepreneurship and Economic Renewal.* Boston, MA: Harvard Business
    School Press.
Kadish, A. and Tribe, K. (1993) *The Market for Political Economy: The
    Advent of Economics in British University Culture, 1850–1905.* London
    and New York: Routledge.
Kellner, D. (1989) *Jean Baudrillard: From Marxism to Postmodernism and
    Beyond.* Cambridge: Polity.
Keynes, J. M. (1936) *General Theory of Employment, Interest and Money.*
    London: Macmillan.
Kirzner, I. M. (1973) *Competition and Entrepreneurship.* Chicago, IL:
    University of Chicago Press.
Klamer, A., McCloskey, D. N. and Solow, R. M. (eds) (1988) *The Conse-
    quences of Economic Rhetoric.* Cambridge: Cambridge University Press.
Kline, S. (1995) 'The play of the market: on the internationalization of
    children's culture', *Theory, Culture and Society*, 12(2): 103–29.
Knight, F. (1941) 'Anthropology and economics', *Journal of Political Eco-
    nomy*, 49: 247–68.
Kolakowski, L. (1972) *Positivist Philosophy: From Hume to the Vienna
    Circle.* Harmondsworth: Penguin.
Kriegel, A. (1978) *Eurocommunism: A New Kind of Communism?* Stanford,
    CA: Hoover Institute Press.
Lane, R. E. (1991) *The Market Experience.* Cambridge: Cambridge Univer-
    sity Press.
Lange, O. (1970) *Papers in Economics and Sociology.* Oxford: Pergamon.
Lange, O. (1994) [1938] 'On the economic theory of socialism', in A. Nove
    and I. D. Thatcher (eds), *Markets and Socialism.* Aldershot: Edward
    Elgar.
Lange, O. and Taylor, F. M. (1964) *On the Economic Theory of Socialism.*
    New York: McGraw-Hill.
Lash, S. and Urry, J. (1987) *The End of Organized Capitalism.* Cambridge:
    Polity.
Lash, S. and Urry, J. (1994) *Economies of Signs and Space.* London: Sage.
Lavigne, M. (1995) *The Economics of Transition: From Socialist Economy
    to Market Economy.* Basingstoke: Macmillan.
Lavoie, D. (ed.) (1990) *Economics and Hermeneutics.* London: Routledge.
Lazar, D. (1990) *Markets and Ideology in the City of London.* London:
    Macmillan.
Leach, E. (1970) *Lévi-Strauss.* London: Fontana.
Leavis, F. R. (1930) *Mass Civilisation and Minority Culture.* Cambridge:
    Minority Press.

Ledeneva, A. V. (1998) *Russia's Economy of Favours: Blat, Networking and Informal Exchange*. Cambridge: Cambridge University Press.

Le Grand, J. and Estrin, S. (1989) *Market Socialism*. Oxford: Clarendon Press.

Leibenstein, H. (1976) *Beyond Economic Man*. Cambridge, MA: Harvard University Press.

Leiss, W., Kline, S. and Jhally, S. (1986) *Social Communication in Advertising: Persons, Products and Images of Well-Being*. London: Methuen.

Lenin, V. I. (1970) [1917] *State and Revolution*. Moscow: Progress Publishers.

Levačić, R. (1991) 'Markets and government: an overview', in G. Thompson, J. Frances, R. Levačić and J. Mitchell (eds), *Markets, Hierarchies and Networks: The Coordination of Social Life*. London: Sage.

Levitt, T. (1983) 'The globalization of markets', *Harvard Business Review*, 83(3): 92–102.

Leyshon, A. and Thrift, N. (1997) *Money/Space: Geographies of Monetary Transformation*. London: Routledge.

Lipietz, A. (1987) *Mirages and Miracles: The Crises of Global Fordism*. London: Verso.

Locke, J. (1960) [1690] *Two Treatises of Government*. Cambridge: Cambridge University Press.

Löwith, K. (1982) [1932] *Max Weber and Karl Marx*. London: George Allen and Unwin.

Lyotard, J.-F. (1986) *The Postmodern Condition: A Report on Knowledge*. Manchester: Manchester University Press.

McCarthy, T. (1984) *The Critical Theory of Jürgen Habermas*. Cambridge: Polity.

McCloskey, D. (1986) *The Rhetoric of Economics*. Brighton: Wheatsheaf.

McCloskey, D. (1994) *Knowledge and Persuasion in Economics*. Cambridge: Cambridge University Press.

McGuigan, J. (1992) *Cultural Populism*. London: Routledge.

Mackay, C. (1995) [1841] *Extraordinary Popular Delusions and the Madness of Crowds*. Ware, Herts: Wordsworth Reference.

McNally, D. (1993) *Against the Market: Political Economy, Market Socialism and the Marxist Critique*. London: Verso.

Macpherson, C. B. (1962) *The Political Theory of Possessive Individualism: Hobbes to Locke*. London: Oxford University Press.

McRobbie, A. (1998) *British Fashion Design: Rag Trade or Image Industry?* London: Routledge.

McRobbie, A. (1999) *In the Culture Society: Art, Fashion and Popular Music*. London: Routledge.

Mäki, U., Gustaffsson, B. and Knudsen, C. (eds) (1993) *Rationality, Institutions and Economic Methodology*. London: Routledge.

Malinowski, B. (1922) *The Argonauts of the Western Pacific: An Account of Enterprise and Adventure in the Archipelagoes of Melanesian New Guinea*. London: G. Routledge and Sons.

Mandel, E. (1976) *Late Capitalism*. London: New Left Books.

Mandel, E. (1978) *From Stalinism to Eurocommunism*. London: New Left Books.

Marcus, G. E. (1990) 'Once more into the breach between economic and cultural analysis', in R. Friedland and A. F. Robertson (eds), *Beyond the Marketplace: Rethinking Economy and Society*. New York: Aldine de Gruyter.

Marcuse, H. (1964) *One Dimensional Man*. London: Abacus.

Marcuse, H. (1972) 'Industrialization and capitalism in Max Weber', in H. Marcuse, *Negations: Essays in Critical Theory*. Harmondsworth: Penguin.

Marshall, T. H. (1950) *Citizenship and Social Class*. Cambridge: Cambridge University Press.

Martinelli, A. and Smelser, N. J. (eds) (1990) *Economy and Society: Overviews in Economic Sociology*. London: Sage.

Martinez, J. and Diaz, A. (1996) *Chile: The Great Transformation*. Washington, DC: Brookings Institution.

Marx, K. (1935) [1875] 'Critique of the Gotha Programme', in K. Marx and F. Engels, *Selected Works*. Moscow: Progress Publishers.

Marx, K. (1959) [1844] *Economic and Philosophical Manuscripts of 1844*. Moscow: Progress Publishers.

Marx, K. (1974) [1845–6] *The German Ideology*. London: Lawrence and Wishart.

Marx, K. (1975a) [1843] 'On the Jewish Question', in K. Marx, *Collected Works*. Moscow: Progress Publishers.

Marx, K. (1975b) [1843] 'Contribution to the critique of "Hegel's Philosophy of Right"', in K. Marx, *Collected Works*. Moscow: Progress Publishers.

Marx, K. (1976a) [1867] *Capital*, vol. I. London: Penguin/New Left Review.

Marx, K. (1976b) [1859] 'Preface to "Contribution to the critique of political economy"', in K. Marx, *Capital*, vol. 1. London: Lawrence and Wishart.

Marx, K. (1977) *Selected Writings* (D. McLellan, ed.). Oxford: Oxford University Press.

Marx, K. and Engels, F. (1973) [1848] *The Communist Manifesto*. Harmondsworth: Penguin.

Massey, P. (1995) *New Zealand: Market Liberalization in a Developed Economy*. New York: St Martin's Press.

Matzner, E. and Streeck, W. (eds) (1991) *Beyond Keynesianism: The Socioeconomics of Production and Full Employment*. Aldershot: Edward Elgar.

Mauss, M. (1973) 'Techniques of the body', *Economy and Society*, 2(1): 70–89.

Mauss, M. (1990) *The Gift: The Form and Reason for Exchange in Archaic Societies*. New York: Norton.

Mead, L. M. (1986) *Beyond Entitlement: The Social Obligations of Citizenship*. New York: Free Press.

Messaris, P. (1997) *Visual Persuasion: The Role of Images in Advertising*. London: Sage.

Meuret, D. (1988) 'A political genealogy of political economy', *Economy and Society*, 17(2): 225–50.

Miliband, R. (1968) *The State in Capitalist Society*. London: Weidenfeld and Nicolson.

Miller, D. (1987) *Material Culture and Mass Consumption*. Oxford: Blackwell.

Miller, D. (1989) *Market, State, and Community: Theoretical Foundations of Market Socialism*. Oxford: Clarendon Press.

Miller, D. (1994) *Modernity – An Ethnographic Approach: Dualism and Mass Consumption in Trinidad*. Oxford: Berg.

Miller, D. (ed.) (1995) *Acknowledging Consumption: A Review of New Studies*. London: Routledge.

Miller, D. (1998a) 'Conclusion: a theory of virtualism', in J. G. Carrier and D. Miller (eds), *Virtualism: A New Political Economy*. Oxford: Berg.

Miller, D. (1998b) *A Theory of Shopping*. Cambridge: Polity.

Miller, D. and Slater, D. R. (2000) *The Internet: An Ethnographic Approach*. Oxford: Berg.

Miller, P. and Rose, N. (1990) 'Governing economic life', *Economy and Society*, 19(1): 1–31.

Mommsen, W. F. (1989) *The Political and Social Theory of Max Weber*. Cambridge: Polity.

Morley, D. (1980) *The 'Nationwide' Audience*. London: Comedia.

Morley, D. (1986) *Family Television: Cultural Power and Domestic Leisure*. London: Comedia.

Murray, R. (1989a) 'Benetton Britain', in S. Hall and M. Jacques (eds), *New Times: The Changing Face of Politics in the 1990s*. London: Lawrence and Wishart.

Murray, R. (1989b) 'Fordism and post-fordism', in S. Hall and M. Jacques (eds), *New Times: The Changing Face of Politics in the 1990s*. London: Lawrence and Wishart.

Myers, G. (1999) *Ad Worlds: Brands, Media, Audiences*. London: Arnold.

Nava, M. (1987) 'Consumption and its contradictions', *Cultural Studies*, 1(2): 204–18.

Nava, M. (1992) *Changing Cultures: Feminism, Youth and Consumerism*. London: Sage.

Nicholson, L. (1986) *Gender and History: The Limits of Social Theory in the Age of the Family*. New York: Columbia University Press.

Nixon, S. (1996) *Hard Looks: Masculinities, Spectatorship and Contemporary Consumption*. London: UCL Press.

Nixon, S. (1997) 'Circulating culture', in P. du Gay (ed.), *Production of Culture, Cultures of Production*. London: Sage.

North, D. (1981) *Structure and Change in Economic History*. New York: Norton.

North, D. (1990) *Institutions, Institutional Change and Economic Performance*. Cambridge: Cambridge University Press.

North, D. (1993) 'Institutions and economic performance', in U. Mäki, B. Gustafsson and C. Knudsen (eds), *Rationality, Institutions and Economic Methodology*. London: Routledge.

Nove, A. (1983) *The Economics of Feasible Socialism*. London: George Unwin and Allen.

Nove, A. and Thatcher, I. D. (eds) (1994) *Markets and Socialism*. Aldershot: Edward Elgar.

Oakley, A. (1974) *The Sociology of Housework*. New York: Pantheon.

Offe, C. (1984) *Contradictions of the Welfare State*. London: Hutchinson.

O'Neill, J. (1998) *The Market: Ethics, Knowledge and Politics*. London: Routledge.

Osborne, D. and Gaebler, T. (1992) *Reinventing Government: How the Entrepreneurial Spirit is Transforming the Public Sector*. Reading, MA: Addison-Wesley.

Packard, V. (1977) *The Hidden Persuaders*. Harmondsworth: Penguin.

Parsons, T. and Smelser, N. J. (1956) *Economy and Society: A Study in the Integration of Economic and Social Theory*. Glencoe, IL: Free Press.

Phillips, A. W. (1958) 'The relation between unemployment and the rate of change of money wages in the United Kingdom, 1861–1957', *Economica*, 25: 283–99.

Piore, M. J. and Sabel, C. F. (1984) *The Second Industrial Divide*. New York: Basic Books.

Piven, F. F. and Cloward, R. A. (1972) *Regulating the Poor: The Functions of Public Welfare*. London: Tavistock.

Plattner, S. (1989) 'Markets and marketplaces', in S. Plattner (ed.), *Economic Anthropology*. Stanford, CA: Stanford University Press.

Pocock, J. G. A. (1985) *Virtue, Commerce and History*. Cambridge: Cambridge University Press.

Polanyi, K. (1957) [1944] *The Great Transformation: The Political and Economic Origins of Our Time*. Boston, MA: Beacon Press.

Polanyi, K. (1977) *The Livelihood of Man*. New York: Academic Press.

Polanyi, K. (1992) 'The economy as an instituted process', in M. Granovetter and R. Swedberg (eds), *The Sociology of Economic Life*. Boulder, CO: Westview Press.

Polanyi, K., Arensberg, C. M. and Pearson, H. W. (eds) (1957) *Trade and Market in the Early Empires*. Glencoe, IL: Free Press.

Poster, M. (1990) *The Mode of Information*. Cambridge: Polity.

Poulantzas, N. (1973) *Political Power and Social Classes*. London: New Left Books.

Procacci, G. (1991) 'Social economy and the government of poverty', in G. Burchell, C. Gordon and P. Miller (eds), *The Foucault Effect: Studies in Governmentality*. London: Harvester Wheatsheaf.

Prout, C. (1985) *Market Socialism in Yugoslavia*. Oxford: Oxford University Press.

Przeworski, A. (1991) *Democracy and the Market: Political and Economic Reforms in Eastern Europe and Latin America*. Cambridge: Cambridge University Press.

Pusey, M. (1991) *Economic Rationalism in Canberra: A Nation-Building State Changes its Mind*. Sydney: Cambridge University Press.

Putnam, R., with Leonardi, R. and Nanetti, R. (1993) *Making Democracy Work: Civic Traditions in Modern Italy*. Princeton, NJ: Princeton University Press.

Putnam, R. (1995) 'Bowling alone: America's declining social capital', *Journal of Democracy*, 6(1): 65–78.

Radway, J. (1987) *Reading the Romance: Women, Patriarchy and Popular Literature*. London: Verso.

Randall, A. and Charlesworth, A. (1996) *Markets, Market Culture and Popular Protest in Eighteenth-Century Britain and Ireland*. Liverpool: Liverpool University Press.

Ranney, A. and Sartori, G. (eds) (1978) *Eurocommunism: The Italian Case*. Washington, DC: American Institute for Public Policy Research.

Ray, L. and Sayer, A. (ed.) (1999) *Culture and Economy: After the Cultural Turn*. London: Sage.

Richardson, G. B. (1972) 'The organisation of industry', *Economic Journal* 82: 883–96.

Riesman, D. (1961) *The Lonely Crowd: A Study of the Changing American Character*. New Haven, CT: Yale University Press.

Ritzer, G. (1999) *Enchanting a Disenchanted World: Revolutionizing the Means of Consumption*. London: Sage.

Robbins, L. (1935) *An Essay on the Nature and Significance of Economic Science*. London: Macmillan.

Robins, K. (1997) 'What in the world's going on?', in P. du Gay (ed.), *Production of Culture, Cultures of Production*. London: Sage.

Romer, P. (1993) 'Ideas gaps and object gaps in economic development', *Journal of Monetary Economics*, 32: 543–73.

Rose, G. (1978) *The Melancholy Science: An Introduction to the Thought of Theodor W. Adorno*. London: Macmillan.

Rose, N. (1992) 'Governing the enterprising self', in P. Heelas and P. Morris (eds), *The Values of the Enterprise Culture: The Moral Debate*. London: Routledge.

Rose, N. (1993) 'Government, authority and expertise in advanced liberalism', *Economy and Society*, 22(3): 283–99.

Rose, N. (1999) *Powers of Freedom: Reframing Political Thought*. Cambridge: Cambridge University Press.

Rose, N. and Miller, P. (1992) 'Political power beyond the state: problematics of government', *British Journal of Sociology*, 43(2): 1–36.

Ross, A. (ed.) (1997) *No Sweat: Fashion, Free Trade and the Rights of Garment Workers*. London: Verso.

Ross, A. (1998) *Real Love: In Pursuit of Cultural Justice*. New York: New York University Press.

Rowling, N. (1987) *Commodities: How the World was Taken to Market*. London: Free Association Books.

Rowthorn, B. (1980) 'Marx's theory of wages', in B. Rowthorn (ed.), *Capitalism, Conflict and Inflation*. London: Lawrence and Wishart.

Ryan, A. (ed.) (1987) *Utilitarianism and Other Essays: J. S. Mill and Jeremy Bentham*. London: Penguin.

Sahlins, M. (1974) *Stone Age Economics*. London: Tavistock.

Sahlins, M. (1976) *Culture and Practical Reason*. Chicago, IL: University of Chicago Press.

Samuelson, P. A. (1955) *The Foundation of Economics*. Cambridge: Cambridge University Press.

Sayer, A. (1997) 'The dialectic of culture and economy', in R. Lee and J. Wills (eds), *Geographies of Economies*. London: Arnold.

Schama, S. (1989) *Citizens: A Chronicle of the French Revolution*. London: Penguin.

Scholten, I. (ed.) (1987) *Political Stability and Neo-corporatism: Corporatist Integration and Societal Cleavages in Western Europe*. London: Sage.

Schudson, M. (1984) *Advertising, the Uneasy Persuasion: Its Dubious Impact on American Society*. New York: Basic Books.

Schumpeter, J. A. (1943) *Capitalism, Socialism and Democracy*. London: Allen and Unwin.

Scitovsky, T. (1976) *The Joyless Economy*. New York: Oxford University Press.

Scitovsky, T. (1986) *Human Desire and Economic Satisfaction*. Brighton: Wheatsheaf.

Sekora, J. (1977) *Luxury: The Concept in Western Thought, Eden to Smollet*. Baltimore, MD: Johns Hopkins University Press.

Seligman, A. B. (1992) *The Idea of Civil Society*. Princeton, NJ: Princeton University Press.

Seligman, A. B. (1997) *The Problem of Trust*. Princeton, NJ: Princeton University Press.

Sen, A. (1977) 'Rational fools: a critique of the behavioral foundations of economic theory', *Philosophy and Public Affairs*, 6(4): 317–44.

Sennett, R. (1998) *The Corrosion of Character: The Personal Consequences of Work in the New Capitalism*. New York: Norton.

Shaw, G. K. (1997) 'Policy implications of endogenous growth theory', in B. Snowdon and H. R. Vane (eds), *A Macroeconomics Reader*. London: Routledge.

Shields, R. (1992) 'The individual, consumption cultures and the fate of community', in R. Shields (ed.), *Lifestyle Shopping: The Subject of Consumption*. London: Routledge.

Sidorenko, E. (1999) 'Neo-liberalism after communism: constructing a sociological account of the political space of post-1989 Poland', Ph.D. thesis, Goldsmiths College, University of London.

Sik, O. (1976) *The Third Way*. London: Wildwood House.

Simmel, G. (1950) 'The metropolis and mental life', in K. Wolff (ed.), *The Sociology of Georg Simmel*. London: Collier-Macmillan.

Simmel, G. (1990) [1907] *The Philosophy of Money*. London: Routledge.

Simmel, G. (1991) [1896] 'Money in modern culture', *Theory, Culture and Society*, 8: 17–31.

Sklair, L. (1994) 'Capitalism and development in global perspective', in L. Sklair (ed.), *Capitalism and Development*. London: Routledge.

Slater, D. R. (1993) 'Going shopping: markets, crowds and consumption', in C. Jenks (ed.), *Cultural Reproduction*. London: Routledge.

Slater, D. R. (1995) 'Photography and modern vision: the spectacle of "natural magic"', in C. Jenks (ed.), *Visual Culture*. London: Routledge.

Slater, D. R. (1997a) *Consumer Culture and Modernity*. Cambridge: Polity.

Slater, D. R. (1997b) 'Consumer culture and the politics of need', in M. Nava, A. Blake, I. MacRury and B. Richards (eds), *Buy This Book: Contemporary Issues in Advertising and Consumption*. London: Routledge.

Slater, D. R. (1998) 'Needs/wants', in C. Jenks (ed.), *Core Sociological Dichotomies*. London: Sage.

Smelser, N. J. and Swedberg, R. (eds) (1994) *The Handbook of Economic Sociology*. Princeton, NJ: Princeton University Press.

Smith, A. (1853) [1759] *The Theory of Moral Sentiments*. London: Henry G. Bohn.

Smith, A. (1991) [1776] *The Wealth of Nations*. London: Everyman's Library.

Smith, C. W. (1983) *The Mind of the Market*. New York: Harper Colophon.

Smith, W. C. and Korzeniewicz, R. P. (eds) (1997) *Politics, Social Change and Economic Restructuring in Latin America*. Boulder, CO: Lynne Rienner.

Snowdon, B. and Vane, H. R. (eds) (1997) *A Macroeconomics Reader*. London: Routledge.

Solow, R. (1994) 'Perspectives on growth theory', *Journal of Economic Perspectives*, 8: 45–54.

Sombart, W. (1902) *Der Moderne Kapitalismus*. Leipzig: Duncker und Humbolt.

Soper, K. (1981) *On Human Needs: Open and Closed Theories in a Marxist Perspective*. Brighton: Harvester.

Soper, K. (1990) *Troubled Pleasures: Writings on Politics, Gender and Hedonism*. London: Verso.

Stallybrass, P. and White, A. (1986) *The Poetics and Politics of Transgression*. London: Methuen.

Stiglitz, J. E. (1994) *Whither Socialism?* Cambridge, MA: MIT Press.

Storey, J. (1999) *Cultural Consumption and Everyday Life*. London: Arnold.

Streeck, W. (1988) *The Social Institutions of Economic Performance*. London: Sage.

Streeck, W. (1995) 'Inclusion and secession: questions on the boundary of associative democracy', in J. Cohen and J. Rogers (eds), *Associations and Democracy*. London: Verso.

Streeck, W. and Schmitter, P. C. (eds) (1985) *Private Interest Government: Beyond Market and State*. London: Sage.

Swedberg, R. (1994) 'Markets as social structures', in N. J. Smelser and R. Swedberg (eds), *The Handbook of Economic Sociology*. Princeton, NJ: Princeton University Press.

Taussig, M. (1980) *The Devil and Commodity Fetishism in South America*. Chapel Hill, NC: University of North Carolina Press.

Taylor, C. (1989) *Sources of the Self: The Making of Modern Identity*. Cambridge: Cambridge University Press.

Thomas, C. and Wilkin, P. (1997) *Globalization and the South*. New York: St Martin's Press.

Thompson, E. P. (1971) 'The moral economy of the English crowd in the eighteenth century', *Past and Present*, 50: 78–98.

Thompson, E. P. (1975) *Whigs and Hunters: The Origin of the Black Act*. Harmondsworth: Penguin.

Thompson, G. (1986) 'The firm as a "dispersed" social agency', in G. Thompson (ed.), *Economic Calculation and Policy Formation*. London: Routledge and Kegan Paul.

Thompson, G., Frances, J., Levačić, R. and Mitchell, J. (eds) (1991) *Markets, Hierarchies and Networks: The Coordination of Social Life*. London: Sage.

Thompson, K. (ed.) (1985) *Readings from Émile Durkheim*. London: Ellis Horwood/Tavistock.

Titmuss, R. M. (1958) *Essays on 'The Welfare State'*. London: Allen and Unwin.

Tonkiss, F. (1998) 'Civil/political', in C. Jenks (ed.), *Core Sociological Dichotomies*. London: Sage.

Tonkiss, F. (2000) 'Trust, social capital and economy', in F. Tonkiss and A. Passey (eds), *Trust and Civil Society*. Basingstoke: Macmillan.

Tönnies, F. (1957) *Community and Association*. East Lansing, MI: Michigan State University Press.

Touraine, A. (1971) *The Post-Industrial Society*. New York: Random House.

Turner, B. S. (1986) 'Simmel, rationalisation and the sociology of money', *The Sociological Review*, 34(1): 93–114.

Turner, B. S. (1988) *Status*. Milton Keynes: Open University Press.

Turner, M. (1984) *Enclosures in Britain, 1750–1830*. London: Macmillan.

Veblen, T. (1953) [1899] *The Theory of the Leisure Class: An Economic Study of Institutions*. New York: Mentor.

Vestergaard, T. and Schroder, K. (1985) *The Language of Advertising*. Oxford: Blackwell.

Warde, A. (1994a) 'Consumers, identity and belonging: reflections on some theses of Zygmunt Bauman', in R. Keat, N. Whiteley and N. Abercrombie (eds), *The Authority of the Consumer*. London: Routledge.

Warde, A. (1994b) 'Consumption, identity-formation and uncertainty', *Sociology*, 28(4): 877–98.

Waters, M. (1995) *Globalization*. London: Routledge.

Weber, M. (1947) *The Theory of Social and Economic Organization*. New York: Free Press.

Weber, M. (1949) *The Methodology of the Social Sciences*. New York: Free Press.

Weber, M. (1958) *The Protestant Ethic and the Spirit of Capitalism*. New York: Scribner.

Weber, M. (1978) *Economy and Society*. Berkeley, CA: University of California Press.

Weber, M. (1991a) 'Politics as a vocation', in H. Gerth and C. W. Mills (eds), *From Max Weber: Essays in Sociology*. London: Routledge.

Weber, M. (1991b) 'Science as a vocation', in H. Gerth and C. W. Mills (eds), *From Max Weber: Essays in Sociology*. London: Routledge.

Weeks, J. (1995) 'The contemporary Latin American economies: neoliberal reconstruction', in S. Halebsky and R. L. Harris (eds), *Capital, Power and Inequality in Latin America*. Boulder, CO: Westview Press.

Weils, R. (1996) *Red Cat, White Cat: China and the Contradictions of 'Market Socialism'*. New York: Monthly Review Press.

Wheelock, J. (1990) *Husbands at Home*. London: Routledge.

Whimster, S. and Lash, S. (1987) *Max Weber, Rationality and Modernity*. London: Allen and Unwin.

Williams, R. (1980) 'Advertising: the magic system', in R. Williams (ed.), *Problems in Materialism and Culture*. London: Verso.

Williams, R. (1985) *Culture and Society: 1780–1950*. Harmondsworth: Penguin.

Williams, R. H. (1982) *Dream Worlds: Mass Consumption in Late Nineteenth-Century France*. Berkeley, CA: University of California.

Williamson, J. (1978) *Decoding Advertisements: Ideology and Meaning in Advertising*. London: Marion Boyars.

Williamson, O. E. (1975) *Market and Hierarchies: Analysis and Antitrust Implications*. New York: Free Press.

Williamson, O. E. (1985) *The Economic Institutions of Capitalism: Firms, Markets, Relational Contracting*. New York: Free Press.

Willis, P. (1990) *Common Culture: Symbolic Work at Play in the Everyday Cultures of the Young*. Milton Keynes: Open University Press.

Wilson, E. (1977) *Women and the Welfare State*. London: Tavistock.

Wilson, T. and Skinner, A. S. (eds) (1976) *The Market and the State: Essays in Honour of Adam Smith*. Oxford: Clarendon Press.

Winch, D. (1978) *Adam Smith's Politics: An Essay in Historiographic Revision*. Cambridge: Cambridge University Press.

Winship, J. (1980) 'Sexuality for sale', in S. Hall, D. Hobson, A. Lowe and P. Willis (eds), *Culture, Media, Language*. London: Hutchinson.

Woolcock, M. (1998) 'Social capital and economic development: towards a theoretical synthesis and policy framework', *Theory and Society*, 27: 151–208.

Wrong, D. (1961) 'The oversocialized conception of man in modern sociology', *American Sociological Review*, 26(2): 184–93.

Zelizer, V. A. (1997) *The Social Meaning of Money: Pin Money, Paychecks, Poor Relief, and Other Currencies*. Princeton, NJ: Princeton University Press.

Zelizer, V. A. (1998) 'The proliferation of social currencies', in M. Callon (ed.), *The Laws of the Market*. Oxford: Blackwell/The Sociological Review.

Zhang, W. (1996) *Ideology and Economic Reform Under Deng Xiaoping, 1978–1993*. New York: Kegan Paul International.

Zukin, S. and DiMaggio, P. (eds) (1990) *Structures of Capital: The Social Organization of the Economy*. New York: Cambridge University Press.

Index

abstract labour 76, 160
abstraction, market 14, 96, 161,
    195, 200–1
Adorno, T. 80, 153, 159, 162–7
advertising 87, 152, 165, 170,
    178–80, 183–5
aestheticization 180–6
Aglietta, M. 135, 178
Agnew, J. 10–11
agora 12
Akerlof, G. 125
alienation 18, 22–6, 30, 34,
    179
    Marxist theory of 65–7, 71–2,
    159
allocation 36–8, 44–8, 52–5, 95–7,
    100, 115, 130, 141, 200
Althusser, L. 128
Altvater, E. 129
anomie 34
anthropological approaches to
    exchange 8, 97–102, 199–200
anthropology, and economics 93,
    97–8
anti-market 14
Appadurai, A. 24, 187–9
Arnold, M. 153
art, and the marketplace 154–8
artificial market 15
Austrian School 37, 51–4

Bakhtin, M. 11
Barro, R. 124–5
Bataille, G. 177
Baudrillard, J. 169, 181–6, 202
Bauman, Z. 68, 141, 184
Beck, U. 184
Becker, G. 59–60, 113
Bell, D. 87, 177
Benetton 179
Benjamin, W. 80, 159, 162, 166,
    171
Bentham, J. 29–31, 33, 44
Blair, T. 86, 132
Block, F. 129, 177
Boas, F. 97
bounded rationality 60
Bourdieu, P. 101, 155–7, 177,
    194
bourgeoisie 68, 153–5
Boyer, R. 135
Braudel, F. 10–16
Brewer, J. 154, 166
bureaucracy 76
Burke, E. 153

calculation 14, 18, 22, 25–8, 31–4,
    39, 46–51, 58–60, 74–7, 101,
    110–12
Callon, M. 90, 94, 110–12, 114,
    116, 193, 195, 200–1

capital 18, 22, 50, 64–73
  definition of 21
capitalism 13–15, 21–5, 34, 41,
    64–73, 79–81, 127–37,
    158–60, 166, 188, 194,
    198–201
  managed 132–7
capitalists 21–2, 50, 64–6, 69, 72,
    129
Carrier, J. 8–9, 192, 194–5
Castells, M. 186, 201
central place theory 9
choice 37–8, 46–51, 58–60, 78
  see also rational choice
class 43–4, 66–9, 86, 158–9
class conflict 43–4, 67, 128
class interests 65–7, 71, 120, 128–9
Clark, J. B. 45
Clarke, S. 43, 57, 86
Classen, C. 190–1
Clinton, B. 86
Coase, R. 107–8, 144
Coca-Cola 190
Coleman, J. 101
collective interests 42, 58, 67
collusion 15, 16, 55
commodification 21–6, 150, 181–3
  of culture 152–4
commodities 22, 160–2, 171
  definition of 23–4, 66
commodity aesthetics 180, 182
commodity fetishism 66–7, 159–60,
    182, 191
communism 130–2
  see also post-communist
    transition
communitarianism 34, 86
competition 15, 19, 23, 43–5,
    51–5, 70, 156–7
  imperfect 54–6
  perfect 39–40, 46, 105
concrete labour 66, 76, 160
conscience collective 83, 85
consumer culture 67–8, 72, 150,
    182–6, 190–1

consumption 15–16, 24, 47, 50, 69,
    72, 170–2, 183–6, 194–5
  cultural 167–72, 178
contract 10, 18, 26, 30, 32, 67, 75,
    82–5, 89, 99, 101–2, 105
contradiction, capitalist 64–5, 69,
    71, 187
co-ordination, economic 2, 36–9,
    46–7, 52, 109, 121
corporatism 134–7, 144, 147
cost/benefit analysis 27, 49–50
costs of production 43–4
Crang, P. 174–5, 186
crisis 34, 84, 135–6
  capitalist 64, 70–1, 135–6
crowds 10, 16
cult of the individual 84–5
cultural capital 156–7
cultural consumption 167–72, 178
cultural economy 176–81
cultural goods 176
cultural industries 170–1
'cultural turn' 150, 174–96, 199,
    202
cultural values, see values, social
    and cultural
culture
  and agency 167–72
  commodification of 152–4
  definitions of 149–50
  high 152, 166
  popular 150, 157–8, 166–72
  and the state 157–8
'culture industry' 164–6

Dalton, G. 97
de Certeau, M. 185–6
demand 38–40, 45–6, 50, 69–70,
    122
demand management 122–5
dematerialization 175, 177, 179–86
department stores 16
depersonalization 26–8, 34, 81
Depression, see Great Depression
desires 11, 31, 47–8, 53–4, 59,
    159, 164, 183

Dickens, C. 19
DiMaggio, P. 93, 101
disenchantment of the world 75–80
distinction 177
division of domestic labour 113–15
division of intellectual labour 2,
    32–3, 37, 92, 149
division of labour 19–21, 30, 41–2,
    70–2, 75, 83–6, 188
Dodd, N. 25, 192–3
domestic production 22, 24, 66
du Gay, P. 171, 177–8
Durkheim, É. 20, 32, 42, 67, 75,
    79, 82–90, 99–100

economic discourse 192–5
economic government 145–7
economic liberalism 15, 53, 117–20,
    138–43
    see also liberalism; neoliberalism
economic man, see homo
    economicus
economic sociology 88–90, 93–4,
    108, 199–200
economics 2, 33, 37–8
    approaches to the market in 2,
    36–54, 92–3, 105
    as culture 191–5
    macro- 120–6, 132, 134
    micro- 69, 123, 125
    neoclassical 2, 39, 51–5, 58, 61,
    107–8, 111, 121, 125, 135,
    192
    as social theory 36–8, 51, 53,
    200
efficiency 19, 28, 47, 51–6, 70, 107,
    139, 142, 147
embeddedness 13, 88, 93–104,
    110–12, 116, 175, 199–200
endogenous growth 104, 126
Engels, F. 128, 133, 141
Enlightenment thought 17, 40, 83
entrepreneurs 22
entrepreneurship 89, 130
Entwistle, J. 178
equality 67, 85

see also inequality
equilibrium 39, 45–6, 52–5, 121,
    125–6
ethic of personality 79–80, 90
Etzioni, A. 60, 86–7, 143
exchange 7–8, 41–2, 80, 83–5,
    198–200
    anthropological approaches 8,
    97–102, 199–200
    gift 26, 97, 101–2
    kinship 97
    kula 97, 100, 192
    market 38, 45–7, 52–4, 74,
    95–6, 100, 161, 181, 202
    non-market 17–18, 95, 97–102
    symbolic 97–101
exchange value 43, 66, 70, 76, 160,
    162–4, 181–3
exploitation 23, 67, 70, 72
    rate of 65, 69
externalities 54–7, 112

Featherstone, M. 78, 87, 155–7,
    166, 177, 182
felicific calculus 31, 76
feminist critiques of economics 22,
    112–16
Ferguson, A. 40
fetishism, see commodity fetishism
firms 70, 106–7, 109–11
Firth, R. 97
flexible accumulation 103, 178–81
    see also post-Fordism
flows 179–91, 202
forces of production 71
Ford, H. 178
Fordism 19, 136–8, 178, 190
    see also post-Fordism
formal rationality 39, 47–51,
    57–60, 73–80, 82, 92, 101,
    149, 197
formalism, in economics 2, 94–5,
    98
Foucault, M. 144–7, 193–4
'framing' of market relations
    111–12, 200

free market 40, 43, 54, 118,
    138–43
free trade 15, 42, 121
freedom 18, 29, 33, 53, 67, 78,
    119, 130, 162
  formal 18, 23, 27, 68, 78
  see also liberty
Friedman, M. 123–5, 135, 138
Fukuyama, F. 102–4, 141
functionalism 20, 88–90

Galbraith, J. K. 22, 43, 177
Gates, B. 55, 158
Gellner, E. 98–9
Gemeinschaft 17, 26
gender 106, 112–16, 171–2
generalized exchange 99–100, 109
Gesellschaft 17, 26
Gibson-Graham, J. K. 8, 201
Giddens, A. 87, 132, 184, 189
gift exchange 26, 97, 101–2
globalization 103, 138, 186–91,
    202
Godelier, M. 89
governance 11–12, 143–4
government intervention into
    markets 55–7, 105–6, 112,
    117–26, 143–4, 194
governmentality 144–7, 194
Gramsci, A. 158
Granovetter, M. 93–4, 100–1, 109
Great Depression 122–3
growth, theories of 125–6
Gudeman, S. 98

Habermas, J. 77, 89, 141, 156
Halévy, E. 30–1
Hardy, T. 24
harmony of interests 30–1, 42–3,
    64, 71
Hart, K. 101
Harvey, D. 136–7, 174, 178
Hayek, F. von 20, 39, 51–4, 61–2,
    130–2, 140
Hebdige, D. 168
hedonism 47
Herskovits, M. J. 97

hidden hand, see invisible hand
high culture 152, 166
Hirschman, A. 20, 42
Hirst, P. 106, 110, 143, 144
Hobbes, T. 29–30, 33, 40
Hochschild, A. 177
Hodgson, G. 3, 36, 106, 108–9,
    131, 201
Hoggart, R. 152
Holton, R. J. 80, 84–5, 88–90
homo economicus 47, 51, 57, 61,
    113–15
Horkheimer, M. 162–6
households 22, 24, 26, 112–13
human nature 31, 61–2
Hume, D. 29, 154
Huyssen, A. 156

identity thinking 163–4
imperialism 20
individual 17, 26–8, 32–4, 40–1,
    53, 61–2, 67–8, 71–3, 78–84,
    89
  cult of the 84–5
individualism 27–9, 80–90, 165,
    200
  methodological 32–3, 73, 86
inequality 23, 28, 32, 35, 65–8, 120
  see also equality
information, in markets 39, 52–6,
    107, 130, 132
  see also price
informational goods 180–1
institutedness, of markets 104–12,
    191–6, 200
institutional economics 94, 106–9,
    144
institutions, economic 93, 106–10,
    195
instrumental rationality 27–8,
    73–80, 162
interdependence 19, 27, 30, 42, 84,
    90, 188
interests
  class 65–7, 71, 120, 128–9
  collective 42, 58, 67

private 2, 31, 38–9, 41–2, 54,
    57–8, 142
self-interest 30, 33, 71, 84
International Monetary Fund (IMF)
    195
Internet 190, 196
invisible hand 30, 42, 44, 54, 96
iron cage 79
irrationality 17, 34, 60, 69, 71, 92

Jameson, F. 16, 174
Jessop, B. 127, 135, 143
Jevons, W. S. 45, 49, 51

Kadish, A. 92, 194
Keynes, J. M. 69, 122–5, 132–4
    neo-Keynesians 125–6, 192
kinship exchange 97
Kirzner, I. 52–3
Kline, S. 190–1
Knight, F. 45, 98
Kolakowski, L. 77
kula exchange 97, 100, 192

labour 23, 67, 69, 72, 160–1, 182
    abstract 76, 160
    concrete 66, 76, 160
labour market 22, 105, 160–1
    in cultural industries 177–8
labour theory of value 43–4, 64–5
Lane, R. E. 3, 36
Lange, O. 131
Lash, S. 87, 103, 135, 178–81, 187,
    192
Lavoie, D. 53, 192
Leavis, F. R. 151, 166
Lenin, V. I. 22, 128, 131, 198
Lévi-Strauss, C. 99–100
Levitt, T. 189
liberalism 29–30, 41, 47, 57, 63,
    67, 71, 82, 146, 194
    economic 15, 53, 117–20,
        138–43
    see also neoliberalism
liberty 11, 29, 31, 50, 119–20
    see also freedom
liminality 11

Lipietz, A. 135
Locke, J. 29, 30, 40
Lucas, R. 124–5
Lukács, G. 80, 159, 162
Luxemburg, R. 22
Lyotard, J.-F. 177

McCloskey, D. 45, 47, 53, 192
McDonald's 17
McGuigan, J. 168
Macpherson, C. B. 29, 86
macro-economics 120–6, 132, 134
Malinowski, B. 97
managed capitalism 132–7
Mandel, E. 22
Marcuse, H. 67, 77, 168, 184, 202
marginal utility theory 44–51, 78,
    123
marginalist economics, see marginal
    utility theory
market
    artificial 15
    clearance 37, 46–7, 52, 55,
        121–2, 125
    definition of 9–10, 14, 32, 38–40
    failure 45, 54–6, 117
    mechanism 45–7, 96
    mediation 24–5, 64, 69–72, 161,
        164
    natural 15
    private 13–17
    process 51–3
    versus plans 38, 53–4, 130–2,
        201
'market idea', the 3, 9, 15
market socialism 130–2
market society 1–2, 6–8, 17,
        34–5, 40–1, 63, 68, 73, 80, 87,
        95, 118–20, 151, 184,
        197–202
marketing 14–15, 178–81, 190–1
marketization 25, 104, 140–1,
        188–9, 200
marketplace 9–16, 96, 172, 187
Marshall, A. 45, 51
Marshall, T. H. 133, 139

Marx, K. 21–3, 44, 50, 64–73,
    75–8, 81, 90, 127–8, 133,
    158–64, 188, 194, 198
Marxist state theory 127–9
mass consumption 19, 178
mass production 178
material culture 25, 150, 159
Mauss, M. 99
maximization 47–8, 50, 55, 59–61,
    110, 113
Mead, L. M. 139
Mead, M. 98
means of production, ownership of
    23, 69, 72, 75
merchants 11, 12, 14, 16, 20, 41
    see also middlemen
methodological individualism 32–3,
    73, 86
Meuret, D. 41, 119, 145
micro-economics 69, 123, 125
Microsoft 55
middlemen 11, 12, 14, 16, 100
Miliband, R. 129
Mill, J. S. 29, 31, 44, 80, 90, 120
Miller, D. 25, 101, 172, 190, 196
Mises, L. von 51, 130
modernity 1–2, 6–9, 27, 87, 155,
    159, 197, 200–2
modernization 13–16, 23, 101
monetarism 123–5
monetarization 25–8, 74, 80
money 25–8, 73–4, 80, 192–3
money supply 123
monopoly 55
Montesquieu, C. de 20, 40
moral community 32, 34, 42, 85,
    102
moral economy 34, 41, 86
Murdoch, R. 158
Murray, R. 179
mystification 35, 64, 69, 162, 184

natural law 29, 121
natural markets 15
natural price 43–4, 48
Nava, M. 170

needs 41–2, 50, 53–4, 72, 76, 81,
    159, 164
neoclassical economics 2, 39, 51–5,
    58, 61, 107–8, 111, 121, 125,
    135, 192
neoliberalism 33–4, 43, 55–6, 86,
    117, 123, 132, 136–41, 144–7,
    192–5, 198–9, 201
networks 11, 38, 53, 93, 101–4,
    109–11, 186, 201–2
Nike 17, 179
Nixon, S. 171
North, D. 106, 108–9
Nove, A. 131, 201

Offe, C. 129, 133
opportunity cost 50
organic community 17, 26, 84
organic metaphor 84, 102
organic solidarity 84
ownership 29, 66, 75
    of means of cultural production
        158
    of means of production 23, 69,
        72

Packard, V. 170
Pareto, V. 45, 47, 51, 57
Parsons, T. 82, 88–90
Pepys, S. 12–13
Phillips, A. W. 123
Phillips Curve 123
Piore, M. J. 177
planning, economic 53, 130–2,
    141–2
Plattner, S. 9, 100
pleasure 31, 47, 51, 183
Polanyi, K. 2, 3, 75, 88, 93–106,
    109, 116, 120, 132, 140, 145,
    191, 201
political economy 40–6, 64, 66, 94
popular culture 150, 157–8,
    166–72
possessive individualism 29
post-communist transition 137,
    141–3
post-Fordism 136, 176–81

post-industrial goods 180–1
postmodern goods 180–1
postmodernism 88, 156–8, 169–72,
    176–86
potlatch 102
Poulantzas, N. 128–9
poverty 120, 132
power 21, 32, 35, 68, 106, 108,
    113–16, 132
praxis 71–2
pre-contractual, the 83, 99
preferences 48, 50, 57–60
price 38–40, 43–4, 46, 48, 53, 56,
    65, 76, 95–6, 130
  market 43
  natural 43–4, 48
price mechanism 39, 52, 96
private interests 2, 31, 38–9, 41–2,
    54, 57–8, 142
private market 13–17
privatization 138–42
Procacci, G. 132–3, 145–6
production 19–21, 41, 64, 66,
    69–70, 74–5, 161, 164, 179
profit 21, 23, 43–4, 50, 65–6, 164
  rate of 65
progress 28, 33
property 18, 23, 29–30, 98, 105
Protestant ethic 75, 79, 87
psychology, of the market 31, 51,
    61–2, 97, 198
Putnam, R. 102

Quesnay, F. 145

rate of exploitation 65, 69
rate of profit 65
rational action 17, 30, 33, 50–1,
    57–62
rational choice 33, 46–51, 59–61,
    114
rational expectations 124–6, 192
rationality 63, 67–80, 90, 92, 95
  formal 39, 47–51, 57–60, 73–80,
    82, 92, 101, 149, 197
  instrumental 27–8, 73–80, 162
  substantive 58–9, 76–80, 149

rationalization 23, 27, 73–80
Ray, L. 174, 176, 194
Reagan, R. 138
reciprocity 95, 99
regulation of markets 11–12, 54–7,
    105, 121, 136, 140
regulation theory 135–6
reification 80, 150, 158, 183
relations of production, *see* social
    relations of production
rent 23, 43–4, 66
Ricardo, D. 42, 44–5, 120–1
Riesman, D. 177
risk 22, 56
Robbins, L. 37, 46–7
Robins, K. 189
romantic critiques of market society
    34, 43
Romer, P. 126
Ross, A. 17, 170
Rousseau, J.-J. 40

Sabel, C. 177
Sahlins, M. 97–100
Samuelson, P. A. 92
Sayer, A. 174, 176, 194
Say's Law 69
scarcity 2, 16, 37–9, 47–8, 54
Schumpeter, J. A. 87, 130–1
self-interest 30, 33, 71, 84
Seligman, A. B. 99, 100
Sen, A. 57–9
Senior, N. W. 44, 50
Sennett, R. 177
Shields, R. 10
shopping 12, 16, 171–2
shopping malls 16–17, 183
shortages 12, 121
    see also scarcity
sign value 181–6
signs 180–6
Sik, O. 131
Simmel, G. 20, 26, 80, 162,
    171
Sismondi, J. C. S. 134
Smelser, N. J. 82, 88–90

Smith, A. 15, 19–21, 29, 30–1, 37,
    40–5, 50, 54–7, 61–2, 69, 71,
    103, 113, 119–21, 129, 143,
    145, 154, 198
social capital 101–4
social contract theory 30, 57
social integration 19–21, 41–5
social order 30–1, 36–7, 40–5, 47,
    63–4, 71, 81, 83–8, 91,
    99–100, 149, 182, 197–8, 200
social relations of production 22,
    24, 65–72, 160–2, 182–4
social reproduction 69, 112–15,
    128–9, 133
social structure 32–4, 64–6, 93
social values, see values, social and
    cultural
socialism 55, 130–2, 200
sociation 80–1
solidarity 41, 79, 83–4, 87,
    99–100, 104
    organic 84
Solow, R. 126
Sombart, W. 21
Soper, K. 77
spectacle 14, 16
stagflation 124, 137
Stallybrass, P. 11
state 29, 41, 75
    and culture 157–8
    and market 117–48
    theory, Marxist 127–9
status 17–18, 23, 27, 184
Stiglitz, J. E. 39, 54–6, 110, 125
subcultures 167–8, 184
substantive economics 94, 98
substantive rationality 58–9, 76–80,
    149
supermarkets 16, 172
supply 38–40, 45–6
supply-side policy 124–6
surplus goods 21
surplus value 64–5, 69–70
Swedberg, R. 45, 93–4
symbolic exchange 97–101
systems theory 88–90

taste 154–9, 177–8
Taussig, M. 26
Taylor, C. 90
Thatcher, M. 32, 138, 198
'third way' 131–2, 202
Thompson, E. P. 12, 106, 201
Thompson, G. 2, 144
time, in markets 52–3
Titmuss, R. M. 133
Tönnies, F. 26
Touraine, A. 177
trade 19–20, 27
    gains from 42
    see also free trade
traditional social order 6, 17, 28,
    40–1, 81, 87, 152–3
transaction cost economics 107–8,
    144
Tribe, K. 92, 194
trust 15, 99, 101–2, 110
Turner, T. 158

unemployment 122–6
Urry, J. 87, 103, 135, 178–81, 187,
    192
use value 43, 66–7, 76, 160, 164–5,
    181–3
utilitarianism 29–33, 47, 51, 63,
    79, 82–5, 88, 200
utility 31, 43, 47–51, 58–60, 74–6,
    183

value 25, 48–9, 69–70, 76, 80
    see also exchange value; use
    value
values, social and cultural 25, 28,
    30, 59, 74, 79, 86, 155, 159
Veblen, T. 108, 177
Venturi, R. 156

wage labour 23, 44, 65
wage relation 22, 65
wages 43–4, 50, 66, 69
Walras, L. 45–6, 52, 55, 121–2,
    125
wants 48, 50

Waters, M. 186
Weber, M. 39, 57, 67, 73–80,
    85–90, 149, 162
welfare 120
welfare state 132–7
    'reform' of 138–9
Wheelock, J. 114–15
White, A. 11
Williams, R. 67, 151–2, 170
Williamson, J. 67, 170, 184

Williamson, O. E. 56, 61, 107–8
Willis, P. 25, 168–70
Winch, D. 41
World Bank 103
World Trade Organization (WTO)
    202
Wrong, D. 57

Zelizer, V. A. 25–6
Zukin, S. 93, 101